THE END OF GLORY

THE END OF GLORY

War and Peace in HMS *Hood*

1916–1941

by

Bruce Taylor

Seaforth
PUBLISHING

Copyright © Bruce Taylor 2012

First published in Great Britain in 2012 by
Seaforth Publishing,
Pen & Sword Books Ltd,
47 Church Street,
Barnsley S70 2AS

www.seaforthpublishing.com

British Library Cataloguing in Publication Data
A catalogue record for this book is available from the British Library

ISBN 978 1 84832 139 7

Typeset and designed by MATS Typesetting, Leigh-on-Sea, Essex
Printed and bound by CPI Group (UK) Ltd., Croydon, CR0 4YY

Contents

Preface

FIVE YEARS AFTER the publication of *The Battlecruiser* HMS Hood: *An Illustrated Biography, 1916–1941* it was suggested to me that the time was ripe for the *Hood* and her world to be brought to a new audience. Hence this book, which represents a substantial abridgement of the earlier volume, as well as an opportunity to incorporate such material as has come to light since 2005. Sheared of much of the technical content that would make it challenging for the general reader, it offers a detailed insight into the life and career of a great warship as seen and recalled by those who made her what she was. And like its predecessor, its aim is to reaffirm the centrality of the human experience in naval life and naval history.

The *Hood* remains the most celebrated symbol of British seapower since Nelson's *Victory*. On her rested much of the pride and hope of the British people for their Navy in its darkest hour and her sinking had a profound and lasting impact on the morale of both, made the more unbearable by the scale of her annihilation. In the years since that moment, the relative decline of Britain and her Navy and the many unresolved questions surrounding the loss of the *Hood* have added ever more poignancy and symbolism to her destruction. But, pertinent as they are, these issues bear less on her life than her legacy. The *Hood* died as she had lived, in the vanguard of the Navy. How she reached that exalted status over twenty years of war and peace is explored in this volume, where possible in the words of those who knew her best.

My debt to the many kind people whose encouragement and assistance made this book possible remains as real today as ever. To them I would fain offer – what some are sadly no longer living to receive – my renewed thanks. My hope is that the result serves to mark and perpetuate their interest and association with the ship in whatever form it has taken. Meanwhile, I have four names to add to those acknowledged earlier: those of my friends Nick Lambert, Christopher McKee and Jon Sumida, and especially that of Deborah Eppolito to whom this renewal is dedicated with love and affection.

Bruce Taylor
Los Angeles, December 2011

Author's Note

A FULL LISTING of sources (published and unpublished) consulted can be found in *The Battlecruiser* HMS Hood: *An Illustrated Biography, 1916–1941* (London: Chatham Publishing, 2005; revised edn Barnsley, S Yorks: Seaforth Publishing, 2008). Citations from documents in The National Archives are Crown Copyright. The copyright of much of the remainder rests either with their authors or their descendants. Credits are given after each photo where it has been possible to establish either the source or the copyright with certainty. Extensive efforts have been made to locate copyright holders in the remaining cases and these are encouraged to contact the author with proof of copyright.

It may be helpful to remind readers of the traditional currency of the United Kingdom before decimalisation in 1971: there were twelve pence to a shilling (known as a 'bob') and twenty shillings to a pound (also known as a sovereign or a 'quid'). Among the many coins engendered by this system was that known as 'half a crown', worth two shillings and sixpence.

Abbreviations

AB	Able Seaman
ACQ	Admiral Commanding Battle Cruiser Squadron
BCS	Battle Cruiser Squadron
BEM	British Empire Medal
Capt	Captain
CB	Companion of the Order of the Bath
CBE	Commander of the Order of the British Empire
Cdr	Commander
CERA	Chief Engine Room Artificer
CO	Commanding Officer
CPO	Chief Petty Officer
(D)	Dental
DNC	Director of Naval Construction
DSC	Distinguished Service Cross
DSM	Distinguished Service Medal
DSO	Distinguished Service Order
(E)	Engineering
ERA	Engine Room Artificer
(G)	Gunnery
HMS	His Majesty's Ship
LS	Leading Seaman
Lt	Lieutenant
Lt Cdr	Lieutenant Commander
Mid	Midshipman
MM	Military Medal
(N)	Navigation
NAAFI	Navy, Army, and Air Force Institutes
NCO	Non-commissioned officer
(O)	Officer's (cook)
OA	Ordnance Artificer
OD	Ordinary Seaman

OOW	Officer of the Watch
OSig	Ordinary Signalman
OTel	Ordinary Telegraphist
PO	Petty Officer
RANVR	Royal Australian Naval Volunteer Reserve
RCN	Royal Canadian Navy
Ret	Retired
RIN	Royal Indian Navy
RM	Royal Marines
RN	Royal Navy
RNR	Royal Naval Reserve
RNVR	Royal Naval Volunteer Reserve
RNZN	Royal New Zealand Navy
(S)	Signals (officer); Ship's (cook)
Sig	Signalman
SODS	Ship's Operatic and Dramatic Society
SS	Steamship
Sub-Lt	Sub Lieutenant
(T)	Torpedoes
Tel	Telegraphist
Temp	Temporary
UP	Unrotated Projectile, Unrifled Projector
USN	United States Navy

1

In the Beginning

THE IMMEDIATE ORIGINS of HM battlecruiser *Hood* can be traced to a note sent by the Controller of the Navy, Admiral Sir Frederick Tudor, to the Director of Naval Construction, Sir Eustace Tennyson d'Eyncourt, in October 1915. In it Tudor requested designs for an experimental battleship based on the successful Queen Elizabeth class but incorporating the latest advances in seakeeping and underwater protection. Central to the Admiralty's brief was a higher freeboard and shallower draught than previous construction, features that would not only permit more effective operation under wartime loads but lessen the threat to the ship posed by underwater damage. Between November 1915 and January 1916 d'Eyncourt evolved five designs, the most promising of which had a greatly enlarged hull and beam in order to achieve the necessary reduction in draught. However, these studies were rejected in a lengthy memorandum by Admiral Sir John Jellicoe, Commander-in-Chief of the Grand Fleet, in January 1916. Whereas the Royal Navy had a marked superiority in battleships over the High Seas Fleet, it had no answer to the large Mackensen-class battlecruisers then under construction for the German navy. Accordingly, six more designs were produced in February, based on the earlier studies but emphasising speed over protection. Of these one was selected for development, resulting in a further pair of designs in March. It was the second of these, Design 'B', which received the nod from the Admiralty Board on 7 April 1916 and upon which the ship that came to be known as HMS *Hood* was based. The final studies had been evolved under d'Eyncourt's supervision by E L Attwood, head of the Battleship section of the Royal Corps of Naval Constructors, assisted by S V Goodall.

What did this design consist of? On a standard displacement of 36,300 tons – over five thousand more than any other ship in the Royal Navy – Design 'B' promised a speed of 32 knots through the use of the lighter small-tube boiler. A length of 860 feet – approaching the length of two and a half football fields – meant that there would only be three graving docks in Britain capable of accepting her bulk, those at Portsmouth, Rosyth and Liverpool. There were to be eight 15in guns in a modified turret design along with sixteen of the new 5.5in mountings. An 8in main belt was believed to offer better protection than the 10in of the Queen Elizabeth class thanks to the introduction of a sophisticated arrangement of sloped armour. However, horizontal protection showed no improvement on earlier designs, being restricted to a maximum of 2.5in, and that only on the lower deck; elsewhere it was no more than 1.5in. On 17 April orders for four ships were placed by the Admiralty, one, eventually called *Hood*, at John Brown & Co of Clydebank. Then came Jutland.

On 31 May and 1 June 1916 an action was fought a hundred miles off the Danish coast which was to have far-reaching consequences for the Royal Navy. Of these only one need concern us here: the fate of the British battlecruisers, three of which blew up under German shellfire. The battlecruiser was a product of the fertile mind of Admiral Lord Fisher, the mercurial genius who transformed the Royal Navy in the years before the First World War. Fisher's intentions are not readily divined, but he evidently recognised that a *guerre de course*, a concerted campaign on British merchant shipping, would form a key element of German naval strategy in the coming war. To counter this he took the principal innovations of his other brainchild, the *Dreadnought*, and created the battlecruiser, a ship which married the size and fighting power of a battleship with the swiftness of an armoured cruiser. However, ship design is a science based on compromise and in order to attain speeds in excess of 25 knots major sacrifices in armour protection had to be made. The first generation of battlecruisers therefore represented a risky and prodigiously expensive solution to the problem of commerce-raiding and cruiser warfare, but the expenditure was vindicated first at the Battle of the Falkland Islands in December 1914 and then at the Dogger Bank in January of the following year. In the first action the main units of Vizeadmiral Graf von Spee's *Deutsche Südseegeschwader* were destroyed by *Invincible* and *Inflexible* 8,000 miles from Britain, thus ending German hopes of a sustained offensive against imperial trade. In the second the armoured cruiser *Blücher* was overhauled and crushed by weight of fire from Vice Admiral Sir David Beatty's Battle Cruiser Fleet. However, there was another side to Fisher's concept, that of fast scout for the battle fleet, and for this role the battlecruiser was to prove significantly less well equipped. Inevitably, the moment came when the battlecruiser began trading salvoes with ships of similar firepower and at ranges which presented a severe danger to her thin horizontal protection. The First World War, it turned out, was fought over ranges far greater than had been anticipated by ship constructors when they designed the armour scheme of their ships. Whereas most capital ships had been optimised to absorb shells fired from four, six, and eight thousand yards, the ranges at which Jutland in particular was fought – ten, twelve and fourteen thousand yards – brought shells to target on a far steeper trajectory than their protection had been designed to resist. This was particularly true of the British battlecruisers, much of whose horizontal plating was no more than an inch and a half thick. The first indication of vulnerability to plunging fire came at the Dogger Bank when *Lion* was disabled after repeated hits from Konteradmiral

Franz von Hipper's battlecruisers. But it was not until Jutland that the inherent weakness of British battlecruiser design and operation became fully apparent. By the time the Grand Fleet turned for home, three of the nine battlecruisers engaged that day had been sent to the bottom with all but a handful of survivors. It is clear that inadequate measures against flash and poor cordite handling contributed to these disasters, but the stark reality is that the British battle-cruiser proved unequal to the demands presented by long-range combat with ships of similar armament.

For all this, the battlecruiser is one of the great offensive weapons in naval history. Though flawed in design, she possessed the quality other vessels of her generation signally lacked: the ability to force the enemy to battle in an age when technical advance made it far easier for a commander to decline action if he chose. Even after Jutland, the fact that the battlecruisers were the spearhead of the fleet gave them a prestige unmatched by any other squadron in the Royal Navy. For the fighting officer burning to engage an elusive enemy, these were the ships to serve in, and in this respect there is little to choose between the mentality with which Beatty and his men went into battle at Jutland and that which governed Vice Admiral Holland's attack on the *Bismarck* twenty-five years later. Whatever the judgements of history, however deficient in tactics or design, however disastrous the outcome, it was in this cast of mind that the battlecruiser was traditionally taken into action.

But for now the Battle of Jutland presented the designers of the *Hood* with a number of severe challenges. Proposals for increased protection were tabled in June and on 5 July d'Eyncourt submitted a revised version of Design 'B', which was eventually accepted on 4 August. The armament was unchanged from the March legend but belt armour was increased to a maximum of 12in and barbettes from nine to twelve. The angled 12in belt now provided the equivalent of 14 or 15in of vertical armour while a 460-foot long bulge packed with steel tubing offered torpedo protection the equal of any prior to the Second World War. However, horizontal protection saw relatively little improvement and was still no better than 2.5in despite the addition of 3,100 tons to the displacement. This might just have sufficed had the *Hood*'s magazines not been placed over her shell rooms as was hitherto the norm in British design. As it was, this amount of protection was regarded by both Jellicoe and Beatty as inadequate and within a few weeks improvements had been made both to turret and deck armour, which had reached a maximum of 3in over the magazines when the final design legend was approved in August 1917. The governing criterion was that at least 9in of armour would have to be penetrated in order for a shell to reach the magazines, but numerous thin decks offered considerably less protection than one thick one. Put simply, the *Hood* did not have an armoured deck and in this lay the fatal weakness of her design, however superior her arrangements to previous construction. Though occasionally classified as a fast battleship, by later standards the *Hood* failed to make the transition from a battlecruiser and ultimately proved incapable of meeting the requirement that had sooner or later to be made of any man-o'-war: the ability to withstand punishment from ships armed to the same standard as herself.

It was long supposed that *Hood*'s keel was laid at John Brown's shipyard on Clydebank just as the battlecruisers were steaming into action at Jutland on 31 May. Star-crossed she may have been, but work did not begin on ship no 460 until 1 September 1916. The keel-laying of the *Hood* was the crowning moment in a programme of warship construction dating back to the turn of the twentieth century. At stake was the preservation of Britain's maritime supremacy against the formidable threat posed by German naval and industrial power. In order to secure victory, British industry had to draw on a wellspring of experience, technique and innovation which makes the 'Great Naval Race' the final expression of the Industrial Revolution. Then, as now, the building of a capital ship was amongst the most challenging of human endeavours. The process required the skills and labour of thousands of men and women, of architects and engineers at the Admiralty, smelters and forgers in Sheffield and tracers and drillers in the yard itself. From across the country the output of dozens of mills, factories, mines and workshops poured in by ship, rail and lorry, over 40,000 tons of materiel from hardened plate to turned cabinetry.

The design of a ship began as we have seen with a brief from the Admiralty to the Director of Naval Construction. Accordingly, the DNC and his team started by calculating the proportions and characteristics of the hull and the balance of propulsion plant, armour and armament which would govern its design. After a preliminary hull form had been worked out, it was tank-tested at the Admiralty Experiment Works at Haslar near Portsmouth to establish the metacentric heights, centres of gravity and buoyancy, wave resistance and coefficients of the vessel as well as the optimum shape of propellers and sub-merged surfaces. Then came detailed plans showing the arrangement of armour and machinery spaces and the projected weights, structure and dimensions of the completed vessel. Once approved by the Admiralty Board these were dispatched to the shipyard contracted to build the vessel so that copies could be made and the preparation of working drawings initiated. It was usual for armament and machinery contractors to produce their own working drawings but where *Hood* was concerned the Admiralty placed far greater reliance on John Brown's own draughtsmen and those of the other three builders than had hitherto been the case. Work began in the mould loft, at John Brown's an immense room over 375 feet long on whose floor the frames of the ship were traced in full size onto black scrieve boards. Each set of scrieve boards contained not only the shape of the frame but also the position of every rivet, bolt, sheer line, buttock line and deck to which it would attach. These were taken to the plate shops where metal for frames and bars of different types was selected, cut, heated and then bent on steel slabs until they conformed perfectly to the prescribed contours. This done, the shipfitters began punching holes in the places indicated so that every frame and bar reached the building slip ready to be bolted and then riveted in place by squads of men. A similar procedure was followed with plates, which were drilled, sheared, planed, flanged, bevelled and pressed to the desired shape and curvature ready for positioning on the hull. Meanwhile, beams were being imparted their correct camber and moulds made for major components such as shaft brackets. The first constructional step was the laying of the keel plate, the backbone of the ship, on a carefully selected and prepared berth. Then the transverse and longitudinal frames were joined to the keel to form the watertight compartments which were the ship's first defence against the sea. The box-like construction which resulted had originated with the Renown-class battlecruisers and over it were fixed the bulkheads that divided the *Hood* into twenty-five watertight sections. Though pierced with huge gaps for funnel uptakes and turrets, longitudinal strength was preserved with girders running the length of the ship, the forecastle and upper decks forming the upper part of a slope-sided box to which the ship owed her structural integrity. While the bow and stern frames were being assembled, the blacksmiths' shop was busy turning out forgings of every shape and dimension as electricians began laying the first of many miles of wiring. Then came the installation of screws, bulges and bilge keels before the paint shop dispatched squads of men to apply the coats of red lead paint which announced the ship as ready for launching.

Though laid down in September 1916, constant design alterations meant that work on the *Hood* would be significantly delayed. On 2 November a shipyard report noted that

> Sufficient information is gradually being obtained from the Admiralty to enable more material to be ordered for this vessel and to employ a few more men on her construction, but in view of the alteration in her design, comparatively slow progress can only be made until beginning of next year.

Alterations were still being made but on 1 March 1917 John Brown & Co was 'Informed by the Admiralty that *Hood* is to be pushed with all despatch'. However, the pressing need for merchant shipping in view of the German submarine offensive against British trade now prevented the yard devoting its full resources to the project. Satisfactory progress was reported on 22 June 1917 but construction of the hull was being hindered by a shortage of manpower. No further shipyard reports are available on the *Hood* until January 1919, by which time she had been launched and was in the process of fitting out. This absence can only be explained by the need to preserve secrecy as requests continued for improved protection in the light of test firings and battle experience. These resulted in May and June of 1919 in the removal of four of the sixteen 5.5in guns and then four of the eight above-water torpedo tubes, the last major changes to be made to a design whose construction was by now far advanced. Already in September 1918 the first barbette plates of face-hardened steel had been lowered into place in the fitting-out basin, part of an armour scheme that would eventually require 14,000 tons of plate. The manufacture of armour plate was a highly evolved process requiring plant of a size and complexity unknown in any other field of steel production. It began with a steel ingot weighing 80–100 tons. Because of the nickel and chromium content in armour plate, extremely high furnace temperatures were required to prepare the ingot for forging. Once heated, the ingot was forged under a 10,000-ton hydraulic press before being returned to the furnaces and rolled in an enormously powerful mill. Heated again, the plate was then straightened under hydraulic pressure and planed down to bring it to the required thickness. These plates, some weighing 30 tons, were then hardened in bogie furnaces for periods of up to three weeks during which carbon was adsorbed onto the face. In the case of barbette or conning tower plates, the armour would be given its desired curvature under the remorseless pressure of another 10,000-ton press.

Urged on by Beatty and others, work on the *Hood* picked up after the Armistice. By the end of January 1919, five months after launching, the final work was being done on the hull. On 27 February the second funnel was reported as up and the 600-ton conning tower under construction. A month later the armour belt was being fitted and the bridge structure taking shape. The turbines were all *in situ* by May Day and the end of that month saw the mainmast erected and the ship largely decked over. After some delay the first 15in turret reached Clydebank from the builders, Vickers, Barrow, on 29 July, the ship being hauled out into the river so that it could be transferred from the coaster *Horden* by the 200-ton fitting-out crane. Delivery and installation of the turrets went on until the beginning of December. However, the Admiralty was increasingly anxious for the *Hood* to be completed and in August the decision was taken to suspend construction of the cruiser *Enterprise* so that she could be expedited without delaying merchant work in the yard. Work proceeded apace with perhaps a thousand men aboard and by the end of October the joiners and electricians were fitting out the living quarters of the ship. Also completed in October was the additional plating on the main deck abreast the magazines requested in May, the final addendum to the *Hood*'s protection. By November the rigging was under way, and on 9 and 10 December basin trials of the engines took place in preparation for her departure for builder's trials in the new year. The work was near done.

The construction of the *Hood* had proceeded with little fanfare and a fair degree of secrecy. Her keel-laying in September 1916 seems not to have been accompanied by the ceremony usually accorded these occasions but it was war and such events were in any case more subdued in commercial shipbuilding than they were in the Royal Dockyards of Portsmouth, Devonport and Chatham. The launching in August 1918 was another matter but even this was tinged with sadness. On the Western Front the Allies were defeating the German army but the previous four years had cost Britain and her empire the lives of a million men. Among the dead was Rear Admiral the Hon Sir Horace Hood, killed at Jutland in the battlecruiser *Invincible*; his American widow performed the launching ceremony. The name *Hood* first appears in a communication from the Admiralty to John Brown on 14 July 1916. She was intended as the lead ship of her class, to include *Howe, Rodney* and *Anson*, four great admirals of the eighteenth century. The man after whom the subject of this book was named was a vicar's son from Thorncombe in Dorset, Samuel Hood (1724–1816). In a career spanning fifty-five years Hood acquired a reputation as a master tactician, making his name at St Kitts, Dominica, Toulon and Corsica before being granted the title of Viscount Hood of Whitley in 1796. Nor by any means was he the last member of his family to distinguish himself in naval service. Samuel's brother Alexander (1726–1814) also made his career in the wars against the French, becoming Viscount Bridport in 1801. Then came their nephews Alexander (1758–98) and Samuel Hood (1762–1814), the former killed leading the *Mars* in a desperate action with the French *Hercule* and the latter one of Nelson's captains at the Nile in 1798. Others followed, including Admiral Lord Hood of Avalon, First Sea Lord from 1885–9.

The Hood family therefore had a record of service going back 175 years and the selection of the name for Britain's latest battlecruiser may have owed something to Rear Admiral Hood's sacrifice at Jutland. However, it was his great-great grandfather the first Viscount whose name, device and motto she bore. The badge was of an anchor supported by a Cornish chough, the rare coastal bird of the crow family with a popular reputation for fire-raising. The motto was *Ventis secundis*, 'With favouring winds'. The *Hood* was not the first ship to carry the name. In 1797, just two years after he had hauled down his flag, the Navy commissioned a fourteen-gun vessel named *Lord Hood* which, however, was stricken in December of the following year. It was not until 1860 that the name was revived, in this case when the 80-gun *Edgar* was converted to screw propulsion during the naval scare of the late 1850s. Rendered obsolete by *Warrior* and her successors, the *Hood* spent a dismal career in the reserve and then as a barracks ship at Chatham before being sold out of the Navy in 1888. The next *Hood*, however, was a first-rate unit, launched in 1891 as the eighth and final member of the Royal Sovereign class of battleships. Though designed by Sir William White, a naval architect of genius, the ship was marred by the insistence of her namesake, the First Sea Lord Admiral Sir Arthur Hood, that she carry closed turrets rather than the open barbettes of her half sisters. These not only made *Hood* the Royal Navy's last turret ship but greatly reduced her freeboard and consequently her effectiveness in anything other than a flat calm. In 1914, to the delight of later generations of scuba divers, she was expended as a blockship at the entrance to Portland Harbour as a measure against German submarine attack. If the name *Hood* had a ring to it, this therefore owed more to famous men than famous ships. But all that was to change.

At five minutes past one on Thursday, 22 August 1918 Lady Hood shattered a bottle over the ship's bows and the *Hood* slipped stern-first down the ways and into the Clyde. Even then she retained a remarkably low profile. As the *Dumbarton Herald* noted on 15 January 1919, 'very few people have hitherto been aware of her existence, and yet the *Hood* is a far more wonderful vessel than the Hush! Hush! ships which made such a sensation [*Glorious, Courageous* and *Furious*]'. However, the ship received the wrong sort of publicity on 19 May when a build-up of gas in an airtight compartment resulted in an explosion which killed two men and injured six more. It was therefore in a curiously muted atmosphere that John Brown's last major warship contract for several years left the yard under her own power on 9 January 1920. Things were different at Greenock later that afternoon, where the *Hood* received the first of many rapturous welcomes from crowds lining Customs House Quay and Prince's Pier. Already advance parties of stokers and sailors had been arriving from the battlecruiser *Lion*, the ship whose company would eventually commission her. The Executive Officer, Cdr Lachlan MacKinnon, arranged for numerous signs to be put up to help them find their way round her labyrinthine decks. Twenty years later MacKinnon would have the misfortune of being commodore of convoy SC7, the first to be subjected to the *Rudeltaktik*, a massed attack by U-boats. For now he had to cope with a different order of chaos as the *Hood* began the long process of becoming a commissioned ship in the Royal Navy. Meanwhile, it had been decided to finish the work at HM Dockyard Rosyth so as to clear John Brown's fitting-out basin for the urgent completion of merchant contracts. The voyage round Scotland was to give the crew an early taste of the *Hood*'s seakeeping qualities as a Force 8 gale buried her forecastle and quarterdeck and vibration made life in the spotting top unbearable at speed. Once at Rosyth the ship had to wait six days before wind and current permitted her to be drawn into No 2 Dock for the fitting out to be resumed. Before the *Hood* departed an experiment revealed her final displacement as 46,680 tons at deep load and 42,670 tons at full load – 1,470 tons above the final 1917 legend and no less than 17.5 per cent above the original 1916 design, most of it armour.

After preliminary testing of her torpedo armament the *Hood* returned to Greenock in early March for full builder's and gunnery trials. These, as both d'Eyncourt and Rear Admiral Sir Roger Keyes were aboard to confirm, were a conspicuous success. All the innovation of her design now stood revealed. Advanced boiler and turbine technology permitted the *Hood* to develop over a third more power for the same weight of plant than the Renown class completed in 1916. During full-power trials off the Isle of Arran the *Hood* reached a speed of 32.07 knots on 151,280 shaft horse power, making her by some distance the most powerful ship in the world. At this speed the four propellers – 20 tons of forged manganese bronze apiece – were making 207 revolutions per minute, giving her a margin of several knots on any foreign capital ship. However, this margin of speed could only be obtained with an extremely high fuel consumption. The *Hood*'s oil capacity was 3,895 tons of which over 70 needed to be burned each hour for her to maintain 32 knots. On the other hand, only 7 tons per hour were required to keep her at her economical speed of 14 knots, which could be reached on a mere 10,000shp, barely 7 per cent of her capacity; she could make 25 knots at only two-fifths power. Needless to say, the ship's endurance varied greatly at these speeds, which extended from 7,500 nautical miles at 14 knots to little more than 1,700 at 32. At full speed, oil consumption was 9 feet to the gallon. Besides her engineering plant the trials, which went on through the whole of March, were designed to test the *Hood*'s fittings and equipment to the very limit of their operational use. Extensive steering and turning exercises were performed in every condition of sea and speed. Her tactical diameter (ie turning circle) was found to be 1,400 yards when the rudder was thrown hard over to 38 degrees. Then there were exhaustive gunnery trials of both the main and secondary armament. Apart from difficulties in two of the shell hoists and a back-flash incident in 'A' turret, the 15in firings were carried out satisfactorily and by the end of March the *Hood* was back in dry dock at Rosyth for a detailed examination of her hull and structure. Though commissioned under Capt Wilfred Tomkinson on 29 March, it was not until 15 May that she was accepted from the builders and officially received into the Royal Navy. Her initial peacetime complement, drawn from Devonport barracks until 1929, came to approximately 1,150. Nor was this all. The trials yielded a series of photographs of the ship at speed which captured the imagination of all who saw them. Here was a warship, the largest and most powerful of her day, possessed of an elegance never before seen and never since surpassed. HMS *Hood* had arrived.

At what price? The final cost to the British government of its greatest ship was £6,025,000, of which John Brown drew £214,108 in profit. This sum is almost twice that of any previous ship, *Renown* having cost £3,117,204, though wartime inflation and the sheer size of the vessel must be taken into consideration. At £142, the adjusted cost per ton made *Hood* 25 per cent more expensive than the *Renown*. To this must be added an annual peacetime upkeep of £274,000 in 1934 rising to about £400,000 by the outbreak of war. Payroll in the 1920s was approximately £6,000 per month. Needless to say, the concept and above all the expenditure invited criticism from several quarters. Writing in *The Naval Review*, an anonymous officer argued that the *Hood*, whose specifications otherwise compared with the Queen Elizabeth-class battleships, had required an additional £2,030,000 to obtain her 7-knot margin of speed. Others, reflecting a view widely held in the years following the Great War, believed the entire sum to have been squandered. The *Australian Worker* had this to say when the *Hood* reached the Antipodes in 1924:

The amount of money expended in building a battleship like the *Hood* would have built 10,000 comfortable cottages for British one-room slum dwellers. The idea that a state of military or naval preparedness is any factor in the security of a nation is A MYTH THAT HAS LONG SINCE BEEN EXPLODED.

But there were other concerns, too. Rear Admiral Sir Ernle Chatfield wasn't joking when he quipped at a meeting of the Institution of Naval Architects in March 1920 that 'if the Director of Naval Construction was going to design a ship to-day he would not design the *Hood*'. Certainly, the G3 battlecruisers projected that same year bore little resemblance to her in either appearance, armament or protection. In his memoirs the DNC, Sir Eustace Tennyson d'Eyncourt, present on that occasion, made plain his own views on the matter:

> The *Hood* had a great deal added to her in the way of protection, but there was more to be done, and ... the Second World War proved her armour to be still inadequate. [...] It was a terrible tragedy that the *Hood*'s improved protection was not fully carried out between the wars.

But this was over twenty years into the future. For now the *Hood* was, to all intents and purposes, the greatest capital ship in the world. The cancellation of her sisters in February 1919 and the limitations on warship construction enshrined in the Washington Treaty three years later saw to it that she would hold this status in splendid isolation while peace lasted. That peace was now hers to enjoy.

2

Cock of the Fleet

ON 29 MARCH 1920 the *Hood* commissioned to full complement at Rosyth in the Firth of Forth. That a high proportion of her 1,150 officers and men should have come from the battlecruiser *Lion* was no accident. Under Vice Admiral Sir David Beatty the *Lion* had become the most famous ship in the Royal Navy, the bloodied veteran of Heligoland, the Dogger Bank and Jutland. Now that she was passing into the reserve there could be no more fitting vessel to receive her mantle than the *Hood*, the promised flagship of the post-war Navy. Before the year was out the *Hood* had assumed that mantle in full and in doing so had traced the pattern of her next twenty years. As *Lion* had been a great ship of war, *Hood* was to prove herself the great vessel of peace.

On 15 May the *Hood* weighed anchor at Rosyth and steamed south for the first time. Pausing in Cawsand Bay to hoist the flag of Rear Admiral Sir Roger Keyes, the hero of the Zeebrugge Raid in 1918, she made her way up Plymouth Sound to her home port for the next decade. No sooner had the *Hood* reached Devonport than she was assigned the first in a long succession of diplomatic missions on which her peacetime reputation would be built. As the outcome of the Russian Civil War became apparent, the policy of the British government became one of preserving the sovereignty of the Baltic states and maintaining its interests and presence in that region. To this end, the Admiralty ordered Keyes to take the *Hood*, the battlecruiser *Tiger* and nine destroyers into the Baltic to alert the Soviet fleet at Kronstadt of the consequences of any offensive activity that summer. In the event, the easing of tensions with the Soviets and ongoing negotiations with her neighbours restricted the Battle Cruiser Squadron to the agreeable cruise of Scandinavia which had been planned as cover for the operation.

In retrospect, the Scandinavian cruise seems very much the beginning of a new era of naval diplomacy which, while it lasted, found no greater emissary than HMS *Hood*, the velvet fist of British sea power. Nearing Denmark on the evening of 31 May, Capt Wilfred Tomkinson held a memorial service on the *Hood*'s quarterdeck for the dead of Jutland over whose graves they were then passing. It was four years since an earlier generation of battlecruisers had met disaster under German gunfire. But the guns were now still, and Keyes' squadron was given a rapturous welcome in Scandinavia. Beautiful as the landscape and people were, there was little doubt that the *Hood* was making an equally lasting impression on all who saw her. Lt Cdr Douglas Fairbairn (1920) describes the passage up Oslofjorden:

> A few miles farther on comes the narrowest part, a strait nearly ten miles long and but half a mile wide, with 600 feet of water under the ship's bottom. With the wooded shore slipping past on either side, the *Hood* pursued her stately way through this narrow channel. At each little village we passed were crowds of cheering Norwegians, some of whom even swam out towards the ship. At every white flagstaff among the trees the Norwegian flag was flying, and dipped in salute to us as we went by: this continued for a whole hour. It was a wonderful welcome, and to those ashore the mighty *Hood*, the largest warship in the world, winding her way through those land-locked waters must have been a magnificent sight.

As a visible symbol of a nation's power the *Hood* can scarcely ever have been equalled.

For the Navy the *Hood*'s role as its flagbearer was matched only by her reputation as the premier sporting ship in the fleet and it was for this that many of her men would remember her. The view is summarised by a member of the 1933–6 commission: 'What a ship! Efficient. Fast. Happy. Beautiful lines. Good at sport. Football. Running ... Good at everything. COCK OF THE FLEET!' Already on her maiden voyage south in May 1920 the foundations were being laid for a great athletic tradition, men being selected to represent the ship in each of the main sports competed for in the Navy. The emphasis on sport was one of the key elements of the Royal Navy between the wars though ironically it was a product not of peace but of war. During its vigil at Scapa Flow the Grand Fleet had turned to organised sporting activity as one of the few outlets for its men in their long confinement. After the war a pinched economy, reduced opportunities for training and the increasing acceptance of the need for physical activity to maintain health and morale led to organised sport being placed on a permanent footing for the benefit of all ranks and rates. In March 1920 the Royal Navy and Royal Marines Sports Control Board was formed as an adjunct of the Admiralty's Physical Training and Sports Branch to provide financial and other support and, with this, sport in the Navy never looked back. A year later the *Hood* received her first Physical and Recreational Training Officer. For the Navy, particularly after the Invergordon Mutiny of 1931, it was a case of *Mens sana in corpore sano* and sporting activity was pursued with increasing vigour as the 1920s unfolded.

The basis of shipboard sport was the inter-part competition, the organisation of games by division, branch or department, in *Hood*'s case usually seamen, marines, stokers, artificers and artisans, and communications ratings. These teams competed in several sports and from them were drawn the sides that represented the ship in fleet events. The organisation of each sport at both inter-part and fleet level was entrusted to an officer, and on his zeal and the morale of his men depended the ship's chances of victory. Among the most popular was football, played both in organised competitions ashore and as a gesture of goodwill at home and abroad. During the coal and rail strikes of 1921 the *Hood*'s seamen had eased tensions with rioting miners at Cowdenbeath near Edinburgh by challenging them to a game. The result of the match is not on record but there were certainly some upsets during the *Hood*'s long sporting career. At Vancouver in 1924 her team was defeated by the Royal Canadian Mounted Police by an undisclosed margin. However, the Battle Cruiser Squadron went down only 7–2 to Brazil's national side in 1922 and Santos, Pelé's future team, they beat 2–1. By the 1930s the *Hood* was able to field a dozen sides for inter-part football from which the ship's team was selected for the King's Cup, the fleet trophy competed for each year. Another important sport was cross-country running in which ships provided teams of thirty men for the Arbuthnot Trophy, known as 'The Bronze Man'. As Rory O'Conor, commander of the *Hood* from 1933–6 and the driving force behind her sporting success, noted, 'Running is a healthy exercise possessing the great advantages of needing no special pitch and of being unaffected by bad weather. It is not everyone's idea of fun, but it has an ever-increasing number of adherents.'

There was certainly no shortage of adherents in the *Hood*, which won the Arbuthnot Trophy three years running between 1933 and 1935. However, as O'Conor indicated, cross-country running was something of a trial and with this twin brothers Fred and Frank Coombes (1935–8) would certainly have agreed. It is the autumn of 1935:

... To make a change, we took the opportunity to get ashore by taking part in a cross-country running race. It was a mistake to be regretted for a long time. All the runners were landed on Weymouth Pier to wait the start and, unfortunately, found a nice fresh water tap which was nectar compared with the flat, stale water aboard, so took in a bladder full which was a mistake as a toilet could not be found before the start. After a lot of milling and pushing about 150 of us set off ... but we soon became separated. Frank thinking that Fred was up in front increased his pace and Fred thinking that Frank was behind slowed down and we never did meet up till it was too late ... Frank, seeing that he had caught up with the ... well known figure of Leading Steward Barnes, the Navy runner, in front, decided that if he stuck near them there was more chance of stopping to relieve himself when the country bit was reached. Unfortunately that bit was never reached and he was still suffering from the effects of a bladder full of beautiful tap water when the finishing line was reached. Also, unfortunately, seeing a sign for toilets he was encouraged to make a sprint for them and in doing so passed a Leading Seaman, Potts, a promotion-seeking experienced runner who took offence at being pushed into 5th place by a common Boy and was heard to be casting parental doubts on a crafty Boy ...

Running was one of the activities in which officers competed alongside the men but others like cricket, golf, squash and polo remained very much the preserve of the wardroom. However, rugby was increasingly played by ratings of the Devonport Division after the Great War, many of whom no doubt saw it as the perfect opportunity to get some of their own back on officers. In this they were not alone. Mid Ross Warden (1940–1) recalls a physical match between the *Hood*'s wardroom and gunroom officers in the autumn of 1940:

> This was a golden opportunity to settle any outstanding scores. Anything goes was our motto, but alas we found our senior officers more than able to return elbows, knees and (when the referee was not looking) the occasional fist. Twice our Commander, who was referee, threatened to call a halt. However, there were no fatalities, and a good time was had by all.

The Navy had a great tradition in Rugby and in 1933 there were no fewer than fifty living members of the Royal Navy and Royal Marines Rugby Union with international caps, among them W J A Davies, constructor commander in the *Hood* in 1937–8.

The other sport offering the chance of beating hell out of an officer was of course boxing. AB Fred Copeman, Invergordon mutineer and champion pugilist:

> Mind you, I was a bit of a boxer and a footballer. I was all sport. And I was well known in the Navy, you see, especially in [the championships]. And I was lucky because in the ... championships I always met a big fat commander. And there's nothing better than the thrill of thumping an officer. And I used to thump them good and proper. I really had a good one there. I used to take a pasting, you know. But once I got that on they didn't last. And they always used to wait for old Fred. 'Right. Up we go!'

Like rugby and football, boxing was one of the few organised sports to survive the onset of war in 1939. On the evening of 29 July 1940 a match took place in the *Ark Royal* at Gibraltar with *Hood*'s men in the green corner and their hosts in the red. The *Hood* won by six bouts to four.

Other sports included fencing, shooting, field hockey, tennis and water polo. The latter enjoyed considerable popularity and games are recorded against the battleship USS *Maryland* at Gibraltar in March 1922, against the Mayor of Hartlepool's XI in September 1932, and at Split five years later against a Yugoslav naval side which swam out to the ship, thrashed the *Hood*'s team and then swam back to shore after tea on the messdecks. Then there was bayonets, a form of fencing in which the *Hood* excelled under O'Conor, her men carrying off the Home Fleet's Palmer Trophy between 1934 and 1936. However, the blue riband events were the sailing and particularly the pulling regattas. On these much of the ship's energies were expended as spring turned into summer.

From the moment of her commissioning in March 1920, rowing was a sport in which the *Hood* had a head start on the competition. Among the men bequeathed her from *Lion* was the cutter crew which had triumphed in the inaugural challenge for the Rodman Cup in 1919. Needless to say, they had little difficulty in repeating the performance at Portland that autumn, or in winning the Battle Cruiser Regatta off Lamlash on the Isle of Arran in August. Enormous prestige was attached to the Silver Coquerelle, the trophy which awaited the victor in the fleet pulling regatta in June each year. Rory O'Conor explains why:

> The Pulling Regatta is the principal sporting event in the Fleet, and for good reason. Eleven men only can represent their ship at football, and at cross-country running the largest team is thirty, but in a big-ship Regatta a team of nearly three hundred officers and men goes forth in the boats to do battle for their ship, and it is no wonder therefore that the Cock is the most highly prized of trophies; it is the reward of arduous training and of massed effort on a grand scale. [...] There is nothing in this world to surpass the heartfelt satisfaction and delight of a ship's company when the Cock comes on board – it is a moment worth living for and worth working for.

Victory, as O'Conor demonstrated in 1935, required an enormous organisation: a large committee chaired by the commander; an officer in charge of each of the twenty boats; picked racing coxswains to drive the men to the limit; a stockpile of oars, and above all weeks of arduous training. Fred and Frank Coombes were among O'Conor's oarsmen:

> At that time ... our only worry was that we had been caught up in the hard work of training to meet the needs of the Boys' cutters' crew. We did not mind the hard work of going out in a cutter at varied times during working hours, ... but [having to spend] at least one hour of each day, in our own time, ... pulling on our length of oar handle to raise the weight was sheer unadulterated hard work, particularly when the Instructor was walking round us giving us the occasional clip across the shoulders with a short length of knotted rope or stonnicky as it was called to encourage us. [...] After what seemed hour upon hour of boat pulling in practice and on the exercise frame came the honour of being named as bowmen in the Second Boys' Cutter's crew ... Almost every single hour of daylight was spent by some crew of the different divisions out in a pulling boat, practising and practising for the big day which seemed never to come.

The gunroom also had its part to play. Vice Admiral Sir Louis Le Bailly recalls the regatta campaign of 1933:

> Admiral James and Captain Binney ... set out to imbue the ship's company with the idea that the *Hood* should win the forthcoming fleet regatta. The gunroom soon discovered that we had a vital role to play in this. Traditionally the fleet gunrooms raced gigs for the Battenberg Trophy the day before the main regatta. A win by *Hood*'s gunroom would be taken as a good augury for the following day. Failure however would be regarded as a bad omen against the ship becoming Cock of the Fleet. Then short and lean I was, I suppose, the obvious choice for coxswain. But for those who were to undertake the hard work we gathered a formidable crew; Beckwith as stroke, Thurstan, Wainwright, Charles, MacFarlane and Gray. [...] But we were young and enthusiastic and how we trained. The chaplain, the Rev J C Waters, himself a notable oarsman was in charge and the new sub, Aylwin, urbane and highly civilised, also took a hand. Even the messman's food improved (subsidised by the wardroom I heard many years later). We practised at dawn and dusk and some afternoons too. I found my duties involved taking charge of the methylated spirit for blistered hands and bottoms. Gig's thwarts, however well polished, were not far removed from sandpaper.

Both attempts were rewarded with victory. Le Bailly:

> *Hood*'s gunroom won the Battenberg Trophy: and next day we raced again and won again. Much money changed hands as *Hood* became Cock of the Fleet. That evening Captain Binney sent down a case of champagne to the gunroom. Later I have a faint recollection of an invading posse of midshipmen from one of the battleships carrying me forcibly to our wardroom and casting me through the door, when I knew no more. The next morning I awoke with the first in a lifetime of hangovers, recovering sufficiently to go over with the rest of the crews to HMS *Nelson* to receive our trophies from the great John Kelly himself.

Even Fred Coombes got in the spirit: 'When [the day finally came] it was soon over but the taste of success and jubilations as we ... proclaimed to the whole Fleet that the Mighty *Hood* was now Cock of the Fleet was to be tasted for a long time.'

Equally, to surrender the Cock was the greatest of disasters. On 19 October 1921 the *Hood* lost the Battle Cruiser Cock to *Repulse* at Scapa Flow. Two days later it was handed over in a funereal atmosphere, the Marine band leading a procession consisting of the ship's goat mascot, Bill, and a party of midshipmen bearing the trophy, all to the strains of Chopin's *Funeral March*. However, once Capt Dudley Pound had received the Cock on behalf of the *Repulse* he was piped over the side to the Squadron's own air, *The Battle-Cruisers*.

However, there were many who believed that athletic excellence was being bought at the expense of fighting efficiency. One of them was Rear Admiral Frederic Dreyer who flew his flag in *Hood* from 1927–9:

> We carried out excellent and instructive practices by day and night, in which we did very well. But we would have done even better if there had been *competition* not merely in each Fleet but for the whole Navy. It seemed to me so odd to say, 'Yes, we will have a terrific competition in our Bisley rifle meetings, but we will not have all-Navy competition for guns of larger calibres as were carried out with great advantage before the First World War.'

It should be noted that Dreyer's tenure coincided with a hat trick of Cock and Rodman Cup victories for the *Hood*'s oarsmen between 1926 and 1928. Rory O'Conor, as can be imagined, took quite a different view in *Running a Big Ship*, the manual on ship husbandry he produced in 1937:

> It is easy to decry as pot-hunting the efforts of the enthusiastic to lead their ship to victory in sporting events, but those who say these things are often the ones who lack the spirit of leadership, or the ability to organise, and the will to carry things through. It is in many cases a facile excuse for slackness or indifference. Opportunities to prove ability to lead are too few in times of peace for any to be neglected. Can there be any reasonable person who would sooner be in a dull and apathetic ship as far as sport goes, as compared with being in one which is keen and spirited? A good ship is one who is always 'there or thereabouts' in the achievement of anything to which she puts her hand. There is no substitute for going all out for your ship whether in work or in play, unless, of course, you are prepared to toddle complacently towards your pension.

More impressive even than his results was the enormous spirit O'Conor was able to instil in his ship's company. No stone was left unturned. The embodiment of this spirit was George, a caricature in singlet and shorts who made his first appearance in the run-up to the 1935 Regatta. Here he is a year later in his footballing persona:

GEORGE

George is the spirit of the *Hood*. Everyone in the ship carries a little bit of him and therefore he is only able to go full steam ahead when all the *Hoods* are present in support. Only eleven men can play for us on the field (not counting the Referee), but eleven hundred can support them! **'Not Eleven – Eleven Hundred'** is the *Hood*'s motto, and when all hands are manning the touchline, George will be there too.

O'Conor's first campaign for the King's Cup in the autumn of 1933 was accompanied by a chough mascot on a pole, borne at all matches. Ties were produced in the ship's colours for officers to wear ashore, green with the chough emblem. To this O'Conor added preferential treatment for his players, the *Hood's* football team being assigned a separate mess with specially designed kit lockers. By the time it was all over George had been transmogrified into a stuffed chough in a glass case, taking his place in a Commander's lobby awash with trophies. For all this, it is clear that by the late 1930s sport had done its work in healing the wounds of the Invergordon Mutiny, and as war clouds gathered far greater emphasis was needed on fighting efficiency. O'Conor's prescriptions for sporting victory would die with him in the bitter waters of the Mediterranean but the spirit which infused them lived on.

Operational demands caused severe disruption to the Navy's sporting calendar as the 1930s wore on, though the mantle of victory was one the *Hood* shrugged off only reluctantly. Patrol duty off Spain prevented her competing for the Mediterranean Fleet Cock at Alexandria in 1938 but the record of trophies accumulated during her career outshines that of any other ship. Between 1920 and 1938, the last full year of competition, the *Hood* won the Rodman Cup at least four times, the Arbuthnot Trophy on at least three occasions and was Cock of the Fleet on no less than five. During the 1933–6 commission she won virtually every competition in the Home Fleet at least once. This success engendered enormous pride in her ship's company, though as the premier ship in the fleet the *Hood* had always been given a more than even chance of succeeding in anything she set herself to. As Admiral Sir Francis Pridham recalled when assuming command in 1936, 'I well remembered how Portsmouth had been cleared of all the best runners, boxers and footballers in order that the *Hood* should excel in any sports.'

But favoured she was from the very beginning. In November 1920 the *Hood's* Marine detachment was called on to supply the guard of honour at the burial of the Unknown Warrior in Westminster Abbey on Armistice Day, the men lining the Mall with bayonets fixed as the body passed on its way. As can be imagined, this did not go down well with the rest of the battlefleet which regarded *Hood* as the only vessel of its number to have escaped service in the Great War. A few pints in the canteen ashore and certain men would be passing loud opinions as to which was the best or worst ship in the fleet as the liberty boats passed on their way. Cdr Neville Cambell was a cadet in *Hood* in the 1920s: 'When I was returning in a launch at Cromarty, an egg was thrown and burst at my feet. Then a voice yelled from a nearby ship: "Yah! And what did the Mighty '*ood* do in the bloody war?"' Frequent brawls reflect a degree of resentment and no doubt the swagger of men who believed their ship to be a cut above any in the Navy. As AB Bob Tilburn (1938–41) put it, 'The majority of people who joined the *Hood* believed they were slightly above average because it was the flagship of the fleet.'

However, much of this rivalry was essentially good-humoured in nature, the result of high spirits, a release of tension and the competitiveness that always existed between ships of different home ports. After months of arduous wartime service *Hood* and *Rodney* viewed each other as 'chummy ships', but this did not prevent a good measure of ribaldry between the crews at Scapa Flow, and not just because the one was manned from Portsmouth and the other from Devonport. Over the winter of 1940–1 a rating in the *Rodney* was court-martialled for committing an enormity with a sheep, an event which naturally persuaded the crew of the *Hood* that, *faute de mieux*, his shipmates all indulged the same proclivity on the windswept braes of Orkney. OD Jon Pertwee (1940–1):

That night in the company of a phalanx of boozed-up *Hood* shipmates, I was weaving down the jetty prior to boarding our liberty boats, when we spied fifty or sixty liberty men off the *Rodney*, waiting to be picked up by their boats. 'Let's see if the sheep-loving bastards can swim,' cried a primed torpedo-man. With unanimous agreement we linked arms and advancing slowly, systematically swept the poor unfortunate men straight off the end of the jetty into the sea. Inevitably a few of us up front went in the 'oggin' with them, as the pushers at the back couldn't differentiate in the dark between *Rodney*'s crew and ours and didn't know when to stop. The drop from the end of the jetty was some fifteen feet and the resulting shouting and general hubbub from the tumbling men was tremendous. Apart from that the water was freezing and we realized that if we didn't get out quick, someone was going to drown. Suddenly the feud was forgotten, albeit temporarily, and everybody started helping everybody else to safety. Strange how immersion in cold water will kill off passion, in *all* its forms. The serio-comic end to the foray was that quite a few of the more drunken participants being capless and therefore unidentifiable, ended up in the 'Lions' Den' by finding themselves aboard the wrong ships. From that night on the crews of *Rodney* and the *Hood* were understandably never allowed ashore at the same time.

All this should of course be taken with a grain of salt but there was one rivalry which assumed a more serious dimension, that between *Hood* and another battlecruiser, the *Renown*. The *Hood* might be the greatest ship in the Navy but only *Renown* could claim for herself the attribute of a royal yacht. In 1919, 1920 and again between 1921–2 the *Renown* had carried the Prince of Wales on his wildly successful cruises of North America, Australasia and finally India and the Far East. In 1927 she took the Duke and Duchess of York on a state visit to Australia, making her at least as eligible as *Hood* to the nickname 'Cook's Tours' which had attached to the latter during the World Cruise of 1923–4.*

*The joke alludes to the package tours for holidaymakers introduced by Thomas Cook in the 1850s.

Though relations were never close, this did not prevent the Battle Cruiser Squadron being welded into a unit of formidable morale and efficiency during the tenure of Rear Admiral William James (1932–4). However, the great falling out came in the spring of 1935 when *Hood* and *Renown* collided following a gunnery exercise off the Spanish coast. The incident reflected badly on James's successor, Rear Admiral Sidney Bailey, who took a thoroughly partisan line in his attempts to exculpate himself and the *Hood's* officers of any responsibility in the affair. This was quite naturally resented in the *Renown* which felt itself the aggrieved party, yet had to carry the can at the subsequent courts martial. As James later put it, 'After the courts-martial would have been just the moment for the Admiral to have gone on board *Renown* ... and shown a big, generous spirit', but it was not to be and the incident served to rekindle the age-old rivalry between Portsmouth and Chatham, which *Renown* had as her home port. In the event, the Admiralty dissented from the findings of the courts martial and shared the blame among them but the damage was done and ill-feeling prevailed between the two ships until *Renown* was taken in hand for reconstruction in the summer of 1936. The falling-out expressed itself in various ways, from *Renown's* failure to offer congratulations to *Hood* on her regatta victory in June 1935 to the petty animosity that developed between the two ships' companies.

However, rivalries of this sort were not confined to the Navy. In the early 1920s the conclusion of the Washington Treaty and the realisation that the Royal Navy had lost the predominant position she had held for over a century was the cause of much tension between it and the United States Navy. To this was added the jealousy of the British matelot for the superior pay of his American counterpart, flaunted now in ports all over the world. Rear Admiral Hugh Rodman USN may have presented the cup which bore his name in recognition of the 'ties of friendship and brotherhood which have been formed and ripened into maturity between the officers and men of the British and American Navies in the Grand Fleet' but the Grand Fleet was no more. Already in January 1921 the Combined Fleet exercises off Gibraltar had pitted the Royal Navy against the 'American Battle Fleet', and not for the last time either. Now in September 1922, just seven months after the signing of the Treaty, the centennial celebrations of Brazilian independence at Rio de Janeiro provided both navies with an opportunity to show which was the first among equals. The first indication that *Hood* had been selected to represent the Navy came during a visit to the ship by King George V at Torquay in July. Soon after it was announced that she and the battlecruiser *Repulse* would be sailing to Rio where a sports competition would be held for the attending navies. Throughout much of July and August preparations went on at Devonport which made it clear that this was to be rather more than a goodwill cruise. National prestige was at stake and neither expense nor effort was spared to equip the Battle Cruiser Squadron for the voyage or to strip the fleet of her finest sportsmen.

On 14 August *Hood* and *Repulse* sailed from Devonport, reaching Rio by way of Gibraltar and Cape Verde on 3 September. On 29 August *Hood* crossed the Equator for the very first time, celebrating the fact with time-honoured relish. Already at Rio were the battleships *Minas Geraes* and *São Paulo* of the Brazilian navy, three cruisers of the Imperial Japanese Navy led by the elderly *Idzumo*, and a pair of sloops representing Portugal and Mexico. Then on the 5th the American representation arrived in the shape of the battleships *Maryland* and *Nevada*. Mid Robert Elkins' journal conveys the bellicose mood of the *Hood*: 'The *Maryland*, which is one of the most modern battleships afloat, looked very small compared to ourselves and *Repulse*. She was also very dirty.' The *Hood* seems to have crossed swords with *Maryland* once already, at Gibraltar in March when the Americans had referred to her as 'some fine picket boat'. So there were evidently a few scores to settle. The first opportunity for getting even came on the 7th when each ship landed a naval battalion for a parade through the city, Elkins declaring *Hood's* to have been 'by far the smartest'. Though no points were at stake, Elkins also judged the Battle Cruiser Squadron to have provided the best illuminations that night 'since we were the only ships which darkened ship before switching on the circuits'. So to the athletics and on the 8th, a day of triumph for the British. Elkins could barely contain himself: 'In every race our competitors walked through, the Japanese and Americans being nowhere. That is the sort of thing which raises British prestige, which has suffered here just lately at the hands of the Yanks.' However, on the morning of the 10th came the first setback for the squadron. In a result that in retrospect could surprise no one, the Brazilian navy defeated the British 2–0 in the football final. Worse was to come. In the regatta that afternoon the Brazilians won the skiffs and, of all humiliations, the Americans took the seamen's cutter race, though a measure of pride was salvaged by the midshipmen's cutter. Things were different in the athletics finals on the 11th, the Squadron winning nine of fifteen events and, crowed Elkins, 'knocking the Yanks into a cocked hat. The tug of war was an absolute walkover.' But it was the boxing competition that brought the 'Naval Olympics' to a truly memorable climax. That same evening four thousand British and American matelots crammed into a marquee pitched on the outskirts of the city. There were eight bouts on the programme and on its outcome depended overall victory in the Games. By the final bout the British were leading by four wins to three. The Squadron had reason to be confident since their last boxer was none other than the Navy and British Amateur champion, Stoker Petty Officer Spiller of the *Hood*. Mid Gerald Cobb (1921–3?) takes up the story: 'Spiller advanced to touch gloves with his rival – as all boxers in previous bouts had done – when the American immediately struck Spiller with a straight left, followed by a right hook. Curtains for Spiller. Uproar!'

Only prompt action by Rear Admiral Sir Walter Cowan, who stepped into the ring and ordered his men to give three cheers for the US Navy, prevented the situation turning ugly. In the event, the bout was declared null and void, Cowan's counterpart apologised and the Squadron won the tourney, but it had been, as they say, a close-run thing. The following day *Maryland* weighed anchor and left for New York, cheered as she went by the *Hood's* company, though what they muttered under their breath is anyone's guess. On the quarterdeck that night the *Hood* hosted a Grand Ball attended by President Pessoa and the cream of Rio society, probably the most sumptuous event ever celebrated in her. The centrepiece was a huge fountain surrounded by a grove of palm trees hung with coloured lights. As Elkins wrote in his journal, 'Preparations were on a most lavish scale and must cost hundreds of pounds'. The following day, having collected three magnificent trophies for their sporting achievements, the Squadron took part in the closing act of the centennial celebrations, an illuminated water pageant in Botafogo Bay in which the *Hood's* chief painter played the part of Britannia. In all the *Hood's* career, in all her great voyages, there can have been few spectacles to match this. On 14 September 1922 the Squadron swept out of the anchorage and into the Atlantic leaving a flotilla of Brazilian destroyers trailing in its wake.

For all its splendour the Brazilian cruise was only a taste of things to come. On 29 November 1923 a squadron of ships embarked on the greatest circumnavigation undertaken by the Royal Navy since Commodore Anson's heroic feat of 1740–4. The World Cruise of the Special Service Squadron as it came to be known was first mooted in the spring of 1923. At the Imperial Conference called for that autumn the Admiralty intended not only to emphasise the dependence of the dominions on British sea power, but to encourage them to participate in its maintenance through the creation of their own naval staffs and by contributing to regional and trade defence with money, ships and base facilities. The World Cruise had therefore a far more overtly navalist agenda than the three cruises made by the Prince of Wales in the *Renown* between 1919 and 1922 which preceded it. It was also far larger and more ambitious than these, embracing not only a large part of the empire but also the United States and South America in an itinerary covering 38,000 miles in ten months. It remained to carry out the immense organisation needed to make the cruise possible: assessing the safety of over thirty anchorages in the season in question; verifying the availability of oil and provisions; arranging events and entertainments in concert with local authorities; above all, budgeting for the enormous cost of sending half a dozen ships and 4,600 men around the world. At an economical speed of 11 knots the squadron's fuel requirement was assessed at 110,000 tons at approximately £3 per ton. Total *additional* expenditure of refitting, fuel and stores above ordinary service, including a generous £8,000 allowance for shipboard entertaining, was calculated at £239,000. There was to be a Squadron 'At Home' laid on by the *Hood* at every major port of call while her companions were to host children's parties, dances and other entertainments at any location visited longer than a week. Sports events were to be participated in ashore. As before the Brazilian cruise two years earlier, the *Hood* was taken in hand for refitting at Devonport, first in August and then in November 1923. The final act was the landing of known troublemakers before the battlecruisers sailed without fanfare on the morning of 27 November. For most it was the beginning of an unforgettable adventure, the zenith of the peacetime Navy. For others like the newly married Lt (E) Geoffrey Wells (1923–4) it was a desperate wrench:

> We were casting off the wires and by 0730 hrs we were clear of No 6 wharf, Keyham Dockyard. As the engines started I felt a pang of realisation of the fact that I was here, Inez in London and that realisation only grew greater as we steamed passed Plymouth Hoe and turned seawards. Just to think of 10 months ahead, 30,000 odd miles steaming! I can't.

The Special Service Squadron consisted of *Hood*, *Repulse* and the 1st Light Cruiser Squadron under Rear Admiral the Hon Sir Hubert Brand, including *Delhi*, *Dauntless*, *Danae* and *Dragon*. With them sailed HMS *Dunedin*, on passage to join the New Zealand Division of the Royal Navy. In overall command of the Squadron was Vice Admiral Sir Frederick Field flying his flag in *Hood*. Field's reputation rests on his disastrous tenure as First Sea Lord during the Invergordon Mutiny but his tact and diplomacy during the World Cruise earned him the headline 'Freddy Field Proves Reg'lar Guy' in San Francisco in July 1924 and he was to prove an inspired choice for this command. A truly gifted speaker, Field's skills as a conjuror (he was a member of the Magic Circle) were guaranteed to break the ice at any dinner party. The initial stop on the cruise was Freetown, Sierra Leone, where the *Hood* received an elephant's tusk, the first in a succession of big-game curios which were to enliven her wardroom for the next fifteen years. Then came Cape Town where the pattern for the rest of the cruise was set: an official reception ashore; the landing of the Squadron's naval battalion for a march through the city with fixed bayonets; banyan parties (picnics) and excursions into the hinterland; an outpouring of generosity and patriotic fervour reciprocated with tours of the ship and lavish entertainments aboard. Introductions made, gifts exchanged, engagements sealed. It was here, too, that the Squadron suffered the first of over 150 desertions, but the cruise as a whole upheld the British matelot's reputation for good behaviour in foreign climes.

After South Africa came the British protectorate of Zanzibar. A small island off the mandated territory of Tanganyika, the Sultanate of Zanzibar was perhaps an unlikely destination for the Special Service Squadron but the Royal Navy had something to exorcise in these waters. On 20 September 1914 the third-class cruiser *Pegasus* had hauled down her colours under heavy fire from the German light cruiser *Königsberg*. Not only was it the first occasion in over a hundred years that a British ship had surrendered, but her humiliation had played out in full view of the citizenry of Zanzibar. The *Königsberg* had been dealt with on the Rufiji River in Tanganyika in July 1915 by monitors sent out from Britain but the Admiralty no doubt felt that prestige needed to be restored. Besides, the

Sultan had loyally stood by Britain in a territory just fifty miles off German Tanganyika. Reaching Zanzibar on the morning of 12 January 1924 the Squadron was received by the Sultan Sayyid Khalifa ben Hamid in his yacht with a string of war canoes in tow. Not for the first time the 3pdr saluting guns on the *Hood*'s flag decks boomed out, twenty-one guns for the Sultan and then fifteen in reply to the light cruiser USS *Concord*, also in harbour. A landing party of Royal Marines and field guns was put ashore for a ceremonial march past and there was instruction for non-swimmers in the Zanzibar Channel. There were trips to the orchards from which came 75 per cent of the world's cloves or, in the case of Lt Wells, a futile attempt to repair the Sultan's electric generator. The Squadron refuelled from a waiting oiler and *Hood* was in receipt of twelve tons of fresh meat and vegetables. Then on the 15th the Sultan arrived aboard for lunch in oppressive heat, the crews of the saluting guns busy once more. The following day he led the Squadron out to sea in his yacht and, after hearing another twenty-one-gun salute, watched it disappear over the horizon.

Next came the tropical splendour of Trincomalee in Ceylon and then Malaya where officers gagged down a Chinese banquet in Kuala Lumpur while their men toured the rubber plantations. Then Singapore where, in token of its broken alliance with Japan, the Navy wanted to build a fortified base for its ships in the event of war in the East. Of the catastrophic failure of British planning in the East, *Repulse* would herself be a victim off the same coasts seventeen years later. On 17 February the Squadron weighed anchor and embarked on a ten-day voyage down the east coast of Sumatra, through the Sunda Strait where the *Exeter* would likewise meet her fate at the hands of the Imperial Japanese Navy in March 1942, past the extinct cone of Krakatoa and at length to Fremantle in Western Australia where Joey the wallaby joined the ship as a new mascot. In Australia and New Zealand awaited the greatest reception for the Special Service Squadron. At Adelaide the Squadron received nearly 70,000 visitors, at Melbourne 486,000. Lieutenant (E) Geoffrey Wells:

> We remained at Melbourne for seven days and enormous crowds besieged us. Numbers unprecedented percolated into every place in the ship. Women fainted on the gangways which almost gave beneath the weight. To get ashore became a feat of no mean skill and elbow power. The *Repulse* also suffered. The little boys of the crowd fared best, they could squeeze where their sisters could not and could deal more rapidly with the ladders.

Half a million people lined Sydney Harbour to watch the Squadron glide in on 9 April. But here, amid the hysteria, sports and festivities, came a major setback for the Navy: the announcement in London that the Singapore base would not be built. Nonetheless, the Australian government ordered a pair of heavy cruisers from British yards and detached the light cruiser *Adelaide* to join the Squadron along with ten midshipmen from the Naval College at Jervis Bay. After eleven days of sport and entertainment Field's battlecruisers sailed for Wellington, their crews exhausted. Mid George Blundell:

> I was running a picket boat, which meant solid work from 6am to 2am or midnight. And on my day off it meant entertaining visitors or being entertained ashore. The shore entertainment was a terrible duty. The official dances were a nightmare at which one had to stay until about 1am. Sometimes I could hardly stand up, having had little sleep for several days. The job of laundering and keeping our clothes spotlessly clean was also a nightmare.

A trying passage of the Tasman Sea left officers and men so drained that all civic functions in Wellington had to be cancelled. However, time and energy was found for one of those shipboard children's parties for which the Navy was famous. Perhaps it was the prolonged separation from their own families, but sailors always went to enormous lengths to entertain children aboard. Merry-go-rounds rigged on the main capstan; slides swishing down from the bridge to a cushioned landing below; a 'flight' in one of the ship's boats dangled from a derrick; the Marine band in full swing; 'Aunt Sally' in the form of a bluejacket dodging missiles being hurled at him from all quarters; tours of the ship and vast teas served out on deck by matelots dressed up as pirates. On 8 May Earl Jellicoe, now Governor General of New Zealand, joined the *Hood* and, hoisting his flag beside Field's, volunteered to ease the burden by taking the Middle watch (midnight–0400) on the bridge for the run to Auckland. Here another 78,000 visited the *Hood* but as Geoffrey Wells noted, the ship's company had had enough of the World Cruise by the time she sailed for Fiji:

> It is very noticeable on board that now passed New Zealand everyone seems to be getting bored with the cruise. I certainly am. Going round the world is alright. In fact being paid to go round and under such circumstances as this is great but one needs a fortnight's holiday at home in the middle of it. Everything moves at such a pace.

Spirits were no doubt revived with draughts of kava, the intoxicating drink of Fiji, and then by the Polynesian beauties of Western Samoa where *Hood* dropped anchor for a few hours on 29 May. But by the time the Squadron reached Hawaii on 6 June a phased suspension of the issue of alcohol had left Field's ships 'dry' in deference to the Prohibition laws of the United States. Still, a dance for 1,100 guests given by the *Hood* at Honolulu, though it toasted the King and President Coolidge in water, was remembered as the finest of the cruise. Then to British Columbia and perhaps Field's most important remit, to encourage Canada to maintain a pair of cruisers on each coast, a suggestion which raised a storm of protest in Ottawa. At San Francisco the Squadron was given a truly remarkable reception, though it must have proved a great disappointment to the apostle of air power, Brigadier General Billy Mitchell. Learning of a plan to use an aircraft to drop a symbolic floral key 'to unlock the Golden Gate' onto *Hood's* quarterdeck, Mitchell took the controls himself, intent on making a further demonstration of the vulnerability of the capital ship to air attack. However, his efforts resulted only in the key pitching unceremoniously into the bay as the guns of Fort Scott boomed out in welcome. It was the first time in forty years that a large British squadron had dropped anchor in American waters and Field's ships made a lasting impression, not only on the city but on relations between their two countries. As Mayor James Rolph put it, 'Your presence with us today will, we trust, make a pact between the British-speaking races even closer. We take a pride in your magnificent ships, which we feel will never be used except in the defense of the world's peace. We surrender our city unto you. We capitulate.'

Meanwhile, it was quite clear that the Squadron's efforts to adhere to Prohibition greatly outstripped those of their hosts ashore. Geoffrey Wells has this memory of the Bohemian Club in San Francisco:

'I guess you boys will have a drink' said one of our hosts producing, as the conjuror does the rabbit, a bottle of whiskey which he passed to the bar attendant who therewith dispensed whiskey and sodas. We received sympathy for our stocks on board being locked up and it became apparent that the only dry community in the district was the British ships. There were some that did not believe we were dry and could not understand that we had no bottles in our cabins. Our reason for not having any was that it was not allowed. This absolutely baffled the American mind!

On 11 July the *Hood* began the longest leg of her journey, the 3,440 miles that separate San Francisco from Balboa and the navigation of the Panama Canal. Almost immediately the 1st Light Cruiser Squadron parted company with *Hood*, *Repulse* and *Adelaide* and steered for Callao, the first stop in a lengthy tour of South America. Field's ships reached Balboa on the 23rd, took in mail and a few stores and then proceeded towards the Canal, which *Hood* would become the largest vessel to traverse. The following morning the Squadron set off down the eight miles of the Culebra Cut. Then came the Gatún Locks with which *Hood* at last reached the Caribbean. The cost of her passage to the Admiralty was $22,399.50 at 50 cents per ton – a little over £5,000 in the currency of the day. In *Hood*, 'General subdued cheers were lead by the Constructor Commander on sighting what he described as 'the same sea as our wives see', but there remained stops at Jamaica, Nova Scotia and Quebec before the *Hood* could return down the St Lawrence to Newfoundland and make for home. At Halifax, Nova Scotia, Field had to deal with the consequences of his early remarks in Victoria, BC, but on 21 September the *Hood*, *Repulse* and *Adelaide* finally quit Topsail Bay, Newfoundland, to the longed-for strains of *Rolling Home*. The wardroom contest to establish the port of call with the most beautiful women placed Wellington first and Kingston, Jamaica, last though voter fatigue may account for this. A week later and with exquisite timing they were reunited with Brand's cruiser squadron off the Lizard, before Field took his ships into Cawsand Bay and thence to Devonport. In his diary Wells wrote, 'Joy such as this is too great to describe by words alone. Ten months ago I left my new possession and now I am with her again.'

Large-scale cruises continued to be made, notably those of *Renown* to Australia in 1927 and *Eagle* to South America in 1931, but nothing would ever approach that of the Special Service Squadron. To these the battlecruiser type was to prove perfectly suited, and for a fleeting moment the World Cruise united technology, treasure, organisation and opportunity in a spectacle never to be repeated, the high point of British sea power between the wars. For the 4,600 men who took part, the two million who visited the ships and the millions more who witnessed their passing, the World Cruise left memories and experiences only now fading into oblivion.

3

Days and Years

THE TECHNICAL ACHIEVEMENT of building the *Hood* was matched by the immense powers of organisation required to give her life, to transform her thousands of tons of steel plating, machinery and equipment into the formidable instrument of war and peace she was meant to be. How this was accomplished and maintained by her crew over a period of months and years, and how her days and nights were filled with constant labour and unceasing vigil is the subject of this chapter.

Battle or mishap apart, no episode in a warship's life could ever be quite as fraught as commissioning day. Weeks or months in advance the commander, first lieutenant and senior departmental officers would come aboard, lists in hand, to prepare for this first and most complex evolution of their tenure. The first priority was fixing the Watch and Quarter Bill by which each of over 1,300 men might know to which division and watch he belonged, what his duties were and where he performed them both on and off watch, where he messed and stowed his hammock and gear, and above all what his action station was. The end product of this fiendish task was the commissioning card handed to each man on arrival. Joining the *Hood* on 31 August 1933, a piece of cardboard told Boy X that he was in Top Division, and that his duties were to be performed in First Part of Port Watch; that he was to reside on the Boys' messdeck and find his Action Station at the Deflection Calculator for the 5.5in guns in the spotting top; that his station for Ammunitioning Ship was in one of the 15in magazines, and for abandoning her by No 6 Carley Raft. And likewise for virtually every man in the ship.

Early on commissioning day fleets of lorries began arriving from barracks, ships and shore establishments to disgorge parties of men and their gear onto the jetty. Mustered in the Royal Naval Barracks, they marched through HM Dockyard behind a seaman band with mace bearer until they found themselves under *Hood*'s immense hull, guns and tiers of decks. Others appeared singly or in groups from training or a spell of leave, all loaded with the hammocks, kitbags, cases, gasmasks and ditty boxes with which they would make their life aboard. At the head of the ship's brow they reported to a regulating petty officer, informing him whether they were 'Grog' or 'Temperance', and then fell in by divisions at their allotted spot on the upper deck.* Once mustered, the divisional officer led them down to stow their kit and sling their hammocks on the messdecks which would in all probability be their home for the next two or three years. Having shaken down, a man would be ordered to find a seat at his cramped mess table and wait for the noisy crush of men settling in around him to subside. As Paymaster Lt Cdr E C Talbot-Booth RNR recalled, it was often a nervous moment: 'All officers and men are feeling rather like new boys at school, unused to their new surroundings and wondering if they will find any old friends; wondering if the ship will be a happy one.' For most the answer to this question would not be long in coming. The arrival of the last contingent permitted the White Ensign to be hoisted, the commissioning pendant to be run up to the masthead and the captain to report his ship as duly commissioned to the commander-in-chief of the port and, if he was aboard, to the admiral whose flag she was flying.

The nature of the relationship between an admiral and his flag captain was one of the nodal points in the life of a great ship. The technical distinction is nicely made by the Rev Beardmore, ship's chaplain between 1939 and 1941: 'The Captain ... looks upon himself as the "Father" of the ship – he commands it; the Admiral is a passenger, in that he is in command, not of the ship, but of the Squadron or Fleet of which the ship is the flagship.' But there was more to an admiral's role than that. Admiral Lord Chatfield:

> The limelight shines more fiercely on an admiral than on his contemporaries in the other fighting services, because he lives continuously among those he commands. [...] His duty in war is to lead his fleet in the forefront of battle and to fit himself to do so he must in peace, also, be among, and personally intimate with, those whom he is going to lead and inspire. As he paces the quarter-deck he is as visible to all and sundry as are the captain and commander. The officers and men value this; they know their admiral, so to speak, intimately, they feel it is *their* flagship, that it is *their* duty to bring honour on the flag she flies.

As a flagship, the nature of the captain's authority in *Hood* was almost always conditioned by the reality of this attachment. The famous naval writer Bartimeus (Capt Lewis Ritchie) captures the essence of the captain's command, dependent on the ship yet curiously divorced from her until the moment of reckoning:

> The captain of a battleship carries the ultimate responsibility for every word spoken by, and for every action of, an individual on board his ship. His also is

*'Grog' or 'Temperance' refers to a man's choice to take up his rum ration or not.

the more immediate responsibility for her safety and war efficiency. For conduct in war he is guided by the articles of war, which enjoin that he shall 'use his utmost exertion to bring his ship into action, and during such action, in his own person encourage his inferior officers and men to fight courageously.' Here you will see that two of his responsibilities, the safety of his ship and the taking of her into action, must be balanced one against the other. [...] In as much as he must take every decision himself, and has to bear full responsibility for it, he is completely alone. The ship is moving through the water at whatever speed he alone has ordered. The guns' crews are all at their stations. When he gives the order they will open fire. When they fire, whether they hit the enemy or not will depend upon the training he has ensured these crews have had, and whether the whole enormously complex mechanism of fire control and guns has been maintained to produce its maximum efficiency at this moment. And lastly he has to consider the moment ahead when the enemy's shells will burst on board his ship. How his ship's company will react to that almost inevitable moment, how much or how little it will affect their morale, will depend upon things almost indefinable, upon 'all their yesterdays', upon the spirit that he has instilled throughout the ship. The loneliness of high command accompanies him wherever he may be, on board, at sea or in harbour, in peace and in war. He lives alone in fact as much as in spirit.

It was the commander's duty as executive officer to deliver into the captain's (and implicitly the admiral's) hands a ship capable of meeting every demand that circumstance and tactical necessity might make of her. To this every facet of her life and the life of every man embarked in her was subordinated.

The ship commissioned, the first full muster of 'Divisions' heralded the stirring of her routine and organisation. If the captain and his officers were the head of this organisation then its heart was the divisional system. By it the *Hood*'s crew was separated into thirteen divisions based on their trade and the part of the ship for which they were responsible, each numbering about a hundred men. Seamen were gathered into three divisions – forecastlemen, topmen and quarterdeckmen – each of which manned one of the ship's 15in turrets, the fourth being crewed by the Royal Marine detachment which formed a division in its own right. There were separate divisions for torpedo and communications ratings, along with those for boys, engine room artificers and mechanicians, the accountant department and another for miscellaneous ratings including artisans, ordnance and electrical artificers, cooks, writers and sick berth attendants. Like the seamen, the stoker complement was split into three divisions, in their case by watches: red, white and blue. And in war a fourteenth division was added: 'Hostilities-Only' ratings. Each division was placed under a lieutenant or lieutenant commander who was charged with its discipline, training, clothing and organisation, and who in turn placed the greatest reliance on the chief and petty officers who made up the heart of the *Hood*'s company. On this system turned the organisation of the entire ship and its ultimate purpose as a fighting unit of the fleet.

So it was that early afternoon on commissioning day found much of the crew mustered once more on the quarterdeck and in the port and starboard batteries. At the bugle call they laid aft to hear the captain's address. AB Len Wincott, who served in *Hood* in 1926, recalls the anticipation which always attended this occasion:

It was an event which set the tone for the future life of the ship's company. 'To be or not to be' was the question, and in this case a much more worrying one than the young chap from Denmark ever faced. The point at issue was whether this would, or would not, be a 'happy ship' – the alternative to which was a 'hell ship'. True, that term was generally reserved for the merchant service and naval ratings rarely used it; but that did not stop them from thinking it.

Reassured or otherwise, the cooks of the mess would then draw their comrades' 'mess traps' or utensils from one of the storerooms and hasten to serve the first meal aboard: tea at 1530. Afterwards the commander would likely drill his men in such evolutions as 'Collision Stations' or 'Fire Stations'. If the ship were already fully ammunitioned then the only call on the gunnery department would be to assume the duty of recording the magazine temperatures. Otherwise the crew would begin the dangerous task of ammunitioning ship from an assortment of barges and lighters loaded with shells, torpedoes, cordite cartridges and detonators. But this was unusual and for most the last official act of commissioning day would be a medical inspection of all new ratings in the sick bay. Then to the messdeck and animated discussion over supper on the prospects for the commission with fellow newcomers or with those remaining from the old. For some 'Pipe Down' at 2230 would confirm their choice or fortune of hammock berth. For others, bumped by heads or tormented by lights or ventilators, the night would provide a somewhat different realisation.

Shortly after 0500 a bugle call would herald the beginning of the first full day of the commission. By 0530 the duty petty officers were passing through the messdecks bellowing the old refrain 'Wakey, wakey, rise and shine. Sun's scorchin' yer bleedin' eyes out', under decks lashed with rain or caked with snow. A mug of 'ky' (cocoa) inside them, 0545 found the duty boys of the morning watch hard at work, to be followed at 0600 by the bulk of the ship's company fallen in to 'Clean Ship'. Over the next hour or so the entire quarterdeck would be scrubbed down from the stern forward to the aft screens, and the brass bollards and other brightwork polished to a brilliant sheen. In the engine spaces, especially on the control platforms, this took the form of cleaning the steel deck plates, whitewashing the more prominent stretches of lagging and polishing the array of brass voice pipes, steel ladders, dials and indicators which filled every space. If, as was often the case, the ship was emerging from a period of refitting then the greatest call on the time and energy of the crew was in getting her to an acceptable degree of cleanliness. Under certain circumstances this might require special measures on the part of the ship's officers. AB Wincott:

> Now, to achieve the high degree of cleanliness desired, an unofficial tradition was practised by some captains which meant, in brief, roping in a large number of men for extra work in their free time. The captain simply passed the word to his commander who ... gave instructions that conditions be created to rope the needed numbers in. Everything was done verbally and nowhere was there written proof, but every man on the ship was aware what was happening. The regulating staff under the command of the master-at-arms moved into action. Not one little infringement was passed up, and if no infringements existed they were invented. Consequently, every day, at commander's defaulters, there was a large crowd of men, mostly seamen of course, waiting to be punished.

Whether this was resorted to or not, the duties themselves were unchanging. Len Wincott (1926):

> ... Scattered round different parts of the ship, some with emery paper, scrubbing away at the dockyard-painted steel deck to make it look like a mirror; some with wash-cloths and buckets of 'suji-muji', a liquid concoction of five parts water and five parts any kind of powerful cleanser guaranteed to remove unwanted marks more effectively than flames; and of course a large body with the inevitable 'holy stone', called by the men 'the sailor's bible'.

To this desultory work the British sailor gave a fair proportion of his existence until time or higher rating exempted him from it. Boy Fred Coombes:

> ... It was no surprise that our lives were to be spent not in being sailors but in endless, meaningless jobs such as chipping paintwork, washing it, and any time-consuming job that could be easily monitored. Of the jobs that we fancied, such as smacking paint about with a brush, the nearest thing we got to painting was to go round on our hands and knees scraping up after the painting party; their time was more important than ours.

At such moments the imprecations came thick and fast: 'Join the Navy and see the world' and especially 'Roll on me fuckin' dozen', a reference to the twelve years of a man's first term of service. By the 1920s a new generation of naval officer was beginning to recognise the senselessness of requiring a man to devote the better part of his time to work of this sort, as the Navy began to fall astern in technology and fighting efficiency. But tradition died hard in the Royal Navy. Admiral Sir Frank Twiss, eventually Second Sea Lord, admitted as much in his memoirs:

The number of officers and men in ships was dictated by the number required to fight ships in action. [...] This meant that when you weren't at war there were far more people living on board than were actually needed to keep the ship afloat, clean and working. It was, of course, accepted as gospel that men must be kept busy. People who weren't occupied became troublemakers; there was nothing else for them to do. So the routine in the Navy, particularly in big ships, was strictly designed to keep men working and keen. Looking back on it now, it was an astonishing performance. For example, a battleship in the Atlantic Fleet before the Second World War, might have nine hundred to a thousand men on board, of which only a proportion could regularly polish all the brass-work, clean all the paintwork, pick up the oil in the engine room or whatever it was, quite easily, in the first couple of hours. So what did they do for most of the day?

The answer is that, in the *Hood* particularly, they continued to polish and clean until the coming war required their skills to be applied elsewhere. Still, there was no denying the pride of seeing an expanse of stained teak decking brought to a lustrous manila finish. A fortnight before his death at the age of ninety-eight in June 2003, CPO Harry Cutler, who went to sea in the *Hood* in 1922, recalled these lines for the author:

> A few drops of water,
> A few grains of sand,
> A sailor with a holystone
> Makes a deck look grand.

The 'holystone', a sandstone block, was supplied by the Admiralty, but the silver sand favoured for scrubbing decks and woodwork had to be obtained in the traditional manner. Among the Coombes twins' first tasks on being selected to crew one of the ship's cutters early in 1936 was to sail her from Portsmouth Harbour to Hayling Island to collect a boatload. The expedition resulted not only in them missing the tide as they returned up the Solent but in their being eaten alive by sand-fleas shovelled up in the cargo as they did so. 'There was always something to learn at sea.'

At 0650, just as the men were drying down the upper deck, a bugle call summoned the cooks of the mess to the galley lifts bearing breakfast for the crew. Ten minutes later a mass piping by call-boys with their bosun's whistles had the men gratefully heading for the messdecks to tuck into the offerings of the galley. Then a chance to wash and change into the 'rig of the day' before the order was passed for 'Quarters Clean Guns' at 0755. At the same moment a party of signalmen was gathering round the ensign staff on the quarterdeck for the first of the Navy's great rituals, morning Colours. On the stroke of 0800 (0900 in winter) the signal was given to a Marine corporal to ring the ship's bell eight times. At the same moment a dozen buglers on 'X' turret sounded 'Attention', as the band of the Royal Marines struck up 'God Save the King'. Men stiffened, officers saluted and all faced aft as the ensign was slowly hoisted up its staff, reaching the gold crown just as the final bars crashed out. Meanwhile, a similar ceremony was being performed with the Union Flag and seaman buglers on the forecastle.

The tolling of eight bells indicated not eight o'clock but the start of the forenoon watch, one of the six four-hourly segments into which the naval day was divided. At noon came the afternoon watch and then at 1600 the two dog watches whose purpose is described below. These were followed by the first watch at 2000, the middle watch at midnight and finally the morning watch at 0400 with which the cycle was completed. Since few men carried timepieces, most relied on the ship's bell to tell them what time it was, which it did by tolling off the half-hours incrementally through each watch. So it was that a man going on duty in the morning watch might well ask a mate to 'shake me at seven bells' of the middle one (0330) so that he could have half an hour to rouse himself for work. The dog watches were divided in order to permit a daily change of watch for a ship working a two-watch routine. This routine, which the *Hood* observed throughout her career, was called 'watch and watch', and under it most of the ship's company was divided into two identical watches, known as port and starboard; the engineering department, however, had three watches: red, white and blue. These alternated duties so that every essential function was being attended to by a full complement of men at any given moment. In most cases this provided an individual with an eight-hour day of work, rising to twelve hours at sea and probably sixteen or twenty in war as need or circumstance dictated. Since a ship on war patrol required her entire crew to go to action stations at dawn and dusk each day regardless of other duties, it will be understood what the impact of sleep deprivation was on their morale and efficiency. But this was exceptional and in the ordinary run of things 'watch and watch' represented a perfectly tolerable lifestyle. Thus, if the divisional system formed the basis of the ship's organisation then the watch system provided the rhythm of her routine.

Colours over, work continued about the ship. For many this meant more cleaning and polishing, a dose of compulsory 'physical jerks' under a PT instructor or, for the more expert seaman, the splicing of wire and rope, maintenance of blocks and tackles and forming of grommets and heaving lines which kept his vessel seaworthy. But for others it signalled the resumption of that other labour which filled the hours of Britain's bluejackets: care of the ship's paintwork. As Fred Coombes said, this was not so much the adding of fresh layers as the scraping, chipping, polishing and scrubbing which provided the perfect surface for paint to be applied. The actual application was left only to the most skilled practitioners. Fine paintwork had to be protected not only from the assaults of the elements but also those of brutality. This translated into punishments for those who wantonly ill-treated paintwork and, more commonly, in the necessity for exterior surfaces to be washed down with fresh water if splashed while scrubbing decks or following rain or periods at sea. The other enemy was rust, which required the surface to be scraped down to the metal and the offending patch treated with oil. About four times a year, ordinary wear and tear, a special occasion or a change of assignment would require the entire ship to be painted. This evolution, which usually took a day for the sides, masts and yards, required the ship to go 'out of routine' and as such was a welcome change for the crew.

In the 1930s it apparently took £135 and four tons of paint to cover the exterior of the ship. The issuing of paint was in the hands of the commissioned shipwright and his men, but its supply was the responsibility of the paymaster commander who presided over that other great edifice of shipboard organisation, the central storekeeping system. On commissioning the *Hood* was provided by the Admiralty with a six-month supply of 10,000 items weighing in at over 400 tons. These items, ranging from bedding to rapeseed oil, were stowed in any of forty stores and compartments throughout the nether regions of the vessel, including the paint store on the lower deck forward. It was the duty of the supply department to keep a permanent tally of the quantity and location of these, the majority of which would eventually be issued from the central store on the main deck. The only items not on the paymaster's ledger were ordnance and engineering spares and equipment, which were looked after by the gunnery and engineering departments respectively. The ship's stores were divided into four broad categories: permanent stores (such as hoses, piping and fittings for which replacement was occasionally necessary), consumable stores (including cleaning gear, cordage, canvas and paint), victuals or foodstuffs of one kind or another, and finally clothing (or 'slops') and tobacco. Clothing was purchased from the issue room (known as the 'slop room') on the upper deck, the men's daily kit upkeep allowance of 3d evaporating in the replacement of worn-out rig, largely as a consequence of the Navy's inability to decide on a practical working outfit for its men. The ship could store up to four months' supply of food, but meat, fish and fresh produce would be purchased from contractors ashore as the opportunity arose. There were, in addition, fourteen days' rations of 'hard tack' – biscuit and corned beef – for dire emergency. Menus for the ratings were drawn up for the approval of the paymaster commander by the warrant supply officer and then prepared in the various galleys by over thirty cooks. Immediate responsibility for victualling rested with a pair of chief petty officers supported by a number of supply assistants and a general mess party of seamen given the task of 'storing ship'. The *Hood*'s last crew produced a couple of memorable characters in this particular fief of the supply department. First the 'Jack Dusty' himself, CPO Supply Geoff Pope, who befriended the actor Jon Pertwee over illicit tots in a victualling office reeking of neat rum, and then a formidable three-badge 'tanky' in the shape of AB W E S 'Darby' Allen, captain of the hold, two men who at the time of their death in May 1941 had given a total of eighteen years' service to the ship. The victualling party was just one of many small groups of men who in their work and society made up the wider community of HMS *Hood*. Throughout her thousand spaces, decks and compartments dozens of such parties performed their duties with varying degrees of competence and enthusiasm, from the glamour of the admiral's barge to the filthy drudgery of the Double Bottom Party. Through their labour and character the ship acquired that distinctive quality which made her what she was, set her apart from all others, and caused her men to remember her for good or ill for the rest of their lives.

To return to the ship's peacetime harbour routine, at 0905 (1005 in winter) the bosun's call sounded 'Divisions', the second daily muster of her company. Fallen in on the quarterdeck and in the batteries, the men were inspected by their officers and reported as present and correct – or not as the case might be – before being led in prayer by the chaplain. It was traditional for the men to line the side, two ranks deep and face inboard, but Cdr O'Conor, ever mindful of his ship's éclat, had different ideas:

> Hands should always fall in facing outboard at Divisions and Evening quarters. Staring at paintwork is a deadly dull occupation, and viewed from outboard the appearance of the ship is enhanced by seeing the faces, rather than the backs, of those fallen in. [...] When the Commander brings the Divisions from the stand-easy position to properly at ease by calling the ship's name, every man should brace up and grow a couple of inches.

The conclusion of Divisions was usually the signal for a spell of competitive drill between the two watches, perhaps the lowering of all boats or the rigging of the ship's awnings. This ended with the 1030 Stand Easy, a ten-minute break during which the men could enjoy a smoke and a breather before resuming their duties until the call for 'Up spirits' at 1115 (traditionally 1100) heralded the end of the forenoon watch. By 1140, just as the rum 'tanky' and his men were bringing the grog up to the forecastle, the decks were being tidied and secured before the men proceeded to dinner. 1150 would find men from each mess lined up to receive the rum ration while the cooks of the mess were in the cooks' lobby collecting dinner from the galley lift. Fifteen minutes later, dinner and grog were being served on the messdecks. Smoking was permitted outside and on fine days the Marine band might well play a medley of popular airs on the boat deck after dinner, the hands sitting about in the sunshine. One day a week – usually Thursday – a 'make and mend' half holiday spared the men any further work until 1540. Otherwise at 1310, while the cooks hurried to clear away the last of the dinner things, the order 'Out Pipes' – extinguish cigarettes – was passed and within five minutes the men were again forming up to be assigned work for the rest of the afternoon watch. Work continued, interrupted by a ten-minute 'Stand Easy' at 1420, until the order for 'Secure' was piped at 1545.

Throughout the ship cleaning gear was being stowed in deck lockers, magazines and storerooms were being locked and lathes silenced for the night. Then at 1600 came the bugle for Evening Quarters.

Until the installation of a broadcasting system ('the tannoy') in 1939, all general orders in the *Hood* were passed either by bosun's call or bugle. The bosun's call was used for the majority of routine orders – 'Divisions', 'Secure' and 'Dinner', to name but a few – these being piped through the ship by a pair of bosun's mates and four call-boys, who trilled their way across decks and along passages. The whistle was also employed on the quarterdeck in the traditional ceremony of Piping the Side whenever a senior officer or dignitary came aboard. In *Running a Big Ship*, the manual for executive officers he published in 1937, Cdr O'Conor ruefully noted that 'Very slovenly drill is often seen at the head of the gangway when receiving officers and in piping the side'. His emphasis on the subject no doubt owed much to the appalling incident at Gibraltar one evening in March 1934 when Admiral Sir William Fisher, Commander-in-Chief, Mediterranean Fleet, arrived unannounced at the gangway and found none to receive him save a solitary Marine bugler. When Fisher emerged an hour later with 'the quarterdeck elite' in tow, the side was of course fully manned, pipes, Marine Guard and all. The bugler in question, T McCarthy, then only fifteen, takes up the story: 'Our visitor was piped over the side and all seemed to end nicely. But no; on reaching the jetty he stopped, turned and faced us all. Then he said "Thank you, bugler, for welcoming me aboard and doing your job properly. I salute you!" And he did just that.'

Apart from its ceremonial function, especially at 'Colours' and 'Sunset', the bugle joined the bosun's call in marking off the *Hood*'s daily routine from 'Hands fall in' at 0600 to the 'Last Post' at 2100. The bugle was also used to pass specific orders with calls such as 'Cable Party', 'Libertymen' or 'Saluting Guns' Crew', the number of 'Gs' added indicating which watch was being addressed. In war, however, its intended function was to transmit vital orders ('Close all Watertight Doors', 'Darken Ship') or alert the crew to imminent danger ('Repel Aircraft', 'Gas Alarm'), for which its range and urgency were better suited than the bosun's whistle.

But night in peacetime held few such terrors, and after Evening Quarters was sounded at 1600 the men either went ashore or shifted out of the rig of the day and into more comfortable gear before settling down to tea. For most their day's work was done. At dusk the quarterdeck played host to the third and most cherished ceremony of the naval day, 'Sunset', when the White Ensign was hauled down for the night. Sunset was reserved for peacetime in harbour because at sea as in war the Ensign flew until it was blown or shot away. The men passed the hours until supper at 1900 writing letters, playing games, mending clothes, painting, reading or studying for higher rating as the mood took them. There might be rehearsals for the SODS Opera or training for one of the *Hood*'s many sports teams. This was also the opportunity for the trades or 'firms' to set up business in lobbies and messdecks as the tannoy broadcast the latest dance and musical hits over the ship. At 2030 the cooks completed their day's work by clearing up the messdecks in readiness for Commander's Rounds at 2100, a brief inspection heralded by the Last Post. It took the commander or duty officer about twenty minutes to thread his way through the *Hood's* messdecks and before he had finished the men were retrieving their hammocks and slinging them for the night. By the time the bosun's mate called 'Pipe Down' at 2200 a good number of his shipmates were either in the arms of Morpheus or counting the rivets in the deckhead.

Although the *Hood* became known for her great cruises, these were the exception rather than the rule. More often than not the pattern of her life followed the ordered routine of the naval year. This began with the Spring Cruise in January which required the Atlantic Fleet, or Home Fleet as it became in 1932, to muster at Portland and proceed to Gibraltar for exercises with the Mediterranean Fleet. After what was often a rough crossing of the Bay of Biscay and a welcome pause at Arosa Bay in northwestern Spain the fleet reached Gibraltar towards the end of January. Admiral Sir Frank Twiss recalls the atmosphere:

> Gibraltar would be the forum for many events and weekly practice programmes. In this period examinations for higher rate would vie with fleet boxing, fencing, running, hockey, football and tennis, to say nothing of a day or two with the Calpe Hunt, visits to Algeciras to sample the Reina [Cristina] hotel, or to La Linea to see a bull fight or for less creditable enjoyment. There was also the Fleet concert to be put on, if not in the coal sheds or even the Gibraltar theatre, then in one of the battleships during a visit to Pollensa Bay in Majorca. But Gibraltar was the busiest period and the time when rivalry was most acute; Commanders of ships were most anxious about their paintwork or the behaviour of their liberty men, while girls, who had somehow arrived out from England, were most active in their search for young men and the excitement and fun of the chase.

However, the main event was the Combined Fleet exercises in March. The aim was to test the training of each fleet and the tactics of their commanders in the expectation of bringing on a major engagement in the Atlantic or the Mediterranean. The exercises, 'of immense boredom to the sailors and Junior Officers but of great interest and anxiety to Flag and Commanding Officers', were performed over a period of days under battle conditions, the ships darkened and closed up at action stations. The exercises usually passed unnoticed by the general public but all that changed in 1934, and not to *Hood's* advantage. In February the senior officers of the two fleets were informed of the tactical problem they were to face that year. The Home Fleet ('Blue') under the monocled figure of Admiral Sir William Boyle, Earl of Cork and Orrery, was to escort an imaginary expeditionary force 800 miles east from the Azores and land it at a point on the Atlantic seaboard of Spain and Portugal. It was the task of the Mediterranean Fleet ('Red') under 'the Great Agrippa', Admiral Sir William Fisher, to prevent this happening. On 10 March Red sailed from Gibraltar to take up patrol positions off Portugal. Fisher and his staff had determined that Blue would make either for Lisbon or Arosa Bay 250 miles to the north. Most regarded the former to be Boyle's most likely destination but Sir William disagreed and dispatched his cruisers and light forces north to cover the approaches to Arosa, which they did in enormous seas. Meanwhile, Boyle had ordered the Battle Cruiser Squadron consisting of *Hood* and *Renown* under Rear Admiral William James towards Lisbon to act as a decoy while the main body of his force, including the convoy, made for Arosa Bay along a northerly route. The weather not only caused severe damage to ships of both sides but prevented aerial reconnaissance playing any part in the affair. With visibility reduced to a quarter of a mile James failed to make a rendezvous with a Blue cruiser squadron and so lost all hope of carrying out an effective sweep for Fisher's battleships, already well to the north. At daylight on the 13th *Hood* and *Renown* were sighted by a Red submarine and subsequently shadowed by four destroyers, Fisher making no effort to engage them. Shortly after, Boyle's main force was reported making for Arosa Bay by a Red cruiser. Fisher immediately steered his battleships north to intercept while Rear Admiral Andrew Cunningham made contact with the bulk of Boyle's force with a flotilla of destroyers. In the early hours of the 14th Fisher closed with the Home Fleet, ordered Cunningham to attack from astern and then opened fire himself from only 7,000 yards. Far to the south, James in *Hood* was making a forlorn effort to rejoin his commander. The press proclaimed Fisher the master naval tactician of the age, though wartime conditions would probably not have afforded him the same opportunity. Still, as Cunningham recalled, 'These bold and masterly tactics not only put an end to the exercise; but settled once and for all the much-debated question as to whether or not British heavy ships could and should engage in night action against corresponding enemy units.' James, for his part, had little doubt where the cause of Blue's defeat lay: 'One of the axioms of strategy was not to employ forces for diversions or feints that could not be spared from the main fleet if the enemy main fleet was encountered. The plan to which I was working ignored that axiom ...'

After a lengthy post-mortem and more junketings the fleets would disperse, individual ships making goodwill visits to a Mediterranean or Atlantic port before returning home at the end of March. In *Hood*'s case home was Devonport in the 1920s and Portsmouth in the 1930s, where varying degrees of refit and repair were needed after the strain of the fleet exercises. This invariably took the form of a month (usually April) refitting at her home port followed in July or August by docking at Portsmouth for the ship's bottom to be scraped and painted and her underwater fittings overhauled. During his tenure as Controller of the Navy (1925–8) Admiral Chatfield introduced an extensive regime of self-maintenance for the fleet which brought many more artisan ratings into the complement of HM ships. The intention was to reduce ships to a single major refit in each commission but this appears not to have had any great impact on the *Hood*, which continued to dock for a month or so each spring and summer. Ian Green of Glenshee, welder at HM Dockyard Rosyth, gives an idea of the work undertaken during these refits:

> Should a repair or major refit be necessary gangs were formed with several shipwrights, some labourers and two or three welders. Sometimes if hull plates were replaced the gang would consist of platers, riveters and caulkers with a burner and welder called in when needed. Whoever was in charge of the gang was responsible for ensuring that no combustibles or vulnerable equipment were the other side of bulkheads or in the line where sparks might fly. A shipwright was always a likely candidate. [...] On the *Hood* I guess there was anything up to 150 workmen on board with probably another 20 on the dock bottom, so it was a veritable hive.

Except for those blissfully on leave the business of refitting caused major disruption to the life and work of the ship, suddenly 'full of noise, pipes and dockyard maties'. Inevitably, there were tensions between dockyard workers and officers in particular. Ian Green:

> There was a certain amount of antipathy between some Navy officers and maties as dockies were called. They thought we were idle. A bit unfair I thought. With that number of people there were bound to be some scroungers and of course it was inevitable that there were times when you had to hang around waiting for work or someone to arrive.

As the war progressed these tensions turned to open resentment at the high wages and comfortable lives led by dockyard workers in comparison with their naval counterparts, but this sentiment the *Hood* and her crew did not live long enough to share.

Between the two refits came the summer cruise, always dominated by the Pulling Regatta at Scapa Flow or Invergordon but for *Hood* particularly a chance to show Britons the Service at its finest. How many boys gazing at her from clifftop, beach or pier must have set their hearts on a career in the Navy? Here is Sir Ludovic Kennedy's boyhood memory of the Atlantic Fleet entering Invergordon in the 1920s:

> But I have left to the end the most thrilling event of the holiday, and one to which I always looked keenly forward. This was the Navy's annual visit to

Invergordon. Early one morning someone in the household would shout out 'They're here!' and we all ran on to the lawn to see for ourselves. There in line ahead, ten miles away across the Moray Firth, standing out sharply against the high ground of the northern shore, and with their grey paintwork glinting against the morning sun, were the ships of the [Atlantic] Fleet – battleships, battlecruisers, aircraft carriers, cruisers, destroyers, submarines, almost like toy ships, all slowly and sedately making their way into the Invergordon anchorage. There were so many that it took them all morning to pass in, and for most of that time, through binoculars and with the naked eye, and with my father at my elbow explaining the function of each type of ship, I watched transfixed.

There were visits to Portrush, Co Antrim, in 1925, to Shoeburyness in 1926 and Helensburgh in 1927, and after her major refit of 1929–31 to Guernsey in 1932 and Oban in 1933. In June 1934 the *Hood's* men laid the name of their ship in stone overlooking Loch Eriboll in the far north of Scotland where it rests still. Then the return to Portsmouth for docking and the great public spectacle of the year, Navy Week at Portsmouth, Devonport and Chatham. First held at Portsmouth over the August Bank Holiday of 1927, the initial aim of Navy Week was to raise money for Service charities by opening the dockyard and its ships to the public. However, the success of the event alerted the Admiralty to the possibilities of increasing public awareness in the life and work of the Navy at a time when it was struggling against reductions in its strength. By the early 1930s, Navy Week had become the main vehicle of Admiralty propaganda and a spectacle to rival the Aldershot Tattoo and the Hendon Air Pageant. The centrepiece in each year she attended was the *Hood*, which received over 100,000 of the 161,000 visitors attending at Portsmouth in 1935. Attendance at Navy Week itself grew from 48,000 at Portsmouth in 1927 to 415,000 at all three home ports in 1938, the last year it was celebrated. Having recovered from this invasion the *Hood* headed north for the autumn gunnery cruise off Scotland, the most demanding part of the naval year. For two months the fleet carried out practices and exercises in increasingly dismal weather with only golf on the links and the King's Cup and Arbuthnot Trophy competitions to distract it. Then it was back to the Channel for further gunnery and tactical exercises, usually off Portland, before the ships retired to home ports for Christmas leave by watches. So ended the naval year.

This routine was of course subject to disruption and over *Hood's* long career the even tenor of her life was frequently broken by protocol, unrest of one sort or another, and then by the onset of war. The Rio celebrations of 1922 replaced the autumn gunnery cruise but the World Cruise had kept the *Hood* from her duties for fifteen months by the time she was ready to rejoin the fleet in January 1925. Even then she and the Battle Cruiser Squadron spent a week in Lisbon representing the Navy at the Vasco da Gama celebrations. The General Strike had her sitting in the Clyde for nearly two months in the summer of 1926 while the Invergordon Mutiny cancelled the autumn gunnery cruise of 1931 altogether. But much worse was to come. The Spanish Civil War upset the training and manning regime of much of the Navy and after 1936 the *Hood* never regained the ordered pattern of earlier years.

Eventually, after two or three years, the day came for the *Hood* to sail for home and pay off so that another crew might recommission her. It was a solemn moment. With the off-duty watch mustered by divisions on deck, the band of the Royal Marines struck up *Rolling Home* and an enormous paying-off pendant unfurled from the main topgallant as she got under way, a bunch of golden bladders secured to the fly to prevent it trailing in the water. The length of the pendant traditionally reflected the duration of the commission or the number of men embarked. The same procedure, to *Rule Britannia*, was followed on entering harbour, crowds lining the shore while families waited on the jetty to be reunited after months, sometimes years, of separation. Within hours the ship had paid off, many of her people scattered to the four winds never to meet again.

4

Life Aboard

ONE OF THE DISTINCTIVE features of life and war at sea is that a ship, however large or small she may be, is at once the home, work and weapon of all who sail in her. More than that, she is their only succour and defence against the remorseless power of wind and water, the common enemy of all seafarers. For this reason, as for the large number of those embarked in her, the life and functioning of a warship has more of the quality of a community than perhaps any other military unit. Whereas a soldier may expect to serve out his time in the same regiment, it is the fate of a ship's company to be scattered by recommissioning or war after no more than a few years. But no matter how short her lease there is always time enough for her distinctive personality to impress itself for good or ill on all her people, and for these in their turn to leave their mark as indelibly on her. In this way the cycle is renewed in the experience of other crews and men until either the violence of the enemy or the breaker's torch fulfils her destiny. Welded in discipline, tradition and war, and yet capable of annihilation in a matter of seconds, it is the transient yet lasting quality of naval life afloat that affords it much of its fascination: short in time, yet rich in memory. This is true of no ship more than it is of HMS *Hood*.

For Cadet Le Bailly, joining his first ship in 1932, his arrival aboard was a solemn and exhilarating moment.

> Thus it was that Dick Litchfield, I and two others foregathered at the Keppel's Head, Portsmouth, one evening in early August 1932. From our modest attic bedrooms we could see the quarterdeck of the great ship which was to be our home. Next morning, clad in our number one uniforms, we duly repaired on board. [...] From the moment we reported to the officer of the watch, the whole rhythm of life was a boy's dream come true. They were all there, as Taffrail and Bartimeus had told us they would be: Guns and Torps, the Springer and the Pilot, the Schoolie and the Chief and the Senior, the Chippie, the Bo'sun, the PMO and of course our lord and master the Sub.*

*Respectively the gunnery, torpedo, physical training, navigator and instructor officers, the chief and senior engineer officers, the ship's carpenter and boatswain, the principal medical officer and the ranking sub lieutenant.

Some, indeed, could say no more of the *Hood* than that her beauty was echoed in the friendly atmosphere they encountered aboard, unusually so for a ship of her size. The Rev Edgar Rea, joining as the ship's chaplain in September 1936, was relieved to discover several familiar faces from earlier commissions, while Paymaster Cadet Keith Evans found himself playing deck hockey within half an hour of stepping aboard. However, for most their arrival was more modest, though no less impressive for that. Hammock and kit-bag over his shoulder and ditty box in his hand, a rating would traipse up a gangway amidships to be received without fuss or ceremony into his new home. Boy Signalman Ted Briggs joined the ship in the summer of 1939:

> Then we were marched up the long gangway to be swallowed by this whirring monster. Everything seemed twice as big as normal. The mess decks were colossal; a series of scrubbed wooden mess-tables reached out at me like massive conjuror's fingers; mess-kids gleamed in imitation of sterling silver; even the overhead hammock bars glinted, while the faint whiff of fuel oil and the constant humming of the air vents engulfed me. This sense of space and clean-cut lines did not diminish in the boys' mess deck, where we were deposited to make ourselves at home.

How different had been the reaction of Boy Fred Coombes, reaching the same messdeck four years earlier. For him and those, including his twin brother Frank, who accompanied him, the reality of life afloat evidently came as a dreadful shock:

> On joining the *Hood* in Portsmouth Dockyard on 31 March 1935, struggling up the long steep gangway with, first, our bags and, after scathing remarks about our slackness, a run back down to fetch our hammocks, we felt like flies on top of a dung heap. After a guided wander down steel ladders, on identical-looking corridors, through huge steel doors, we ended up somewhere in the bowels of what seemed like an inhuman, airless and windowless white-painted mass of long passageways and boxes, in what was, in reality, a barracks. We felt more like the maggots underneath the dung than the flies on top. [...] After being led through some deserted messdecks and enclosed compartments, we found all our bags and hammocks heaped at the bottom of a steel ladder after being thrown, a deck at a time, through three decks to the lower level, which led to our mess deck. That rough handling of our hammocks was to be the first indication that life was rough at sea and on ships.

The seamen's messdecks in which Briggs and Coombes were to make their home for the next few years differed little from those in other capital ships of the Royal Navy. Ranged on the upper and lower decks were fifteen enclosed messes for senior ratings and eleven open ones known as 'broadside messes' for the bulk of the ship's company – over 1,100 men in peacetime. In a typical open mess, such as that of the torpedomen and the quarterdeckmen on the port side of the upper deck amidships, accommodation was provided for about two hundred men in a space up to 70 feet long and 30 feet across. The main feature of each was a row of long wooden tables lying athwart the ship and supported either on folding legs or else suspended from the deckhead by means of a series of highly polished steel bars. On either side wooden forms provided seating for up to twenty men per table. Each of these tables constituted a 'mess' in its own right and it was here that a man ate his meals, read his mail, played games and spent much of his life cheek by jowl with his comrades. Every mess had its number, even to port and odd to starboard, the numeration beginning forward and proceeding down from the upper to the main deck. The atmosphere of a large messdeck is nowhere better described than in the following passage by Lt Cdr W B Harvey, who began his career on the lower deck:

> At one end of the table a game of solo, euchre, brag or any other of the innumerable card games was in progress, usually with slightly resented 'advisors' hovering in the background; Spoff Hammond who ran the 'goffer' shop would be mixing a concoction in a bucket to sell as lemonade; 'Brigham' Young would be writing to one of his many girls, sorting out their photos in his ditty box; 'Nobby' Hall, prospective Med Fleet light heavyweight champion, doing his shadow boxing; cooks of the mess peeling spuds and over all a buzz of conversation, jokes, taunts and cat calls making a noisy, happy background, repeated in all sixteen broadside messes.

For Divisions each morning the white linoleum cloth that covered the tables was rolled back to reveal the scrubbed deal wood beneath and the mess cutlery artistically arranged on top. At the gangway end the 'cooks of the mess' polished and stacked the assortment of 'fannies' (food containers) with which each was equipped with military precision. Fred Coombes:

> At the other end of the table was another highly polished tin box holding some tea and sugar in separate compartments, which we were advised was to make tea in a large, odd-shaped tall teapot with removable tea strainer, with a small lid, the only recognisable thing being the spout to pour from. Neatly arrayed in front of the box, with the teapot on top, was a mess kettle and lid alongside a round, wire-handled, flat-bottomed can and lid, all highly polished, which, with a large soup ladle, were to be our mess utensils. Underneath the table was a highly polished and clean bucket, even though it was to hold any leavings such as the tea leaves from the teapot.

Along its length a series of shallow racks fitted to the underside of each table provided space for shoes and so forth, while no doubt adding to the general sense of cramped discomfort. The opposite end of the table was usually hinged to the ship's side, along which ran stowage for ditty boxes, boots and other items. Just above the table was a lamp – traditionally oil-burning but in *Hood* always electric – together with the mess number neatly done in black paint, and a small noticeboard containing special orders and the duty roster for cooks of the mess. Higher still was additional stowage for ditty boxes and the rack for 'mess traps' (assorted utensils) that completed the culinary outfit of each mess. Fred Coombes:

> On the ship's side was fixed a wire-framed mess cupboard with separate and safe stowage for the standard crockery and cutlery, and underneath a highly polished box lid which fronted the bread barge – bread bin to us novices – who, from custom, were looking for something to eat and finding that, as on all Boys' mess decks, there was never any leftovers.

Along the internal bulkheads were ranges of gleaming steel lockers for the rest of the men's equipment. Against the deckhead a confusion of kinked hammock bars, beams, cabling, ventilation trunks and fittings for hammock stowage completed the austere panorama. Amidst all this the Coombes twins and their companions sat disconsolately waiting for something to happen. However, help in the shape of food and messmates was at hand:

> Having had a taste of finding our mess deck after stowing our hammocks, we all decided to stay put in our messes until Cooks to the Galley was piped about 4 o'clock, when two duck-suited youngsters came rushing into each mess, one to put a handful of tea into the pot, the other to show us how to roll the usual white lino table cloth on the table, scatter a few knives before dashing off to join the queue at the Servery and be handed a numbered tray containing just the correct number of rations required in the mess. [...] Of food there was no sign until the duty messmen came running down the steel ladders, their backs to the rungs, an impossible method of descending without a lot of practice, but the only way to carry our food down to our mess, some three ladders down, using the back of our ankles pressed against the preceding ladder rung to balance ourselves and with our heels pressed firmly on the next rung down. It was the only way to carry a dish that at some time would have to contain liquids such as gravy. After a bit of practice we were soon to run down ladders in this way, a much quicker method when we couldn't use our hands to balance and the only way when we had to carry a dish without spilling its contents.

A drink of tea and a slice or two of bread and things looked much rosier: 'After tea, which was more often bread and jam, we sat around sipping our strong, sweet tea and talking to our new messmates, who were waiting their turn to go on leave, and found new advisors, already veterans of six months' service on the *Hood*, coming from our home town and taking us under their wings.'

Even for those not subject to the terrible hunger pangs of the Coombes twins, food was a significant and indeed contentious part of naval life. On commissioning in 1920 the *Hood* became the first ship in the Navy to adopt the dual systems of 'General Messing' and 'Central Storekeeping'. Traditionally, each mess had been given a monthly allowance of food which was drawn and prepared by two of its members, the cooks of the mess, who performed this task on a daily rota. Once prepared, their pies, joints and vegetables would be taken up to the galley to be baked in the ship's ovens until dinner or supper. This system, which was known as 'Canteen' or 'Broadside' messing, had its supporters among those on the lower deck who favoured their own concoctions, but as ships' companies became larger the wastage and inefficiency implicit in requiring the 'cocoa bosuns' (galley staff) to cook as many dishes as there were messes began to call for change. The Navy's answer was the General Messing system devised by Warrant Officer Alphonso Jago, after whom it was named 'Jago's' by the lower deck. Under this scheme the paymaster and his victualling staff assumed responsibility for all lower-deck catering, undertaking to provide three meals a day to a pre-arranged weekly menu against the deduction of a daily allowance from the men's wages. This allowance amounted to 1s 1d in 1937 rising to 1s 3d in 1940. The introduction of General Messing placed a corresponding need for improved food-storage facilities aboard, which in *Hood*'s case included large refrigerated meat and vegetable stores on the lower deck forward. In all, some 320 tons of provisions could be laid in to keep the ship supplied for up to four months. This scheme, which saved the Navy a lot of money, was for some time the source of much suspicion and resentment on the lower deck. Telegraphist S Donovan: 'We accepted it reluctantly. No longer could we collect mess savings at the end of the month as a result of economies we made in each mess by not catering for those on leave and ashore.' Nonetheless, others took quite the opposite view. Gunner 'Windy' Breeze, Royal Marine Artillery (1920–2): 'The *Hood* was the first ship to start general messing. This was under a Paymaster Commander and instead of being in debt every month we soon had a huge surplus which was used to entertain the visitors to tea and cakes (rock cakes, stone hard).' For a member of the *Hood*'s first crew, AB Leo Brown of Newbury, the clincher was fried fish and chips from the galley range and 'tiddie oggies' – pasties – every Friday. Indeed, most came to appreciate not only the greater variety but also the improved quality of meals that had earlier been left to the questionable culinary talents of their messmates. Even so, for OD Norman Wesbroom, aboard in 1931, 'general messing was never very popular'.

Though preparation generally improved out of all recognition, the meals served remained much as they had always been. Breakfasts of bacon, tomatoes, tea, bread and butter, or issued in sandwich form after a rough night at sea. A roast or 'pot-mess' stew for dinner or supper with the eternal 'duff', or steamed pudding, for afters. But whatever the quality of the preparation, the journey from servery to mess still greatly imperilled the offerings of the ship's galley. For Fred Coombes, tea was 'a quantity of bread, butter and perhaps jam which, if the ration carrier had remembered, would be on the plate and not in the bottom of what might be a greasy dish'. AB Bob Tilburn (1938–41) took a still more cynical view: 'Our food was very, very good, when it was in the fridge. But by the time the chefs had had a go at it, and it was on your plate, it wasn't too good.' After the meal came the clean-up. Fred Coombes:

> All the time learning, we soon had to have the pots washed, the mess cleaned up, and perhaps the one who had the job of emptying the gash bucket over the ship's side down the steel gash chute (which prevented the ship's side becoming marked) would hear the familiar tinkle as an item of cutlery went down too, and often heard the remark 'Tinkle, tinkle little spoon, knife and fork will follow soon'. The oceans of the world must be marked by small items of Sheffield-made Royal Navy cutlery ...

It was surely *Hood's* misfortune that, having been in the vanguard of General Messing, she did not survive long enough to savour the next development in naval culinary organisation, the cafeteria-style 'Centralised Messing' introduced during the Second World War.

At nightfall the men retrieved their hammocks from compartments or stowage nettings under the deckhead and slung them fore and aft over the mess tables to minimise the effect of the ship's motion on their slumber. Each 'mick' contained a mattress and a series of rope 'nettles' by which it was lashed to hooks fitted to the deck beams specially for this purpose. Fully extended it measured all of eleven feet, though required very little width. By moving a wooden 'spreader' bar along the nettles the hammock could be opened or closed as the user's need for privacy, warmth or comfort dictated. Fred Coombes explains the procedure:

> The long day finished with us slinging our hammocks for the first time for real, holding the nettles open at our head end by a short length of stick, unfolding our one heavy woollen blanket lengthways across our opened hammock before swinging our bodies in with the help of the conveniently placed hammock bar of the next sleeping billet. Landing feet first on our blanket and lowering our shoulders and blanket beneath us, it was easy to draw each side up in its turn and wrap ourselves in. A comfortable bed when you got used to it and if we had made our boots and clothing into a comfortable pillow, held in place by the head nettles. Though the curvature of the spine suits the sag of a hammock, supported only at either end, sleeping on our backs was not natural though we soon got used to it ...

Sleep when it came was at best fitful that first night:

> The steady subdued roar of machinery that came down those fan trunkings
> above our heads might have helped us to sleep but the lights … were not
> dimmed till after 'Lights Out' at 10. Fitful sleep came to most after a lot of new
> and odd movements as we wriggled about and tried to, at the same time, keep
> our blankets wrapped around us … our hands between bent knees and not
> protecting our privates as now seemed necessary. Our long troubled night,
> broken by odd bumps underneath as passers-by headed our perhaps too-low-
> slung hammock as they went about their duty … was ended at what seemed an
> early hour by the switching on of all the lights and the raucous shouting of the
> ill-tempered … Petty Officer who was on duty.

The order to 'Lash up and stow' hammocks may have been received with chagrin
by some, but for others on the Coombes' messdeck it was a case of the early bird
catching the worm:

> The time being 5.30am gave us little time to lash up and stow our hammocks,
> get dressed and find our mess for a promised cup of ship's ky [cocoa] and
> biscuits, only to find that the established messmates had turned out early to
> draw the rations before lashing their hammocks up and disposing of the rations
> in comfort. We were only caught the once as, like all things learnt the hard way,
> only fools get caught twice.

However, for many there was every reason to remain ensconced as long as
possible. During his tenure Cdr Rory O'Conor took steps to enforce the standing
orders requiring every hammock in the ship to be lashed up and stowed away
by 0645 each morning:

> It is bad enough for a man to have to turn out and scrub the decks at six o'clock
> in the morning, but it is still worse if when he comes down to breakfast he finds
> someone from Guard and Steerage just getting out of a hammock slung over
> the mess table, and getting mixed up with his breakfast. It is unpleasant and
> causes unpleasantness.

O'Conor's remarks touch on the central issue of messdeck life, the question of
maintaining respect and comradeliness between men in an environment that
was not only fraught and overcrowded but also devoid of privacy. Beyond the
confines of his hammock or caboose, the only shred of privacy left to a man in
a world subject both to official inspection and the intimate scrutiny of his messmates was his ditty box – traditionally a hinged white-wood container which
from the 1940s was replaced by a small briefcase with a spring lock and handle.

Under such conditions there were inevitably moments when one had had enough of one's messmates, when exhaustion, discomfort and frustration would fray nerves or tempers to breaking point. The view of OD Jon Pertwee, a 'Hostilities Only' rating in 1940–1, is typical of the more sophisticated men that war brought into the Navy: 'Time spent with my mates on the mess-deck was fine, but in small doses only; for any long period, the noise and the subject matter of general conversation was one of boring and monotonous repetition, "parties" [girlfriends], poking and booze, booze, poking and "parties".' For a bored and seasick actor like Pertwee the antidote was to be found among friends elsewhere in the ship, in this case CPO Geoff Pope of the Supply Branch:

> 'Sit down, lad, and have a tot,' said Geoff, and from that moment on we became the best of friends. When work was slack and the sea was flat, I would call in for a grog and a chat, but if it was rough, Geoff let me crawl in under his desk with my jam tin, and seemed quite impervious to my noisy discomfiture.

However, for regulars recruited before the war it was the norm to socialise only with those in the same mess or duty area. Stoker Dick Turner (1936–9): 'Being such a large ship it was impossible to mix socially with many of the crew so you tended to find yourself with a small group of close friends.' This homeliness no doubt owed something to the prolonged separation from family that was the lot of all sailors. Len Wincott (1926): 'To me it was obvious that I had joined a band of men who were in the first place sober, sentimental home-lovers, whose frequent absence from their closest bred in them a firmer tie with their homes than many people who come home from work every day care to show.' But for many intelligent men there was something enervating about life at sea. AB Bob Tilburn had recourse to astrophysics: 'I always thought it was tremendous, the sea, but mentally, life at sea was numbing. I started reading navigation handbooks and I got some books about the stars. I would write down how far a star was away, multiplying the speed of light by so many million miles. Just to keep the mind going.'

Though truly negative accounts of life aboard are rare, their scarcity should not blind us to the disagreeable realities that occasionally asserted themselves. Every so often a breakdown in relations or other circumstances would require an individual to be transferred away from his mess. O'Conor:

> Care is needed to ensure that a man's part of the ship and his mess are never changed unless it is absolutely necessary, or for some good reason it is to his advantage. Quarrelling and mutual antipathies sometimes make a change desirable, and cases occur when a fresh start in a new environment and with different associates will turn a youngster from wrong ways.

Equally, the anguish when a thief was found to be at work in the midst of a community that laid such reliance on trust is to be imagined.

> The incidence of petty theft on the messdecks is a difficult and disturbing problem. It is difficult because a thief is seldom caught red-handed, and it is disturbing because it engenders an unhappy atmosphere of suspicion among messmates. Unless he is a kleptomaniac, the man who steals from a shipmate must be the meanest of mortals. Experience shows that he is also, usually, most cunning, and, regrettably, he is seldom laid by the heels.

The moral integrity of the lower deck improved markedly after 1900, but with the Second World War came many dubious characters or 'skates' into the Navy. As OD B A Carlisle (1940–1) discovered to his cost, theft was rife on the messdecks of most big ships:

> Conditions below deck were by modern standards primitive and to wash one had to leave one's clothes outside the washroom and go in and sponge down. I foolishly left my belt, which held my worldly wealth of £7 (representing 70 days' pay), and when I came out the money had gone. I reported the loss to the Master-at-Arms who was sympathetic but naturally said there was no remedy.

Small wonder OD Bill Hawkins (1940–1) always took care to bring his clothing with him into his hammock when he turned in for a kip.

For such moments – and there were many – when only complete solitude would do, the caboose, or cabouche as it was sometimes called, came into its own. Jon Pertwee:

> The most heartfelt want of any sailor at sea was privacy and a man would go to any lengths to find it. Behind a cupboard, on top of a cupboard, or in a cupboard, he would lay out his hammock mattress and make himself a little home-from-home. I was luckier than most on three counts. First, I was in charge of a rope-locker on deck. This was about seven foot long, four feet high and with the ropes coiled and piled up at one end, left sufficient room for my mattress, ditty box and 'things'. With a pusser's torch suspended from the deckhead I spent many a happy hour reading, writing letters and generally revelling in the privacy this minuscule iron cell afforded me. With the locker catches down, I was unassailable. Photos of my dear ones were stuck on the bulkhead allowing me to dream undisturbed of peace and tender loving arms enfolding me. These 'cabouches', as such havens were traditionally known, were quite accepted by the Officers and Petty Officers and could be occupied during daylight hours without fear or hindrance, although two men in a 'cabouche' with the door closed and locked off, was likely to be frowned upon. You wouldn't

believe how many of my mates were able to get themselves into that ridiculously confined space for a smoke and a 'crack' (chat).

A caboose between decks lent itself to even greater improvement and redecoration, many going to the lengths of painting and fitting their retreat with a permanent light, pictures, some sticks of furniture and even a bed. Taking one's night's rest in a caboose was discouraged and some were locked against buggery, but officers frequently turned a blind eye. To deprive a man of those hours of privacy and solitude that, in war particularly, might occasionally mean the difference between survival and insanity in the cockpit of messdeck life was not a step to be taken lightly.

The open messes were presided over by the 'Leading Hand of the Mess', a leading seaman or 'killick' who was but one promotion away from sharing the enclosed messes of the petty officers. There was a clear hierarchy on each messdeck, the leading hand being followed in seniority by those ratings whose three Good Conduct badges signified at least twelve years' service in the Navy. It was the endurance, skill and mordant humour of the long-service rating that shaped a messdeck's character in peace and stiffened its inmates to the trials that beset them in war. However tendentious his other views, when the Invergordon mutineer AB Len Wincott described his companions of the inter-war Navy as the 'finest body of men in the world' he meant it. Responsibility for individual messes was also given to leading seamen, after whom time served on the deck was the determining factor where it came to allocation of lockers or a decent berth to sling one's hammock. Rank also exempted leading hands from the duties of food and mail collection and of course the daily mess cleaning, during which the tables were hoisted to the deckhead and the forms cleared away so that the corticene flooring could be scrubbed and every surface buffed to a gleaming finish. Each mess would then be reassembled and its utensils and equipment laid out in the prescribed manner.

Despite a near obsessive concern for cleanliness, conditions aboard often militated against hygiene. Though a considerable improvement on older capital ships and fitted with amenities unknown in smaller vessels, *Hood*'s lower-deck bathrooms still left a lot to be desired. Ted Briggs: 'The drains and scuppers could seldom cope with the ablutions and laundering of scores of naked matelots, and the result was a constant flood of four inches of murky water on the floor. Hence the old expression: "For you I swim the stokers' bathroom in full flood backwards."' Ejectors were fitted to drain the bathrooms but a shortage of pressure prevented them being left permanently open. In addition, a chronic shortage of boiler feed water required most washplaces to be closed for several hours each day – longer in wartime – while the ship was at sea. As ratings were not allowed on the messdecks in their grimy working rig this often made for severe overcrowding when large parties of men came off watch. The men performed their ablutions in a galvanised tub 30in wide and 10in deep which they filled from large taps set into the tiled bulkheads. In heavy seas, the flood of water sloshing from side to side might well send a tub, matelot and all sliding right across the bathroom to the consternation of its occupant. Meanwhile, the absence of designated laundry rooms obliged men either to bring their washing into the tubs with them or else do their scrubbing in the basins found there, so adding to the mess and congestion. In war particularly, many found themselves with neither the time nor the inclination to undress at sea, leaving the overdue task of changing and 'dhobeying' their clothes to the return to harbour. When not done at the washplace basins, dhobeying was often performed in a bucket of water from the galley with a bar of 'pusser's hard', the waists on the main deck amidships being a favourite spot. Scrubbed clothing would then be deposited at the drying room or, in the case of stokers, taken below for the heat of the boiler rooms to deal with over the course of the next watch. 'Pusser's hard' was a form of currency by which the Navy maintained the cleanliness and tidiness of the messdecks. Telegraphist Dick Jackman (1937–9) explains:

> If detergent existed in those days it certainly never reached *Hood*, and all non-personal washing was done with large bars of yellow soap about 2.5 x 2.5 x 6 inches which could be purchased from the ship's stores. If one left belongings lying around they were picked up and put in the 'Scran Bag', and in order to retrieve them one was fined a portion of a bar of soap, size depending on the amount left lying around. This requisitioned soap was then used to keep the ship and mess clean.

Although regarded as a most comfortable vessel on completion, the issue of habitability became more pertinent as time passed. Certainly, the *Hood's* amenities and general standard of comfort seemed less remarkable towards the end of her career than they had at the start. As Mid H G Knowles reported during a brief stay in June 1939,

> Exploring the *Hood*, full of noise, pipes, and dockyard maties, amazed me that such a contrast and change could have occurred since I went over her at Malta. There she had been my ideal in polish and efficiency. Now I began to realize how small and airless are the messdecks: indeed there is hardly a single scuttle below decks.

By the late 1930s heating of the messdecks had become impossible because the tubing leaked so badly that the evaporators could not supply both it and the ship's boilers with the water necessary. The absence of scuttles and poor air circulation meant that light and smell deteriorated the further one penetrated into the ship. The *Hood* had never been well ventilated but the tendency to dampness of a vessel whose messdecks were frequently awash was increasingly blamed for the high incidence of tuberculosis (TB) aboard. As Cdr E W Roberts (1933–6) recalled,

'With hatches battened down, the forced air ventilation was inadequate to meet requirements. The atmosphere between decks became fetid and one had difficulty in breathing normally. The ship's side plating was constantly wet with condensation. With a full crew on board, *Hood* was an unhealthy ship.'

The matter was first brought to the attention of the Admiralty after an able seaman and a midshipman had been invalided off the ship with TB in 1932. These concerns were brushed aside by the Admiralty which noted that £5,000 had been spent on habitability during the 1929–31 refit and that incidence of the disease in the *Hood* compared favourably with the rest of the Fleet and the civilian population. However, by the late 1930s the *Hood* had earned an unenviable reputation as 'the TB ship' and the Admiralty could no longer ignore a disease that, in the Navy at large, had twice the mortality rate of civilians and was as prevalent as it had been thirty years earlier. Cases of men with chest problems were reported weekly in the Mediterranean during 1936–8 and a regime of exercises on deck instituted. Appropriately enough, Vice Admiral Andrew Cunningham had been chairing a committee looking into problems of ventilation and habitability afloat at the time of his sudden appointment to the *Hood* in June 1937.

Equally, in a society that was so fastidious about cleanliness it comes as a surprise to read Captain Francis Pridham's comments regarding the grime and filth he discovered aboard on assuming command in February 1936. Whereas the carrier *Glorious* acquired a huge colony of rats that succumbed only with the loss of the ship, the *Hood*'s frequent sojourns in tropical climes made her a particular haven for cockroaches. At Gibraltar in April 1936 *The Chough*, the ship's magazine, proposed a 'Cockroach Week' of planned extermination. But it was a losing battle, and when the *Hood* returned to Scapa Flow freshly stocked from her Mediterranean interlude in August 1940, the gunroom adopted a different approach. Mid Ross Warden RNVR remembers:

> One member of the gunroom hit on a novel idea – Cockroach Races! We had a small colony and there seemed to be no reason why they should live a life of ease. The green felt covering for the gunroom table made an excellent paddock; chalk lines were drawn, the contestants were kept in matchboxes; and some others even went to the extreme limits of giving their prodigies special diets. Bets (small) were laid and at the shout 'They're off!' nothing would happen. The next step was a lit match applied to the rear extremity which was conducive to forward motion.

But while cockroaches never quite assumed the status of mascots, they had the virtue of not discriminating as to rank and came to be regarded as part of the ship's character. Decades later an anonymous boy seaman of 1933 was to answer the question 'What do you remember most about HMS *Hood*?' with 'The cockroaches which outnumbered us 100 to one'.

In shipboard life the Royal Navy acknowledged rank and promotion by conferring two of its most signal privileges, additional space and enhanced privacy from subordinates. So it was with the enclosed messes of the chief and petty officers, which might consist of no more than a curtained-off partition on a larger messdeck or an entirely separate compartment with easy chairs at one end and an adjoining pantry. Whatever their structural arrangements, each mess enjoyed the services of at least two 'messmen' who performed the same duties as the 'cooks of the mess' on the open decks. The messman was often a junior rating of the branch to which the mess belonged, his labour entitling him not only to a monthly stipend from the mess fund but also a number of privileges which made it a much sought-after position. The food served to petty officers was supposedly the same as that consumed by the rest of the lower deck, but of course in practice this was some way from being the case. Petty officers slung their hammocks with the rest, but there were compensations, not least the privilege of taking their rum issue neat, and consequently of being able to store it illicitly for future consumption. Then there were the warrant officers, the dozen or so men – true masters of their craft – who, more than any other, ran the ship, from whom neither she nor her men held any secrets. In recognition of their status, warrant officers were granted a private mess, galley and stewards to attend them as well as shared cabins on the main deck aft complete with bunks, though doubtless many had cause to regret this when it came on to blow and the motion of the ship threatened to deposit them on deck. The position of the warrant officer, half way between the lower deck and the wardroom officers, no doubt made for a demanding position requiring great tact and professional skill, but in them and their kind lay the backbone of the *Hood*'s company. Vice Admiral Le Bailly:

> For a few chief petty officers there was the big jump to the warrant officers' mess. Here were the barons, men of vast experience who knew all there was to know about sailors, who lived a very private life off duty in a mess into which few wardroom officers penetrated. Infinitely kind to midshipmen, but set in their ways, they were rightly regarded with awe by junior lieutenants.

On their shoulders and those of the chief petty officers the wartime transformation of the Navy was borne. In quiet expertise and steadying courage they were among the finest it had to offer.

No overview of the *Hood*'s lower deck would be complete without mention of the boy seamen of whom around eighty were embarked. The majority reached the ship in drafts of up to twenty or thirty from the boys' training establishments, from *Impregnable* at Devonport until 1929, and thereafter mainly from *Ganges* at Shotley or *St Vincent* at Gosport, with a few from *Caledonia* at Oban between 1937–9. Rated Boy 1st Class, they constituted the Boys' Division aboard and lived in a segregated mess on the main deck forward under the authority of four petty officer instructors. Among those responsible for their welfare were the so-called 'sea daddies', those leading seamen selected to initiate the boys in the minutiae of shipboard life. Along with the rest of the crew, the boys worked 'watch and watch', usually four hours on and eight off, but though life was generally much easier than in the training establishments they were often assigned the most menial and arduous duties. Morning routine was particularly unpleasant. Boy Jim Taylor, who served his apprenticeship aboard in 1939–40, remembers:

> A big difference in the daily routine was that every morning first thing – before 7 am – we boys had to scrub the decks. The ship's company in charge had seaboots but we boys were barefooted. A hosepipe was basically thrown over the side of the ship and seawater pumped over the decks until it was nearly ankle deep. The water was dark and very cold, and as it washed into the scuppers got colder still. Eventually one was left on a damp deck that was colder than you could imagine. If your toes were knocked, as they frequently were, they were too cold to bleed. This deck washing was probably my pet hate in the Navy.

However, there were easier tasks, including those of officer's messenger, of lashing or unlashing hammocks, service with the ship's boats or even membership of a crew. Budding specialists like Ted Briggs kept watch on the flag deck with a dozen other Boy Signalmen. Apart from their shipboard chores of cleaning and polishing, boys had to submit to two hours' instruction in the schoolroom flat on the main deck aft, together with an hour's homework each day. Smoking and shore leave were greatly restricted, as was pay which in 1939 amounted to 8s 9d per week for a Boy 1st Class. Of this the boys received a weekly allowance of just 1s 6d, the balance being paid in a lump sum (without interest) on promotion to ordinary seamen at the age of eighteen. Discipline remained harsh, with caning by warrant for the most serious offences and the 'stonnicky', a length of knotted rope, wielded by petty officer instructors to encourage the laggardly.

To be drafted from the *Hood* meant being severed from a unique community, one that could never be recreated except in the mind's eye. For many, of course, the news must have come as a blessed relief but for others it was undoubtedly a source of great sadness. Whatever their emotions, very few can have been left unmoved by the experience, particularly those whose service took them across the rubicon of war. For Lt Louis Le Bailly, completing his second commission aboard in November 1939, the time had come to move on, though not without a measure of nostalgia for all that had passed:

> Although both wardroom and gunroom contained many delightful people with whom I had become fast friends, I was conscious that I had been in *Hood* overlong, too apt now to look back to earlier and easier days. I spent some of

my remaining hours touring the ship. It was a sad if, in the chief stokers', artificers' and chief petty officers' messes, a singularly alcoholic parting which the wardroom completed: I was thankful for the taxi that bore me to North Road Station.

PO Len Williams, drafted in February 1941 after five years aboard, also found himself torn between memory and anticipation:

> I received the draft with mixed feelings. Due to my long service in *Hood* I had grown attached to her. We had travelled many thousands of miles and had visited many distant places together; besides which I liked my shipmates, most of whom, like myself, had served a very long time in the ship. On the other hand I wanted, eventually, to qualify as a Torpedo Gunner's Mate and Instructor and to do this I must first of all clear the hurdle of the Leading Torpedoman's Course, which was the next step.

But when the moment of departure came there was no doubt where his feelings lay:

> As our train passed over the Forth Bridge, we looked across to the dockyard and saw the 'Old Lady' lying alongside the basin wall. I would not be honest if I did not admit that I was very close to tears as we watched her pass out of sight, as our train sped onwards towards Edinburgh. I had joined her a very humble Seaman Torpedoman and had left a Petty Officer. I owed *Hood* a lot and I was grateful.

Nor could there be much ambivalence in the memory. The sentiment of Stoker Jim Haskell, a veteran of 1934–8, echoes the enduring conviction of a generation of men who sailed in her: 'To me *Hood* was always my Navy, the finest ship I ever served in'.

5

Crossing the Line

FOR LONG-SERVICE REGULARS as much as erstwhile civilians it was the camaraderie and friendship that men remembered from their service. AB Len Williams of Portsmouth, a torpedoman aboard between 1936–41, puts it eloquently:

> Living as we did, cheek by jowl, in close contact with each other, often led to strong friendships. The sort of relationships not found amongst men in civilian life, where friends meet only occasionally, and where lives are lived in separate houses. Here we lived together as a giant family. We knew each other's failings and weaknesses, and liked each other in spite of them. We slept in close proximity, in swaying hammocks. We even bathed together in the communal bathrooms. In fact we lived candidly with one another, accepting the rough with the smooth. This sharing and living together, forged a comradeship which one can never find in civilian life.

Out of this community would come one or two special friends. In the Mediterranean between 1937–8 Williams enjoyed the unforgettable companionship of a rating his memoirs refer to only as Doug:

> About this time I became on friendly terms with Doug, who was a wireless operator. The 'Sparks' mess was on the same messdeck as ours, and sometimes we would take a walk on deck together. Whether there was something about me which invited confidences I do not know, but Doug used to pour out all his troubles in my ear, and gradually we got on shore-going terms. [...] He was more like Snowy than Harry had been, preferring the bright lights and cabarets to the quiet places. It was like old times again. We went swimming together at weekends, followed by an evening down the 'Gut'. In Doug's company I began to enjoy life again. [...] On nights we were not ashore, Doug and I slept on the upper deck under the huge forecastle awning. We both had camp beds and we would lie and watch the signal lamp, high up on the mast of the Castille Signal Station, flashing its messages to the fleet lying in the Grand Harbour. It was the

limit of our vision before the awning blotted out the stars. It was pleasant lying there, listening to the bells of the horse-drawn carozzins or gharries, as we usually called them, and watching the lights of the waterfront bars and cafes ashore and the bobbing lights of the dghaisas [boats] going about their business. We would talk until the lights ashore began to go out one by one, and soon we ourselves would grow tired and fall asleep. [...] Doug and I had a couple of pleasant months together, going ashore and enjoying ourselves before the Spring Cruise began ... Shortly before we sailed, Doug was drafted to the destroyer leader *Hardy*, and I saw very little of him afterwards. I missed him of course, but thereafter, when going ashore, I usually picked a casual friend to go with. It was not quite the same, since Doug and I had been together a year and we each knew the others' likes and dislikes, and we always got on so well together, but navy life is like this; friends come and go, and one has to make the best of it.

Despite the predominantly heterosexual and indeed homophobic sexuality that characterised the lower deck, homosexuality was a perceptible undercurrent in naval life – no surprise in a community that was both exclusively male and set apart from ordinary society. Confidential fleet orders in 1929 and again in 1940 expressed dismay at the number of 'unnatural offences' being reported in the Navy. The Admiralty's emphasis on the steadying influence of the older man in curbing this perhaps reveals its ignorance on the subject since it was the 'Sea Daddy' himself who was as inclined as any to seek sexual favours of his younger shipmates. Joining *Hood* in November 1940, OD Jon Pertwee was befriended by a three-stripe able seaman of the peacetime Navy:

He was a real mother to me, and as I was reliably informed by my hammock lasher, would've been a lot more, if I'd given him half a chance. There was nothing really homosexual about him, said my informant. It was just that when at sea, having a young 'oppo' to 'care for' was an old Navy tradition. It was further said that the expression 'chuff (carryings-on) for duff' (pudding) was not without a certain element of truth. Perhaps food was the only article of barter left to those young men unlucky enough not to have a tot to bargain with, but to me bartering with pudding seemed a bit beyond the pale.

Pertwee is not the most reliable of commentators but there is ample anecdotal evidence for arrangements of this sort in the *Hood* and elsewhere. Equally, in this as in so many other areas the war served to erode existing sexual barriers. Terri Gardner, called up in 1940 and trained as a Navy cook, was discharged for suspected homosexuality after service in a corvette:

One was young, and sex is very much a thing in your life when you're in your twenties – you're out to get every bit and have as much fun as you possibly can. The married man away from home and in the Navy as far as I could see, was the worst sort of man – he would go out of his way for a bit of nonsense. The difficulties were finding somewhere to be intimate.

The psychology of homosexuality lies well beyond the scope of these pages but there can be no doubt that, ashore as afloat, homosexual activity was by no means the preserve of homosexual men per se. It was occasionally partaken of by frustrated heterosexuals in the confines of shipboard life, men for whom a secluded caboose or a night ashore when the ship entered harbour offered temptations impossible to resist.

Until the mid 1930s the stoker complement of the Royal Navy was composed largely of men in their twenties, many of them miners from the north of England. However, at this moment a change of recruiting policy for the first time brought numbers of teenage stokers into the engine room departments of HM ships, a development with which neither they nor the Navy proved sufficiently prepared to cope. Vice Admiral Sir Louis Le Bailly, Lieutenant (E) and a divisional officer in the 1936–9 commission, recalls the upset caused by their arrival in the *Hood*:

> The advent of young stokers onto the stokers' messdecks posed problems. Many were under 18, yet there were no separate bathrooms and being young and some, good looking and attractive, were fair game for homosexually inclined older men. So steps were taken to billet them into separate Messes and to integrate them in 'Dog-Watch' schooling with the Boys. Further, in some cases the Boys' Divisional officers agreed to permit them to take part in subsidised and supervised 'runs' ashore, sightseeing and picnics. On the whole the writer's view is that the measures taken for both seamen and stokers certainly diminished and possibly abolished 'romances' and rape. But in a big ship with innumerable corners and 'cabooses' and fan flats, concealment was not difficult.

Although Boy Fred Coombes (1935–8) evidently subscribed to the homophobic tendency shared by most of the lower deck, his concern to protect his genitals during his first night aboard was not perhaps as absurd as it seems on a prima facie reading of his memoirs. The issue of homosexuality was clearly a pertinent one in the *Hood* during the mid 1930s, Coombes and his pals on the Boys' messdeck spending much of their time ridiculing their petty officer instructor and his 'bum boy' and speculating on whether their divisional officer was himself 'a bit of a puffter [*sic*]'.

As a product of the Royal Naval College at Dartmouth, a community based on the English public school model, it would not have been altogether surprising had the officer in question indeed been 'a bit of a poofter'. Le Bailly, a cadet at Dartmouth between 1929 and 1932, has these comments on the College between the wars:

... Naval Term officers [were] forbidden to have wives within 30 miles and many of the old masters [were] delightfully 'bent' bachelors. There was ... segregation by age-group of 'Terms' except perhaps in the mid-Thirties under the influence of two over-enthusiastic Cadet Captains, when the consequent 'romances' reached almost scandal proportions. Some of the elderly Masters hastily married their Housekeepers. The policy, if there was one, seems to have been 'Cadets must get it out of their systems'.

Sometimes, however, it was asking too much of an officer to 'get it out of his system'. At about 1130 on the morning of 29 June 1939 as the *Hood* lay at Portsmouth a boy seaman reported an indecent advance by the newly joined First Lieutenant. At noon the executive officer, Cdr William Davis, received a message in the wardroom anteroom to the effect that the master-at-arms needed to see him urgently. By 1230 the first lieutenant was under arrest in his cabin with a Marine sentry outside and it was here, before two bells of the afternoon watch had struck, that he blew his brains out with his own shotgun. Though dark rumours persisted into 1941, the evidence was quickly disposed of in one of the ship's incinerators, the matter declared a tragic accident and the deceased accorded a full naval funeral. So ended a brilliant career. He lies in the cemetery of RN Hospital Haslar, a victim perhaps of weakness and incontinence but more certainly so of the honour code and repressed sexuality of his age.

Great as the impact of homosexual incidents were, it would be a mistake to regard them as anything other than occasional frissons in the life of the ship, though no doubt much went undetected. The following comment by Telegraphist Dick Jackman (1937–9) puts it all in perspective:

... The Old Man and 'Winger' (the younger person) was a general reference to a friend without any sexual connotation, someone perhaps only a year or so younger and usually being a run-ashore chum. My own particular friend was a Chief Ordnance Artificer ... while I was a junior Telegraphist. I don't know his age but he was older than me, we had much in common, principally because we both came from the Isle of Wight and many hours were spent talking and walking the forecastle as well as runs ashore. This caused some ribald comments, but like most of them they were not meant seriously. I flatter myself that I was a reasonably good looking Boy Telegraphist, but during my two years plus aboard *Hood* I never encountered any homosexual approach, nor was I aware of any elsewhere. Perhaps I was naïve?

In peacetime the sounding of Evening Quarters at 1600 heralded the end of the working day for most of the crew and, for a proportion of them, an evening's run ashore with perhaps night leave until morning. By 1645 the 'libertymen' had changed into their No 1 suit with gold badges and 'tiddley' accoutrements and were fallen in for inspection on deck. A reading of the pertinent sections of the

King's Regulations and Admiralty Instructions and they were boarding the ship's boats or drifter for shore. It was said that 'England's best ambassador' was 'a British Blue-Jacket walking ashore in a foreign port' and this was certainly borne out during the great cruises of the 1920s when 'Jack's' behaviour was usually found to be exemplary. But it was often a different story in home ports or at Gibraltar and Malta. Particularly Malta; AB Len Williams:

> Malta provided some pretty hilarious nights which will long live in my memory and, no doubt, in the memories of hundreds of thousands of sailors the world over. We owe a lot to the patience and kindness of 'Joe', the average Maltese lodging house and bar keeper, who on numerous occasions would help the worse-for-wear matloes to bed.

For the officers a typical run ashore might consist of a blow-out at the Rock Hotel at Gibraltar or an evening in the Union Club in Valletta. Louis Le Bailly:

> Usually the senior engineer, Lancelot Fogg-Elliot, too busy on board to be anything but a bachelor, would dine with us weekly at Valletta's Union Club. This had a men-only entrance, but through a peep-hole one could jealously watch the poodle-fakers as they disported themselves with their damsels in the presence of some rather forbidding mothers. From frustrated voyeurism it was but a step to the long bar and a gimlet (still the in-drink) and so to the magnificent room, where the knights of Malta had once dined, and an excellent but economic meal.

Though officers occasionally partook, the *Hood*'s ratings were often in search of more prurient entertainment. Len Williams:

> In our runs ashore, Doug and I always included a visit to the 'Forty Three' club in Floriana. We usually started here before proceeding along the Strada Reale to the Gut. This club was run by a man of about 40, known to all the fleet as 'Charlie'. He was a female impersonator, who, when dressed up resembled Mae West and took that famous lady off to a T. [...] Sometimes we would take a bus or taxi over to Sliema and visit one or two of the bars. These were mainly patronized by the destroyer men, since Sliema Creek was the destroyer anchorage. One bar in particular, the 'Empire', staged a female boxing contest as their cabaret show, and we sailors would be treated to an orgy of boxing contests. The contenders, dressed in one-piece swim suits, wore a coloured sash across their chests indicating a 'Miss England' or a 'Miss Austria', or some other nationality. Although to watch two buxom wenches knocking each other about seemed pretty revolting to us, most of us cheered them on as we sipped our iced beer, but the atmosphere was so clouded with tobacco smoke that it was sometimes difficult to see the contenders at all!

As in British society generally, attitudes towards sex in the Royal Navy were, for officers at least, a curious mixture of awareness and denial. To this outlook the lower deck often lent its tacit support. Capt George Blundell, then a midshipman, recalls the efforts of his West Country coxswain, PO A W Jeffrey, to preserve his moral integrity during the *Hood*'s second Scandinavian cruise in the summer of 1923:

> On another occasion I was driving my picket boat along what was then called 'Christiania Fjord' [now Oslofjorden] in Norway. On one side of our route was a ladies' bathing pool. It was summer and all the ladies were bathing in the nude. Each time we passed, my dear Jeff directed my attention to some feature on the opposite side of the fjord. Obviously he considered it improper for his young officer to gaze on a naked female form.

In its own way, PO Jeffrey's discomfiture reflects that of the Admiralty itself which failed to include sex education in the curriculum of its officer cadets and midshipmen. A few might be taken aside for a fatherly chat by an officer or chaplain, but as Rear Admiral Edmund Poland recalled, 'a majority of young midshipmen had their first sexual experience in a brothel'. And not just their first. Paymaster Cdr Keith Evans has this reminiscence of a bordello in Malta in 1938:

> Strada Stretta commonly known as 'The Gut'. Wrexford's 'Aunty' a bit of a hag I think from Northern England. Bella and Tessa may have been Maltese but I think more oriental, comfortable numbers. As Gunroom officers, most of us aged 18 or 19 (not quite under age), I think our leave expired at 1900 (later on occasions), so we had to make way for our 'elders' from the Wardroom and Warrant Officers' Mess.

As a result, incidence of venereal disease (VD) – or 'Wardroom lumbago' as it was euphemistically known on the lower deck – was a concealed but not unknown reality among the officer corps. At least one of the *Hood*'s officers 'caught a dose' during the 1936–9 commission. Confined to his cabin, he was dispatched home at the earliest opportunity.

Attitudes were rather less inhibited on the lower deck where VD remained common despite the fact that improved hygiene and education reduced incidence by more than half between 1912 and 1932. Common enough, indeed, for Chief Ordnance Artificer 'Brigham' Young to give OA Bert Pitman a word to the wise on his first visit to Gibraltar in the summer of 1940:

> When we went to our first foreign port, Gibraltar, he sent for myself and another youngster and he said 'I want you two to go over the border to La Línea tonight and I want you to go to a brothel, one that also has a bar. Now

go into that brothel, pick the girl you'd most like to go to bed with, but don't. Get yourself a drink, in fact, have several drinks and just sit and watch her.' Well, I picked on a beautiful-looking girl, but having seen her go up and down the stairs with a couple of matloes I lost any desire to get off with her.

But the temptation was always there. Walking along 'The Gut', the red-light district of Malta, sailors were wont to have their black 'silk' scarves torn off by girls eager to entice them into a brothel. Even a stroll though the Alameda Gardens at Gibraltar might lead to an unexpected liaison with a lady 'hawking her pearly' in the bushes. Equally, there was great pressure from old-timers for young sailors to prove their manhood through sexual initiation in a brothel. In the handbook for naval chaplains he published in 1944, the Rev Harold Beardmore, *Hood's* chaplain from 1939–41, dilated on the situation his readers might encounter:

> One finds a number of men who are not hardened to loose living. Sometimes the lapse took place after a party where the man had too much to drink, and his resistance to strong temptation was weakened awhile: frequently one comes across a comparative boy who has it pressed upon him by some old-timer that he could never call himself a sailor until he had been with a woman. Thus it was in the form of an adventure that he went wrong, probably with some girl who, for want of a better term, might be called an 'amateur,' and who in the eyes of the young man was probably safe as far as disease was concerned. The important thing is to get hold of the patient before the hardened sinner endeavours to comfort him by saying, 'That's all right, mate; we all get our unlucky runs; no need to take it to heart.' This is first-class propaganda on the part of the devil.

And so yarns were spun of the buxom harlots of Trinidad and St Lucia, of the 'White House on the Hill' at Arosa with its long queues of white-uniformed sailors, of the Oriental beauties of Singapore and Honolulu and of course the varied delights of Southsea and Union Street in Plymouth. But occasionally an encounter with a prostitute in foreign climes might end badly. In September 1937 an official visit to Yugoslavia to celebrate the birthday of King Peter II afforded the *Hood's* crew a week in the port of Split and its hinterland. A first run ashore found the Coombes twins and their pals in one of the harbourside cafes:

> It was all very pleasant. We sat there sipping and trying to get used to their local wine or whatever it was and being served by two young and good-looking, clean and smart girls. The next thing, one of our party was seen slipping through the small door following one of the girls. The remainder could only guess what was happening but were alarmed when, a bit later, some Police and

Gardia of some kind burst in the little door and could be heard storming up the stairs. Wondering what to do, we could only go outside and wait for developments and soon, after a lot of shouting and commotion, the Police bundled the girl downstairs, knocking hell out of her just as the window went up and the fourth member of the chums came to the window, looked out and dropped his shoes out before starting to climb down a drainpipe that came down near the window. [...] Quite a few people were passing and all the rest of the lads could do was to pick his shoes up for him and help him back across the lane into the cafe ... He told us he had just finished 'emptying his kitbag' when the commotion on the stairs had started and had just got out of bed to put his trousers on when the door burst open. This gang entered and grabbed the girl and started shouting at her and giving her a good hiding. He was petrified and when they had gone looked for the best way out which was the window ... After he had recovered [we] decided that the best thing was to get the hell out of it ...

Evidently, the pair had fallen foul of King Peter's draconian laws against prostitution.

Return to home port invariably brought pleasures of a different ilk, perhaps a reunion with wife and family or, in the case of the Coombes twins, a visit from their girlfriends after a lengthy train journey from Sheffield. It was Navy Week 1936 and, amidst a carnival atmosphere, the *Hood* lay awash with visitors in dry dock at Portsmouth. For Fred and Frank there were certain naval traditions to be lived up to if possible:

After ... a good look round the ship, both above and below decks, except for not daring to offer to show the girls the Golden Rivet, which was reputed to be riveted into every RN ship, normally in some secluded part, well out of the way of prying eyes, we [spent the evening] passing the time away and smooching on Southsea Common and promenade, which was later to be converted into a vast, grass-covered bed. The popular tune at the time was 'Chapel in the Moonlight', but Southsea became renowned for the number of girls' knees, bent not in prayer but only earning their railway fare, and the words 'Bobbing Arseholes in the Moonlight'.

As in every other sphere, the onset of war brought with it a quickening of amorous life. While the *Hood* was refitting at Portsmouth in the last summer of peace, Jim Taylor and his companions on the Boys' messdeck were given strict instructions to avoid the cafe at no 12 Great Southsea Street, the petty officers' brothel. Condoms were issued free and in quantity but 'Rose Cottage', the ship's VD ward with the legend 'Only those who have been purified can be pure' posted on its door, continued to have its patients, despite the red-ink entry on a man's medical history and damage to his prospects that followed. In the quarterly report he submitted on the medical condition of the ship in April 1940, Surgeon Cdr K A Ingleby-Mackenzie, the Squadron Medical Officer, listed four cases of gonorrhoea and one of syphilis, though two of the former were to the same man. Despite being diagnosed and discharged to hospital, the syphilitic not untypically denied all exposure to infection, whereas the others admitted contracting theirs during the ship's brief stays at Greenock. In his report for the next quarter, which the *Hood* spent largely at Plymouth and Liverpool, Ingleby-Mackenzie recorded nine fresh cases of gonorrhoea and the installation, complete with framed instructions, of an ablution cabinet in the urinals near the port battery in which the men could discreetly take prophylactic measures after an encounter ashore. Still, this shows a decided improvement on 1932, when the ship recorded a total of seventy-five cases of VD, many contracted during a spring cruise in the Caribbean.

Needless to say, such liaisons occasionally brought consequences other than disease. With due allowance for post-war embroidering, the following aside by OD Jon Pertwee is worth citing:

> Lieutenant [Horace] Davies also had the well nigh impossible task of running to earth those lusty lads who had given *noms de plume* and aliases to various female conquests in port. Among the favourite names to be assumed was Able Seaman Derek Topping. When the arm of a derrick or crane is about to reach the perpendicular, the operator would shout 'Derrick Topping' meaning the crane arm had almost reached its limit. This pseudonym was frequently given after a night of love and passion, to minimise chances of identification should the sound of tiny mistakes be heard pattering up the companionway. Another much-used name was Able Seaman B M Lever. The initials B M standing for breech mechanism, and lever referring to the lever on a gun that opens and closes the breech. So pathetic letters of remarkable similarity would arrive with envelopes marked S.W.A.L.K. (sealed with a loving kiss), possibly reading:

> > Dear Derek,
> > You said you was going to rite but you never. I am now three months gone. I am disparate has I am beginning to show – wot are you going to do about it? Rite soon.
> > I.T.A.L.Y. Doris.
> > P.S. H.O.L.L.A.N.D.*

> These impassioned pleas were posted on the ship's notice board and brought forth little response other than cruel laughter. Derek Topping and Basil M Lever should've felt very ashamed of themselves.

*I.T.A.L.Y. stands for 'I trust and love you' and H.O.L.L.A.N.D. 'Hope our love lives and never dies'.

On the other hand, certain matelots nurtured the hope of fetching up with a wealthy widow ashore, and in this endeavour not a few went adrift on foreign service. During the 1936–9 commission none pursued this goal more ardently than 'Tiny' Fowler, one of the ship's divers. Here is Fred Coombes' version of events. The date seems to be January 1938 and the place Marseilles:

One of the best yarns was started on that visit when Tiny Fowler, our huge … diver went adrift. Whether or when he had met his friends before could only be guessed at, but he clearly knew where to meet them because he went ashore the first night at anchor and that was the last we saw of him 'til just before we sailed, when a smart, medium-sized motor yacht came alongside. They must have known what they were doing as they came to our forward gangway … where a glamorous grandma came on the bottom platform with Tiny Fowler to do a bit of snogging before the Regulating Crushers came running down to Tiny to run him back up into custody.

Three months later at Golfe-Juan on the Côte d'Azur Fowler was at it again:

Lofty Fowler was not allowed ashore this time but had worked them a flanker by hiding in the forepeak of the picket boat that had been used by the officers to go ashore. He went by nipping out when the officers had gone and before the crew could stop him was off. The crew swore blind that they did not know that he was aboard … but that was the last we saw of Tiny 'til the day we sailed. […] The next day when we went in to fetch the few stragglers … one of our first customers was Tiny Fowler, drunk too, but with what looked like a dowager duchess on one arm, a bunch of flowers and a basket full of eggs, some of which had got broken and were running down his trousers, on the other. If his lady friend had intended the eggs to restore his vitality she was unlucky as Tiny returned peacefully.

Fowler had ample time to savour the memory in the army detention quarters at Corradino, Malta. The remainder, with wives or partners a world away and perhaps little inclination for adventure, had to find contentment in the privacy of their cabin, hammock or caboose and await a reunion all the sweeter for the length of its parting.

Of course, there were activities ashore beyond mixing with the opposite sex. Proverbially, there was unrestrained consumption of 'the Demon Drink', however much the Navy might try to discourage it. Jon Pertwee has this wartime reminiscence:

When at anchor in Scapa Flow, off duty liberty men used to go ashore to taste the pleasures of Lyness night-life. This, for the majority of the men, meant going to one of the enormous NAAFI canteens and, armed with Naval issue coupons, imbibing their allotted two or three pints of beer. Clever barterers, however, always managed to collect a pocket full of additional coupons, which allowed them the long-looked-for opportunity of going on a monumental 'piss-up'. After several such outings I sold my beer coupons and opted for other joys of the flesh.

Getting them back on board was no mean feat. The Coombes twins had the misfortune of crewing one of the boats sent to bring the men off after a night's carousing on the Côte d'Azur in May 1938:

A lot, as drunk as newts, were stood on the wooden jetty with their girlfriends and others and would not climb aboard us. We struggled to carry some of them aboard the launch, only to see some of them crawl on their hands and knees to the other end and out again so eventually we went back to the ship with whoever would stay and went back with six big marines to get the others aboard. It went on a long time and it ended up with the cells on the ship that full of drunks that they had to release the more sober to find room for the more drunk.

One of the drunks was Stoker Harry Holderness:

No one was interested in returning until a stoker petty officer, who had drunk his fill, said he was going aboard – and soon we were all following him. When the boats arrived at the *Hood*, which was three miles out, the officers were furious because the ship had not sailed. Most of us were singing and waving long French loaves. Commander Orr-Ewing called for us to be quiet and ordered the coxswains to take the boats round the ship until we were silent. But that set us singing 'Side, Side, Jolly Ship's Side'. Once round, however, we all quietened and filed aboard. The stoker petty officer, who had drunk too much, got a recommend for getting us all aboard.

No wonder the task of returning a boatload of drunken sailors was among the sternest tests a midshipman could face in his time aboard. There were severe punishments for the drunk and disorderly, but with the outbreak of war came recognition of the importance of allowing the crew to let off steam and thus a more tolerant attitude towards inebriated libertymen. AB Len Williams remembers the *Hood* at Greenock in early 1940:

There was a considerable difference in height between high and low tide in the Clyde area, and when the lads began to come back from leave, some of them the worse for wear and singing their heads off, it proved quite an evolution to get them safely down the steep ladders and into the boat. Captain Glennie, being a wise gentleman, and knowing the ways of sailors, had told the ship's company that he did not mind how his lads got back on board, provided that they DID get back. 'I do not wish to go to sea in an emergency with any of my crew missing' he warned us. Consequently, many and varied were the conditions the sailors were in when we finally got them on board. On one occasion we lowered a steel provisioning net into the liberty boat, and loading the helpless ones carefully into it, hoisted them inboard with the main derrick. However, I cannot remember us ever letting the skipper down. We always sailed with a full crew.

This, however, was not always the case. At no time in the *Hood's* career did more men desert than during the World Cruise of 1923–4. Evidently, the chance of a life in the sun for a man who was otherwise committed to another eight or ten years in the 'Andrew' was well worth the remote possibility of recapture, and by the time the Special Service Squadron sailed for Hawaii six months into the cruise, 151 had deserted from her seven ships, all but ten in Australia.

Needless to say, the Navy lived and worked to a harsh code of discipline, one that came down heavily on those who infringed it. Mindful of Invergordon, Capt Rory O'Conor made no bones about the constitutional framework under which every man served: 'Those in authority can afford to act calmly, seeing that they are backed by the authority of the whole Service and the Naval Discipline Act, with the Lords Spiritual and Temporal and all the Commons in support.' The point was not lost on the majority of men. As CPO Harry Cutler put it, 'We knew what to expect. Those who got into trouble were those who kicked over the traces and refused to submit to discipline.' The structure of this discipline mirrored the organisation of the ship herself. LS (later Cdr) Joe Rockey of Plymouth: 'The routines were quite strict and well laid down and if you did not carry them out you expected to be penalised, and if you disobeyed of course it meant that you were passed further along the chain of command, dependent on the error you'd made or what offence you'd committed.' Enforcement of the King's Regulations and Admiralty Instructions by which the Navy was governed was entrusted to the master-at-arms and the ship's three regulating petty officers or 'crushers'. The master-at-arms, or 'Jaunty' as he was known, was a man to respect. An experienced petty officer selected for toughness and intelligence, the lower deck held few secrets from him. As the senior chief petty officer in the ship he was the only rating afforded a private cabin and thus the privilege of sleeping in a bunk. His influence on the lower deck was enormous:

The Master-at-Arms in a ship is a man whose co-operation and friendship one should cultivate. He is as a rule most helpful when he sees you are all out to encourage him in keeping the ship free from such things as leave-breaking, theft and immorality. A good Master-at-Arms can probably do more than any other member of the lower deck towards making a ship's company happy and contented.

But if the master-at-arms chose to wield his considerable power with a heavy hand then life for many on the lower deck could be made intolerable, as indeed it would be for any unwise enough to 'get athwart his hawse'. Occasionally, the need for men to be detailed for disagreeable duty required the crushers to trawl the lower deck for volunteers and for such occasions it behoved one to be on the right side of the Jaunty and his men. But their main duty was in keeping discipline and enforcing observance of naval and shipboard regulations both ashore and afloat. This meant patrolling the messdecks for illicit drinking or proscribed games like Crown and Anchor, or against the bullying, violence and intimidation that occasionally reared its head. It might also mean landing with a shore patrol to monitor the behaviour of libertymen and counting them back on their return to the ship. In his capacity as head of the ship's police, the master-at-arms was always in attendance at 'commander's defaulters', the miscreants and their crimes enumerated in a large book carried under his arm. During the regime of Cdr Rory O'Conor (1933–6), commander's defaulters took place at 0820 each morning save Sunday. It was a duty to which he gave the utmost importance:

> The Commander needs to be in a consistently judicial frame of mind for his magisterial duties … Appearances are often misleading, and when they are unfavourable to the accused one may be misled into an injustice. Remember the old Chinese proverb: 'A man may be a teetotaller, but if his nose is red, no one will believe it.'

Some three thousand defaulters having passed through his hands during the 1933–6 commission, O'Conor was able to offer readers his accumulated wisdom on the dispensing of justice:

> The majority of small offences are committed by thoughtlessness or mischance and not by intention, and after one solemn warning most men are careful not to reappear as defaulters. [...] In dealing with defaulters a Commander comes face to face with an endless variety of motives and mischances which bring men to his table, cap in hand. It is a central truth of human nature that men's faults are the corollary of their virtues, and that without our faults we should be different men for good, as well as for ill. Justice is most just when tempered with mercy.

Where punishment was concerned, the following measures were recommended for leave-breakers:

> First offence: – If reasonable explanation – Caution
> – If no reasonable explanation – Scale
> Second offence: – Scale
> Third offence: – Captain's Report

'Scale' here meant stoppage of leave, though stoppage of pay was an additional consequence of going adrift. Other infractions would receive one of the many punishments in the naval inventory, from No 16, an hour's extra work, to No 10a, two hours' rifle and bayonet drill after tea. Of course, if one had an identical twin aboard it was possible to mitigate the worst effects of a punishment through artful substitution. Two sailors in this ambiguous situation were Fred and Frank Coombes, boy seamen with a knack for getting into trouble:

> We had become well accustomed to doing plenty of jankers, but Gib added a further dimension as in the Med awnings were generally left rigged, which gave us the advantage of not being seen by the higher decks or the bridge. We soon came up with the idea of sharing the punishment by changing places at some place in our hour-long trot around 'A' and 'B' turrets. From our time at *St Vincent* we had always shared our loads in punishment by taking turns to do the mustering and the evening drill.* The fact that we now had two huge turrets to screen [us] from the Instructor and four convenient hatches leading to a lower deck to choose from made things much easier for us. No matter at which point our keeper stood to keep an eye on us, there was always one hatch not in his vision where we could change over ... The other boys under punishment, who we had thought might object to our swapping over, made no secret of the fact that they were as keen as us to see our tormentors taken out for a trot. Though a lot were aware when one of us was on punishment and poor old [PO] John Bunney tried to catch us at it by nearly doing as much running as us ... we were never caught doing our vanishing act as one ran up [onto] the upper deck and one went down to the lower ...

In the event of a serious or repeated misdemeanour the offender would be sent before the captain for jurisdiction under the Naval Discipline Act. Captain's defaulters usually took place around 1100, the master-at-arms once again in attendance. The captain was the only officer aboard who could punish a man by warrant, that is either by confining him to the ship's cells for a maximum of fourteen days or by stripping him of his rate, his good conduct badges or his Good Conduct Medal if he had more than fifteen years' service. In the case of boys or midshipmen this extended to authorising a caning, administered by the master-at-arms to the former and the sub lieutenant of the gunroom to the latter. Officers were tried by court martial, a tribunal composed of their fellow officers acting under naval law but over whose judgements the Admiralty reserved plenary power. Really serious cases, men whose crimes fell beyond the punitive jurisdiction of the captain, were discharged to the detention quarters ashore for periods up to ninety days. Others, like *Hood*'s mutineers in 1931, would find themselves ejected from the Navy 'Services No Longer Required' or subject to criminal prosecution.

*HMS *St Vincent* was the boys' training establishment at Gosport.

6

Of One Company?

IF THE MOMENT of his arrival aboard might well provide a boy seaman with his first inkling of the rigours that awaited him in his chosen profession, a few days would quite likely add a taste of its frequent drudgery and occasional injustice. On his second morning aboard Fred Coombes (1935–8) and his companions were ordered to scrub the upper deck. Maybe the weather was worse and his subsequent experiences more bitter, but there can be no denying the disgust and disillusion in Coombes's account:

> The next day we mustered at 6, still trying to crunch with our teeth the hard ship's biscuit before someone robbed us of it. On mustering with the rest of the upper-deck part of the ship's company, we were all reported to the Duty Officer who gave the usual order to scrub decks. The only difference that morning was that, in the unusually cold weather for Portsmouth, when the sea water was pumped and hosed on the decks the water froze and turned to icy slush as it ran on deck and over the side. As normal in the RN, the last order was always obeyed and, as normal, the lower end in the pecking order, those with no boots and socks, [took] off boots and socks, rolled our trousers up and, on the orders of the leading seaman in charge of our small section, were told to grab a long-handled heavy scrubber and 'scrub aft'. Of those who did not own or have ... a pair of seaboots, most seem to have vanished or faded away as soon as the icy slush was seen and felt on bare feet to set us all hopping and heading for a still dry part of the deck. The Duty Officer, who was no doubt still wearing his uniform jacket and trousers over his pyjamas and heavy woollen scarf, was sat in his nice warm cabin, sipping nice warm tea as he waited for his nice hot bath to be run for him, was wondering why different leading hands and petty officers kept running to his door to tell him that it was freezing up there. Don't know how long it took him to get back on deck but do know that, when he did, all he could find was his senior ratings and those wearing seaboots still washing the decks but, instead of scrubbing them, trying to broom the slush over the side before it froze solid. Can well imagine what the ship's commanding officer said to his juniors when he saw the dirty slush frozen to his freshly-painted lovely

ship's side, but by that time he had it all to himself and his senior ratings as we were all below in the muggy warmth getting thawed out and into heavier underwear before breakfast.

For the Coombes twins, however, poor leadership was as nothing to the demoralising effect of petty discipline:

> The first time that we were both rattled for a very minor offence was by a young midshipman, of about our own age but educated. We found out why these snotty-nosed youngsters were called snotties and began to realise why all those who hoped for [promotion], whether officer or man, were fighting each other to bring their names to the attention of our seniors. Such as us, with no ambition and very little interest, were thought to be good food to feed on. Even the maggots would have had better taste but it suited them and that was all that mattered. We went to build the mound of their ambitions.

The opinions of Fred Coombes are unusual in their vehemence, particularly in the *Hood* which is remembered as a happy ship throughout most of the 1930s. But they encapsulate much of the resentment and frustration that at one time or another burned in the hearts of all ratings who went down to the sea in ships in the inter-war period. To be sure, the Coombes twins were, on their own admission, hardly whiter than white; in fact, they were notorious for always being in trouble. But their sentiments, expressed in vivid sailor's language, would have been shared by many in their more desperate moments. As Coombes recalled, 'It was explained to us by the odd older members of the crew – a lot of whom were survivors of the wartime fleets, now drastically reduced – [that they] only put up with the poor conditions and pay to avoid the mass unemployment that awaited them if they did not achieve Pension Age.' Where officers and morale were concerned the view of Telegraphist Dick Jackman (1937–9) was perhaps more typical of the younger rating:

> I cannot comment on life in the wardroom, except that it was of a very high standard and very much resented by the lower deck for whom very little was done to make life enjoyable. Petty restrictions such as making the wearing of uniform compulsory at all times, ashore and afloat, with the exception of banyan parties when sports wear was worn, could have been relaxed. One needed to be a contortionist to get out of, and back into a sailor's uniform ...

Cdr Rory O'Conor (1933–6), that most reform-minded of officers, gauged the issue of morale in rather simpler terms. Seen from the opposite end of the spectrum, the whole problem boiled down to nagging by officers and superiors:

> The tendency to nag arises from human fretfulness, and there is nothing to surpass

it for making an intelligent man feel insubordinate. Injustice is far easier to put up with than any form of bully-ragging. The Commander has to make it clear early in the commission to all those set in authority under him that, no matter what is done or left undone, he will not have things aggravated by nagging. [...] If a man is sulking, the chances are that someone has been nagging him.

Equally, it was as well for someone in authority to avoid any sort of confrontation with the men. The Rev Harold Beardmore, chaplain aboard between 1939–41:

When visiting the messdecks see that you don't get involved in an argument: *(a)* when a rating takes an opportunity of getting at you or your job, or *(b)* when he gets 'hot under the collar' about some social or service matter. It is best to send for the man at some convenient time, and discuss the matter thoroughly over a cigarette in your cabin. One finds that when the man is by himself he is much more reasonable than when surrounded by his messmates, before whom he may like to pose as a bit of a sea-lawyer.

Coombes, for his part, eventually reached the conclusion that 'the uneducated, too-thick-to-think lower end were not at a disadvantage by being uneducated if they made up their deficiency by using their common sense'. Time and a DSM earned off Normandy in 1944 would amply vindicate this view. As he lived to discover, the coming war would alter the sailor's lot beyond all recognition. Though Coombes and his companions could not know it, they and their ship were living in the twilight years of the old Navy.

Where opinions on the men were expressed at all these were usually full of respect, affection and admiration. That of Vice Admiral Le Bailly is typical:

Above all we learned about sailors: from our hammock boys, who lashed up or unlashed our hammocks each morning and evening, the only people on board younger and financially poorer than we were (despite the small subvention we gave them); from our boats' crews, from the lordly chief and petty officers, from the cooper, still plying his trade, from that now unhappily extinct dinosaur, the Royal Marine gunner and from his fellow warrant officers; from them all more than any formal lecture or book could teach us.

Even so, such views were often underpinned by a strong measure of suspicion. In the handbook for naval chaplains he dedicated to the *Hood*'s company in 1944, the Rev Beardmore warned his readers against the age-old subterfuges of which sailors were capable.

I once had to 'vet' the case of a certain rating who requested to change from C of E to Methodist. As the Methodist Church Party had to walk two miles to their church, and the walk included a steep hill, my suspicions were aroused. After a chat in my cabin, I realized that this rating had a particular longing to quench his thirst on a Sunday morning about 1000 when the sun was really hot. In the walk to church the party had to pass the Recreation Room where good beer was obtainable. The trick was to get in the last section of fours, and as they passed this welcome spot, just slip out and slip back again by mingling with the congregation outside the church later when the party fell in to return to the ship. The captain smiled when this was explained to him, and the request was not granted. We should be men without guile, but see that you are not 'sold a pup' by the old-timer who may think that because you are new to the Service he may be able to 'work a swindle' as the saying is on the lower deck.

There is, of course, more than a hint of condescension in Beardmore's comment that 'They think these things out very carefully'. This attitude did not pass unnoticed. AB Len Wincott, Invergordon mutineer and *Hood* veteran of 1926: 'If a sailor tried to explain the cause of a minor misdemeanour, the officer's foregone conclusion was always that the man was lying. Equally, it was accepted without evidence or question that the men were dull-witted.' Yet, as Wincott continued, 'It is greatly to the credit of the officer corps of the RN that a considerable number of them discarded this attitude, developing instead an approach based on a simple, humane principle: firm but polite.' This attitude owed much to the enhanced concern for the plight of their men that the Invergordon Mutiny brought to the upper echelons of the Navy. Even so, 1938 still found Capt Francis Pridham having to exhort his officers to 'Learn all you can about how your men live in their ship. Details of the serving of his food, where he writes his letters, the true extent of the facilities (or lack of them) for washing, shaving, keeping his kit tidy etc. Study life on the Mess Deck. Discover their recreations.' And above all, 'Keep in mind the very narrow financial margin within which many men and their families have to live.'

Concerned interest there may have been, but there were still ratings, twenty-year veterans of the Navy, for whom cynicism was the ultimate lesson of their experience. Fred Coombes: 'Of the others, survivors of the previous generation, most were tough old nuts with nothing to lose, their Good Conduct badges having gone with the wind many a time, and toughened up by periods of detention. [Together, this] made for a tough old navy that required tight control.' Needless to say, most officers were under few illusions as to the type of man they were dealing with here. Capt Pridham made no bones about it:

There are of course various kinds of 'black sheep'. The chap who is 'grey black' through his own foolishness, gets drunk on shore and makes himself a noisy nuisance, is no great anxiety. The really 'black' ones, the Bolshies, the coarse, the lecherous and the surly gaol bird are the dangerous ones. I have no compunction in saying that the risk we run in carrying this type justifies us hounding him down, and out, when we find him out. The Navy is not a reformatory.

But there were other considerations. For most officers, iron-hard discipline served not only to restrain the unruliness and aggression that made the British sailor the formidable man he was, but also to harden him against the day when the sea or the enemy might mete out more than irksome labour or petty discipline. Fred Coombes admitted as much in recounting the following incident on the Detached Mole at Gibraltar in the autumn of 1935:

Though not very pleasant places to hang around, the toilets ashore were much sought after by some as a place to skive or perhaps read the newspaper, which at busy times in the mornings meant that queues were formed at some of the blocks. Some anxious person, crossing his legs and stamping his feet, had the idea and was given the opportunity to crumple a sheet of newspaper up, wait for the flush to run, light the paper and drop it on the outflow. The resulting yells as posteriors were singed soon meant that at the first yell everybody stood up and watched for the party piece to float past before sitting down again. This harmless form of amusement went on for weeks, perhaps months, and caused many a laugh. But there is always someone to go too far, as happened when someone used petrol to catch the lot and not the first to shout. Letting the petrol be poured slowly till it had reached the other end, he threw in his match, resulting in a huge flash which engulfed the culprit as he was the only one singed round the face and head, all others being scorched at the other end. We heard the thudding explosion from aboard and saw a line of matelots staggering to the Sick Bay in various forms of undress, mostly walking like cowboys, to have their scorch marks soothed. It was to be the last time that amusement was to be found in that form, though some wit sealed it off by putting on the notice board a notice that a delicatessen meal would be served that evening in the Sick Bay, the menu being Roast Beast Cheek, Grilled Swinging Steak and Curried Dusters. The culprit was found to be a stoker in the motor boat where the petrol had come from. It was a foolhardy trick, but if the Navy wanted crews with plenty of fire in their bellies who played hard, backing their King's Regulations and Admiralty Instructions by rigid discipline, they had to expect small explosions as devilment fired up.

The challenge of harnessing this energy as war beckoned was Capt Pridham's special concern in 1938:

[The] endeavour to bring out the fighting qualities of our men should be our constant consideration. As their leaders it is our business to inspire enthusiasm and confidence. A 'clean shoot' should be regarded as a step towards emptying the shell bays into the guts of the enemy. It is no easy matter to bring into proper significance in peace time the importance of our fitness for fighting – our sole purpose and great responsibility. Yet few of us remember it as such for long at a time. We are inclined to forget that even in these highly mechanised days superiority in battle is far more a matter of fighting qualities in ourselves and our men than of calibre of guns and thickness of armour.

To the majority of men, the *Hood*'s officers seemed, in Ted Briggs's words, to be 'like God Almighty'. AB Bob Tilburn describes the attitude of most: 'In those days you were not necessarily frightened of those officers, you were in awe of them. Because they were so far above you, not only in the mental scale but in the social scale as well. It was still very feudal.' Typically, Fred Coombes took a rather more jaundiced view, though it was one shared by many:

The way of the RN [was] that when we went to sea on exercises we, the lower end, were too thick to understand why we did what, for [which reason we] were never informed. Steaming round the ocean was for the officers' benefit; if we were involved, the only information was that which we read on the notice board and not why [...] There was still a lot at the top end who still thought that education and breeding were the be all and end all of Service life.

Despite Coombes's remarks, considerable efforts were made after Invergordon to keep crewmen informed of the ship's movements and the diplomatic context of her activities. William James, who flew his flag in *Hood* between 1932–4, was surely the first admiral to clear lower deck to explain forthcoming exercises to the men. In the *Notes for Newly Joined Officers* he prepared during his tenure, Capt Francis Pridham (1936–8) made it quite plain where the advantage of doing so lay:

It is not difficult to give your men some idea of the duty the ship is being employed upon. The purpose of the exercises about to be carried out, why the ship is about to visit Arzeu or Barcelona, why the paravanes are being got out early in the morning watch, etc. etc. The more you can interest the Ship's Company in what is going on the better. Moreover, you will thereby short-circuit the disgruntled man who spreads the yarn that they are being bully-ragged and driven unnecessarily.

But though the Invergordon Mutiny ushered in a significant change in officer attitudes, there can be no doubt that arrogance and thoughtlessness lay at the root of much disgruntlement and disaffection on the lower deck. O'Conor tacitly admitted as much: 'All men, young and old, are sensitive and it does not do to speak roughly, or someone will be burning with indignation from a neglect of courtesy, of which you may remain profoundly unconscious.' In most instances the men could draw on a subtle and evolved language to express their disgust or disappointment at those given command over them. A tone of voice, a nuance of body language, a show of reticence, all spoke volumes to those on the receiving end. There were moments, however, when extreme aggravation called for more direct means of communication. Shoddy or listless work, mass leave-breaking and desultory performances in fleet sporting events were a sure sign of poor morale and failing leadership. The tenure of Rear Admiral Sir Walter Cowan and Captain Geoffrey Mackworth in 1921–3 rivals the Invergordon Mutiny as the most unhappy period in the *Hood*'s long career. Both fell victim to pranks by their subordinates. One fine day somebody pushed Bill, the ship's goat mascot, through the skylight of Cowan's sleeping cabin and into his bed. On another occasion Mackworth, who was fond of asking for working parties of six Marines, received a box of toy soldiers in the mail along with an impudent note which resulted in the entire detachment being subjected to a handwriting test. Neither culprit was ever discovered. But there were gentler ways of letting off steam. The pukka accent in which much of the wardroom spoke was the subject of ridicule on the lower deck and many was the officer who acquired a nickname. Len Wincott:

> The nicknames that men give to their officers are more informative than many people think. If an officer is given a number of nicknames, and more and more are conjured up, it is a sure sign that he is far from popular. If on the other hand he gets one which sticks to him, one can be certain that he is respected.

Equally, the officer whose men called him a 'gent' was being paid their very highest compliment. But most were glad to keep their distance and generally had as little contact with officers as possible. Nowhere is this attitude more exquisitely captured than in the following exchange between Mid George Blundell, then in command of the *Hood*'s first picket boat, and his West Country coxswain. The year is 1924.

> I have often reflected on what a lot the petty officers tactfully taught me on how to behave. One day we landed a number of officers just after lunch: the ship's company was still at work. On return I asked the coxswain (Jeffreys was his name; he was a darling man) 'What do the men think of the officers going ashore in working hours?' Jeff looked at me with that 'three badge' twinkle in his eye. 'Lor' bless you, Sir,' he replied, 'We likes to see them out of the way.' I have never forgotten that wise remark.

Other junior officers received more detail than PO A W Jeffrey would perhaps have been willing to share. Louis Le Bailly served both as a midshipman and as a sub lieutenant (E) in the 1930s:

> As a midshipman of a picket boat, often sitting snugly in the forecastle with its

crew in Queensferry or Tangier or Malta's Custom House Jetty, with perhaps 30 minutes to wait [...] before the late night officers' leave boat was due, one heard things that one should not have heard and learned lessons. [...] What amazed me and has continued to amaze me is how cheerful and relaxed most sailors seemed to be despite their living conditions and how, on the whole, they admired the officers, although prepared good humouredly to 'take the Mickey' out of some.

The *Hood*'s wardroom numbered around forty-five officers out of a peacetime complement of about 1,150 men. As was the case throughout the Navy, the ship's officers were divided into two branches, executive and civilian. The distinction is important because it was not until after the Second World War that officers of the so-called 'Civilian Branch' could aspire to their own seagoing commands. Among the 'Executive Branch' were the specialists in gunnery, torpedoes, navigation and signals together with the 'salthorse' officers who were content to make their careers without advanced training in any discipline. This branch was, of necessity, completed by the captain and his principal executive officer, the commander. Officers of the civilian branch wore the same uniform as their executive colleagues, though their particular specialisations were distinguished by coloured cloth between the gold stripes on their cuffs. In the case of engineer officers this was purple. Paymasters wore white, instructors blue, shipwrights and constructors silver-grey, surgeons red and dentists orange. Unusually for a capital ship, the *Hood*'s officer complement was remembered as a friendly and homogenous body throughout much of her career, 'probably as happy as a big ship could ever be'. However, this cannot disguise the tensions and snobbery that occasionally surfaced in the wardroom, particularly between executive officers and the engineer branch which was stripped of its executive status by the Admiralty in 1925. Executive officers derided engineers as 'plumbers', 'dustmen' and 'dirty fingernail types', to which the latter responded with 'dabtoes', 'crab wallahs' and 'fish heads'. In 1937 Sub-Lt (E) Louis Le Bailly, fresh from the Royal Naval Engineering College at Keyham, found himself greeted on the quarterdeck by Cdr David Orr-Ewing, a gunnery specialist, with the words, 'Are you another of these pacifist subs from Keyham?' The notion that the technical disciplines were at odds with the spirit of a fighting service and their practicians ill-suited to seagoing command remained deeply engrained. Evidently, there were many in the Navy who had as yet failed to grasp the technological realities that the coming war would so ruthlessly assert on it.

The gunroom to which, as a sub lieutenant, a chastened Le Bailly repaired on arrival was the domain of the midshipmen, the Royal Navy's officers in waiting. Until 1932 it was part of his training as an officer that every cadet emerging from the Royal Naval College at Dartmouth should serve up to two years aboard a capital ship, and the *Hood*'s gunroom complement was never less than twenty-five. Thereafter, cadets spent a year in the training cruiser *Frobisher* before being promoted midshipmen and let loose on the fleet, a development which caused the *Hood*'s gunroom complement to drop to around fifteen with a turnover of half a dozen or so every four months. The gunroom was a large and austere compartment on the port side of the upper deck served by an adjoining pantry. Sub-Lt Le Bailly, returning after a four-year absence, was relieved to find things much as they had been during his earlier occupation:

> With some trepidation I entered the gunroom door at the armchair end reserved for sub-lieutenants. The brass stove, which I had assiduously polished, was still there and to my delight I was welcomed by a near-contemporary as the co-ruler of his little kingdom. I soon discovered that the gunroom was still a place where laughter mostly prevailed and the food as bad as ever with the same grinning, but now even more pear-shaped, messman peering through the serving hatch; where the same tin lockers in which I had kept my journal and sight book were still used by the midshipmen; where the only daylight came from the skylight. The same leather-coated cushions on the benches at the ship's side were even more worn as were the two leather armchairs of which I could now claim one.

The gunroom was mostly taken up by a large polished mahogany table at which the 'young gentlemen', suitably attired, were waited on at dinner by a pair of mess stewards. During the 1930s at least, catering for the *Hood*'s gunroom was, by choice, left in the hands of a civilian messman. Louis Le Bailly:

> Dinner, as with our other meals, was dispensed by the same wily Maltese messman and his acolytes who took a shilling a day from our pay. Our wine bill was limited to 10 shillings a month as cadets and 15 shillings as midshipmen. On this we could treat ourselves to a sherry, a glass of beer on guest nights and an occasional glass of Marsala when we returned, cold and shivering, with our boat cloaks and uniforms wet through from a rough boat trip. Spirits, had we been allowed them, were almost unknown to us and few could afford or wished to smoke.

Though the bullying made notorious by the novels of Frederick Marryat and Charles Morgan was largely a thing of the past, the gunroom remained a spirited community which, like its public-school equivalents, deferred to authority yet frequently took pleasure in the misery of its inmates. Equally, it was often a forcing ground for lifelong friendships between officers. Ragging, especially on gala nights, was a popular and often violent diversion to which senior officers traditionally turned a blind eye, though in 1938 the gunroom created something of a stir by including inflated condoms among its Christmas decorations. Rear Admiral Peter La Niece (1940) recalls some capers off Scotland early in the war:

It was a high spirited gunroom and one evening we went ashore to Helensburgh, on the northern side of the Clyde, to see a film; on leaving the cinema we 'borrowed' a framed picture of the film star Loretta Young; this was borne back on board, signed by all concerned, and hung in the gunroom as a trophy. Later on it was captured by a raiding gunroom from another ship; in due course it was recaptured. It was then replaced by a Barber's Pole also acquired from Helensburgh. Suffice to say the Barber's Pole went from ship to ship until after the end of the war when I rediscovered it. [...] I still have the picture of Loretta Young ...

The prevailing atmosphere is captured by Paymaster Lt Cdr E C Talbot-Booth RNR:

Although discipline is probably stricter than in any other force in the world, there are times when the bounds are loosed to an extent which cannot be understood by foreigners. There are occasions when the junior members of the Ward-room Mess will make a swoop or raid on the Gun-room, or midshipman's mess and a tremendous scrap will ensue. The compliment may be returned and a fierce combat ensue on the floor of the senior mess to the detriment of boiled shirts and winged collars. Five minutes later perhaps the junior midshipman is knocking at your cabin door his hand raised to the salute while he gravely informs you that your boat is alongside.

The sub lieutenant of the gunroom could be delegated the authority to administer up to a dozen cuts with a cane or dirk scabbard for minor offences, though this form of punishment was forbidden by O'Conor during his tenure as commander in 1933–6. As he later wrote, 'The old argument, that a Snottie preferred half a dozen to having his leave stopped, is disposed of when it is realised that neither treatment is suitable for an officer'. O'Conor also stamped out both early-morning gym and the degrading rites of 'creeping for Jesus' and 'fork in the beam', the gunroom punishments that sub lieutenants had inflicted on their juniors since the days of the sailing navy. The time was ripe for change:

Punishments that are suitable for schoolboys are not suitable for adolescents of the ages of 18 to 21 whom it is intended to regard as officers. We must have it one way or the other. Either treat them as schoolboys – messengers, truants – or else make up our minds that they are officers and that we are going to treat them as such.

With O'Conor the midshipman of the Royal Navy finally came of age.

In most cases life as a midshipman afloat gave an officer his only taste of sleep in a hammock. With no designated sleeping compartment, midshipmen usually slung their hammocks in one of the flats on the main deck aft, sub lieutenants enjoying the comparative luxury of a shared cabin. The large white chests with which generations of midshipmen had gone to sea were stowed in the chest flat on the port side of the main deck aft. Nearby was the subordinate officers' dressing place and an adjoining bathroom, the former fitted with stowage for clothing and equipment and the latter with a steam main that provided just enough hot water for the sub lieutenants' baths and no more; their juniors maintained the acquaintance with cold-water bathing struck up at Dartmouth. Touring the ship in January 1926 Major General Sir George Aston RM, who had first gone to sea in the Victorian navy, was mightily impressed at the improved conditions for midshipmen since his day:

> In my time he had only a chest (for which he paid) to wash in and to keep all his clothes in. Then he was given a 'bathroom', so called, with flat tin baths. Still only the chest flat to dress in. Now he has a chest, provided by the Government, a chest of drawers and part of another one, a bathroom as on shore, with hot and cold water, and a dressing place with lots of room to keep his gear – in *Hood* long lines of hooks and spreaders for coats etc. etc. Nowadays he has his sextant supplied, instead of paying for it.

On the basis of a fortnight spent aboard while the ship was refitting at Portsmouth in June 1939, Mid H G Knowles would certainly not have agreed.

> The gun-room's only ventilation is a solitary skylight, while the chest flat and sleeping flat lack even that. The chest flat, recently a thieves' paradise, has always to be kept locked, while nine of us try to keep our clothes in our trunks, no chests having been supplied, most of the hanging room already taken up by the coats of other midshipmen in a space far too small, where everything disappears unaccountably amongst a maze of trunks and boxes.

Austere as it was, life as a midshipman in *Hood* was taken with stoicism and humour, a common sentiment of difficulties shared and challenges surmounted in the formative phase of one's career. Louis Le Bailly: 'I and my group (1932) lived quite happily in the Flat around the X turret barbette as there was no room in the chest flat. Much clothing was common and one of my messmates had a large stamp made which inscribed his handkerchiefs with "Stolen From…"'. Above all there was pride. Lord Moran captured it perfectly in *The Anatomy of Courage*: 'That a boy has set his heart on this tough service goes for something. He has initiative; he is a cut above the ordinary. Long before the Hitler Youth was thought of, the Navy caught him young and soaked him in the pride and joy of a great tradition.'

The midshipmen's education, welfare and leave arrangements were entrusted to a lieutenant commander known colloquially as 'snotties' nurse'. The incumbent was often a sympathetic figure who had assumed this duty by choice, but, as O'Conor lamented, his brother officers tended to regard midshipmen either as gofers or, in the worst cases, 'as schoolboys and their natural prey'. Ross Warden, who served aboard as a midshipman RNVR in 1940–1, puts it in perspective:

> The rank of midshipman is very precarious and one learns to treat certain ranks with suspicion, especially that of Lieutenant-Commander. Commanders and above (the majority) seem to mellow with seniority: it may be the start of a second childhood, but when they hand out justice you can almost sense them thinking: 'Well, I was once a midshipman myself.' By and large we were exceptionally fortunate with our Lieutenant-Commanders: there was just one snake in the woodpile, who apparently enjoyed making our lives miserable.

Warden and his companions were able to take their revenge on Lt Cdr Snake with a packet of Ex-Lax on the *Hood*'s return from the Mediterranean in August 1940, but such *Schadenfreude* was not always possible. More often than not the snotty, or 'wart' as he was often known, had to accept his lot with only the lower deck to console him. Looking back on the early 1920s, Capt George Blundell recalled how 'ships' companies of those days seemed nearly always kind and sympathetic to the "middies". Perhaps they saw in them a kindred "depressed class".' They did to a degree, and often went to great lengths to cover up for young officers in trouble, though not always for the reasons Blundell thought. All the same, as Rear Admiral Edmund Poland recalled of his three-man motor-boat crew in 1935, 'they owned me, wouldn't let anybody be beastly to me'. While it was never entirely reciprocated, the lasting respect engendered for ratings by those who were later to command them remained one of the greatest strengths of the Royal Navy.

As future officers, midshipmen were assigned important duties afloat, chief of which was that of midshipman of the watch. As deputy to the officer of the watch he was expected to assume control of the ship's routine, discharging his duties on the quarterdeck in harbour and from the bridge at sea. This involved taking sun and star sights and assisting him in keeping the deck log as well as running errands of one sort or another. The most coveted responsibility, however, was command of one of the ship's boats, a skill upon which the Navy placed the greatest emphasis. The business of boat handling not only gave a midshipman a feel for command and seamanship but allowed him to make his mistakes in a relatively controlled environment; as O'Conor put it, 'a picket boat smashed may one day mean a battleship saved'. Most mornings began with physical training followed by Morse, flag-hoisting or semaphore exercises before breakfast, after which he might be told off for duties by his divisional officer.

Beyond his ordinary duties, a midshipman's week was filled with classes and study for the sub lieutenants' exam. In the midshipmen's study on the main deck right aft and in turrets, engine spaces and elsewhere around the ship, an instructor officer and a range of warrant and petty officers gave theoretical and practical classes in gunnery, torpedoes, wireless, navigation and engineering. The sub lieutenants' exam consisted of a number of written papers, exercises and evaluations culminating in 'the Board', a viva voce grilling on seamanship by a panel of senior officers. The concluding part of a midshipman's qualification rested in his journal, which he was required to keep daily and illustrate with maps, pictures and technical drawings of naval interest. Infinite care and attention was lavished on these, which remain a valuable source of information on the daily life of the ship. For Latham Jenson of Calgary who joined *Hood* as a midshipman RCN in December 1940, his journal was nothing less than a hobby. During the sub lieutenants' exam held aboard in April 1941 it got the only perfect score in the Home Fleet and Jenson went on to become a distinguished illustrator after a career in the Royal Canadian Navy. The completion of the four-day exam was greeted with jubilation by the successful candidates. Ted Briggs, then a boy signalman, recalls the celebrations of Jenson's group, the very last to achieve promotion from the *Hood*:

> I remember this particular session because after it was over there was a riotous party in the midshipmen's gunroom, of which the ship's company got to hear. After the gin, beer and 'el torpedo' and 'depth charge' cocktails had flowed, bottles began to fly – and trousers, too. One lieutenant was cut by a piece of shattered glass, before all the popular officers were debagged by the 'mids'.

For a time boys and midshipmen might share duties and instruction, but on promotion the enormous social gap asserted itself and their ways parted forever. As on the lower deck, an officer's status was denoted by his accommodation, which ranged from a shared cabin on the main deck aft to the extensive apartments for the admiral and captain on the forecastle and upper decks. Officers' cabins had always been a case of 'multum in parvo' – much in little – but, as on the messdecks, the first impression seems to have been of airy spaciousness in comparison with other ships. A typical cabin, 15 feet long, 10 feet wide and 12 feet high, was entered through a door fitted with louvre windows which slid behind a rifle rack facing the lobby. Lit by a scuttle and a lamp at the deckhead, its furniture consisted of a bunk bed set on a unit of drawers laid fore and aft along the ship's side, an upright wardrobe for uniforms, further drawers, a foot locker for shoes, and a desk and chair. A pair of shelves, a mirror and a small stand attached to the painted bulkheads completed the fittings. The only semblance of permanent decoration lay in the two laths of teak that ran along each bulkhead and to which pictures could be secured with screws. Because the officers' cabins aft were prone to flooding, the corticene flooring was rarely mitigated by any carpeting while a set of rails on each bunk bore witness to the occasional need to wedge oneself into bed in heavy weather. Even so, efforts were made to beautify the surroundings with chintz curtains and lampshades and the usual selection of family or risqué pictures as the taste and attachment of the inmate dictated. In larger cabins the decor extended to framed pictures, ornaments and perhaps a ship model under glass for the mantelpiece. Sub-Lt John Iago, who joined the ship from civilian life in September 1939, brought his skills as an electrical engineer to bear in the decoration of his:

> I've had the same cabin all the time. It looked very bare to begin with but now I have improved it. I have made the spare bunk into a sort of sideboard and have framed and put up pictures, mainly from magazines. This evening I have been fixing up a system of indirect lighting, which is very fine. All lights are concealed and shine up on to the deck head and I have a bed light and a dressing table light. It all looks very pleasing and I am thinking of having some yellow or red bulbs in a few of the holders. Altogether there are 12 small bulbs now. Also there is a special shaving light, which comes on with my razor!

After lights out Iago no doubt drifted off to sleep to the same chorus that had lulled generations of officers at sea:

> On one's first night in a warship there are many strange sounds to wonder at, for in addition to the customary creakings and groanings of an ordinary ship, the rifles in their racks add their clatter to the din of the steering gear; a battleship wallows with a long slow roll and the rhythmic rattle of the small arms which accompanies each change becomes a pleasing tattoo which lulls one to sleep.

What distinguished the Royal Navy from many of its foreign counterparts was the degree of personal service an officer could expect on board. All from the rank of lieutenant onwards were assigned a Marine servant to rouse him in the morning, fill his tub in the officers' bathroom, see to his clothing and laundry and keep the cabin and its contents clean and tidy. The same level of service was expected with rather less justification during wartime. On 6 July 1940, three days after the attack on Mers el-Kebir, one officer felt moved to issue the following complaint in a letter home:

> Have been having a bit of domestic trouble! My new man is always too busy to clean shoes, or to make my bed before teatime – I may change him for one of my torpedo men.

The Marine in question presumably had his hands full as the *Hood* beat back to Gibraltar after covering the *coup de grâce* on the battlecruiser *Dunkerque* at Mers el-Kebir. Despite the many black and Filipino stewards engaged by his own navy, this level of service came as something of an eye-opener to Lt Cdr Joseph H Wellings USN:

> My servant calls me at 0800, brushes my clothes, shines my shoes and lays out the rest of my clothes. Right this moment my *bed* is turned down, pajamas laid out evenly, slippers under the bed. I take my bath before dinner in order not to go out afterwards and possibly catch cold – (yes, the tub is drawn – or rather the water is drawn and just at the correct temperature).

Personal attention of this sort more than made up for the comparatively primitive washing facilities aboard. All cabins were fitted with hot and cold running water but the wash basins drained into copper receptacles which had to be emptied by hand. In the largest captain's and admiral's compartments the ultimate touch before they were replaced with electric stoves was a coal fire kept regularly stoked by a Marine servant.

The heart of the officers' world was the suite on the forecastle deck amidships known as the wardroom. First came the anteroom, lit by a large skylight on the boat deck and furnished with a pair of leather-upholstered settees and a club fender round the stove. Here, under a large bookcase holding the wardroom library, officers gathered for drinks before lunch and dinner. A doorway, later converted to an arched opening guarded by a curtain, led into the wardroom proper, a lofty space lit by further skylights and a row of scuttles overlooking the port battery. The wardroom was dominated by the four large mahogany tables at which the officers ate their meals waited on by Royal Marine attendants. Unlike *Iron Duke*, *London* and *Sheffield*, the *Hood* had never been presented with a great silver service, but in cabinets about the room, on its walls and tables were the mementoes and trophies of her voyages across the world: the silver-mounted elephant's tusk given at Freetown in December 1923 and the trophy heads of lion, tiger, bison and moose presented thereafter along with countless cups, salvers and centrepieces in silver and gold. All were landed in August 1939, to be destroyed in the Portsmouth Blitz. A third settee filled one corner while a kneehole desk opposite allowed officers to compose letters on the ship's crested stationery. The furnishings of what was by earlier standards a somewhat austere space were completed with a piano – much used on guest nights, a pair of stoves under mirrored mantelpieces, sundry cupboards and a large buffet from which attendants served food passed through a hatch in the wardroom pantry.

As in the other officers' messes, wardroom catering lay at the discretion of its members. Throughout much of her career the *Hood*'s wardroom appears to have left the matter in the hands of a messman who provided three meals a day plus tea against a monthly deduction from officers' pay. Generous as it was, no opportunity was lost for adding to wardroom fare. On Sunday, 18 May 1941 a last fishing trip on the shores of Scapa Flow brought Lt Cdr Roger Batley a 2lb sea trout and the wardroom a catch of fifty fresh lobsters which he relieved from an old fisherman for two shillings apiece. Breakfast was served between 0730 and 0900, lunch between midday and 1300, tea at 1530 and finally a formal dinner at 2000 sharp. At sea, and especially in wartime, a more relaxed routine prevailed, with meals being largely on a self-service basis. The food prepared in the wardroom galley was expected to be of an extremely high standard and even in wartime was the equivalent of a good restaurant. Indeed, Sub-Lt John Iago RNVR is unlikely to have been the first wartime officer to question whether such lavishness was appropriate in view of the dearth on the Home Front:

I don't think it would hurt us to have a great deal less, especially in view of shortages elsewhere. Breakfast: Porridge or cereals followed by grilled herrings or some other fish. Next course, eggs and bacon, then toast and marmalade or honey to finish. We have a three- or four-course lunch, small tea (just tea and cakes) then we round off the day with a four-course dinner at sea and six courses in harbour.

Even Lt Cdr Wellings of the US Navy, a service known for its generous fare, was taken aback at the range of foods on offer, though he was perhaps not the first American to be stunned at the sight of a monumental English breakfast:

The food is much better than at the main office. Grapefruit every morning so far, cereal or rolled oats, ham or bacon and eggs, toast, marmalade or butter (or both) and coffee. How is that for a breakfast? I have given up afternoon tea as I don't want to gain on this job which is much easier than my last one.

For his part, John Iago found his expanding waistline a matter of some embarrassment while his relatives in suburban London subsisted on wartime rations: 'Have gained 1 st 4 lbs since joining the Navy, which explains why my reefer jacket would not meet and has had to go back to Gieves for adjustment!'* However, wardroom catering was not without its mishaps. Some consternation was caused in 1935 when it was discovered that PO Cook Sultana, a Maltese, had been using his armpit to shape the beef rissoles that were a wardroom favourite.

In the 1920s at least, the atmosphere in the wardroom, particularly where meals were concerned, had something of the character of an English country house or a gentleman's club ashore, with all their quirks and mannerisms. Sailing in *Hood* during the world cruise of 1923–4, the writer V C Scott O'Connor noted 'a little fad in the Navy ... that no one is very fit to talk to at breakfast', though Aston and later Wellings found their messmates cheerful enough. The fact that O'Connor was on record as saying that all naval officers were 'born idiots' can't have endeared him to the wardroom. It was supposedly taboo to discuss women, religion and politics, though the drift to war presumably meant that at least one of these topics was frequently broached.

*Gieves was the principal Navy tailor.

Clinking glasses was regarded as a portent of death, the threat usually warded off by fining the culprit a bottle of port. Drinks were served before and during lunch and dinner in harbour, but the restrictions on alcohol at sea were strictly adhered to. There was no ban on drinking at sea, and indeed non-watchkeepers were entitled to three tots of alcohol a day, but it was 'not done' for any watchkeeper to partake. It was a different matter in harbour, but even there consumption was regulated with monthly 'wine bill' allowances of £5 for officers, each drink being entered in the wardroom wine book and subject to regular scrutiny by the captain. Even at official parties the amount drunk was recorded and tabulated against the 'monthly mess share'.

As the admiral and the captain usually dined alone there was no special seating at table except for the mess president and vice president who held office for a week at a time. Officers dressed for dinner, which consisted of mess jackets, winged collars and bow ties in peacetime but no more than reefers in war, though a stiff collar would be added in harbour. Officers of the Royal Marines wore the tight breeches that were traditional in the Corps, some like Lt A H R Buckley of the 1923–6 commission exercising their right to don the blue mess dress of the defunct Royal Marine Artillery. Grace would be said if the chaplain were present, all standing until the mess president had taken his seat. Then course after course would be served by a phalanx of attendants in white mess tunics, twice weekly to the accompaniment of a Royal Marine orchestra in the anteroom. As Wellings, unaccustomed to this luxury, put it, 'music at dinner does aid one's digestion', though his contentment no doubt owed something to the alcohol which was never served in his own navy. In keeping with the tradition of the Royal Navy, the Sovereign was toasted while officers remained seated, followed by a toast to the relevant potentate if foreign guests were aboard. So it was that the *Hood*'s wardroom found itself drinking the health of Chancellor Hitler when officers of the *Deutschland* came aboard at Gibraltar in June 1937. At Scapa three years later it was the turn of the President of the United States to have his health drunk, Lt Cdr Wellings observing protocol with a toast to King George VI.

Relatively little has survived to record the mood of the *Hood*'s wardrooms in either peace or war, though one thing was quite clear: it didn't do to be a teetotaller in such society. The following advice given by the Rev Beardmore to aspiring naval chaplains speaks volumes.

A teetotaller certainly starts scratch in any mess, and finds life rather difficult, especially on a foreign station, where there is a lot of entertaining to be done, and where each officer has to do his bit. I think the average Naval officer considers a padre to be a good messmate if he has learnt how to drink sensibly; they look upon him as a normal person, and looking back, I can remember getting inside the shell of many a 'reserved' or difficult messmate over a glass of wine, and making a valuable contact.

As in the gunroom, there were times when alcohol and high spirits turned the normally august surroundings of the wardroom into something of a melee, particularly Thursday evenings in harbour – Guest Night. Beardmore, who had no doubt sat through all too many during his two years as the *Hood*'s chaplain, felt moved to issue this warning:

> The Chaplain who thinks it is a popular thing to be broadminded, and accepts everything that is said and done in a Wardroom Mess, doesn't *really* command respect. Officers expect the Chaplain to be different from them, and if at rather a late party he joins in, or condones, the more vulgar songs that are sung from time to time, he lets the side down in their eyes, to say the least of it.

Officers who stayed up drinking were often only a step away from out-and-out rowdyism. In what was perhaps the last letter he ever wrote, the ship's First Lieutenant, Lt Cdr John Machin, confessed with ill-concealed pride that he had cracked a rib during a guest-night caper in May 1941. But there were times when matters got really out of hand. One night off the Yugoslav port of Split in September 1937 Lt Gresham Grenfell, creeping on all fours under the wardroom tables, stalked the row of trophy heads on the forward bulkhead with a loaded shotgun. Selecting the moose as his target, he calmly emptied both barrels into it, blasting off an antler to the consternation of those present. Unfortunately, some of his shot passed through a scuttle and lodged in the hammock of a sailor sleeping in the passage outside. The antler was glued back on and the sailor fobbed off with beer, but, as Fred Coombes said, 'if the Navy wanted crews with plenty of fire in their bellies who played hard ... they had to expect small explosions as devilment fired up'. Evidently, this was as true of the *Hood*'s officers as it was of her men.

The *Hood* was the finest ship in the Navy and it can come as no surprise that her wardroom should have included several whose accomplishments past, present and future place them among the elite of a great service. To describe the wardroom of 1936–9, the *Hood*'s last peacetime commission, is therefore to give a flavour not only of its character over the previous twenty years but of the calibre of men who made up the officer corps of the British Navy. The executive officer for most of the commission was Cdr David Orr-Ewing, later captain of the fast minelayer *Abdiel* when she was mined and sunk at Brindisi in September 1943, and eventually Commander-in-Chief Home Fleet after the war. Among his many accomplishments was the ability to drink beer standing on his head. Lt Cdrs H A L Marsham and C H Hutchinson had distinguished careers in the Submarine Service during the coming war, the former as CO of HMS/M *Rover* and the latter in command of HMS/M *Truant*. Hutchinson ended the war as Chief of Staff to Admiral Sir Bernard Rawlings in the British Pacific Fleet and became captain of the Royal Naval College at Dartmouth. Lt Roger Hill, who hated big-ship life, went on to win a DSO assisting the crippled tanker *Ohio* into Malta while in command of the destroyer escort *Ledbury* in August 1942. His *Hood* messmates, however, would remember him chiefly for his devastatingly beautiful Swedish wife and her equally entrancing friends. Among the engineer branch were Cdr (E) Peter Berthon, already Dean of the Royal Naval Engineering College at Keyham and the moving spirit behind the foundation of its successor at Manadon. His future son-in-law, Lt (E) Louis Le Bailly, survived the sinking of the cruiser *Naiad* off Sidi Barrani in March 1942 and went on to become naval attaché in Washington DC and finally, as Vice Admiral, Director General of Intelligence. It was a truly exceptional officer who could get on in the Navy as a teetotaller and a non-smoker, but one such was Constructor Cdr W J A Davies, capped twenty-two times for England in rugby and remembered as one of the greatest half-backs in the history of the game. Davies's international career was interrupted by service in *Iron Duke* during the First World War but he went on to lead England to two famous Grand Slams in 1921 and 1923. The steadying influence of a distinguished paternal figure of Davies's stature was a priceless asset in the young and boisterous wardrooms of the inter-war years. A messmate, the Rev Edgar Rea, was to remember him thus:

> Although old enough to be father to many of us, he was humble, approachable and quite unaffected by the great name he had made. Even the most junior officers were permitted to tease him and no one enjoyed it more than Davies. The number of parties and receptions which he attended during his great rugger days must have been legion and yet I think I am right in saying that he remained throughout, both a teetotaller and a non-smoker. Unlike so many people on social occasions, he never looked uncomfortable without a glass in his hand. He could sit or stand in any circle, he alone without a drink, and join in the conversation and laughter without appearing ill at ease. In every respect he was a fine example to the young, with whom he was so very much at home.

The gunroom of the time also contained a number who would distinguish themselves in later years, including Mid D C 'Bull' Wells, eventually Vice Admiral Commanding, Royal Australian Navy. But if the *Hood*'s wardroom was one of accomplishment it would prove also to be one of sacrifice, and there were many, destined no doubt for high rank, who were not to survive the Second World War. Lt Cdr (later Cdr) E O Unwin, Squadron W/T Officer first on Cunningham's and then Layton's staff, suffered a harrowing death in the Atlantic after the light cruiser *Dunedin* fell victim to *U124* in November 1941. Lt Cdr (E) Lancelot Fogg-Elliot, then a commander, perished together with his entire engineering staff when the cruiser *Galatea* was torpedoed and sunk by *U557* off Alexandria in December 1941. Mid O S V Waterlow, a holder of the DSC, was listed as missing, presumed killed after the submarine *Talisman* failed to return from a patrol off Italy in September 1942. Of the five Australian midshipmen shipped in 1938 only one survived the 1940s. Two of them, T E

Davis and I T R Treloar, were serving in the cruiser HMAS *Sydney* when she was lost with all hands following a punishing engagement with the German raider *Kormoran* off Australia in November 1941. Another, Mid B M McFarlane, perished when the midget submarine *X22* collided with HMS/M *Syrtis* in the Pentland Firth in February 1944. A fourth, K A Seddon RANR, died in the destroyer HMAS *Nestor* in January 1947. For the *Hood*'s officer complement as for the ship herself, the price of admiralty was to be exacted in full.

Naturally, the *Hood*'s wardroom was not without its share of timeservers, failures and non-entities, those who, in O'Conor's words, lacked 'the spark of leadership, ... the ability to organise, and the will to carry things through'. Nor could its society very well be described as a 'band of brothers'. The 'community of sentiment' preached by Admiral Lord Fisher prior to the First World War would not be realised until the Navy finally embraced the technical realities of its calling in the 1950s. But, as on the lower deck, the *Hood*'s wardroom was imbued with a certain spirit which her officers would carry with them in the trials to come – of pride, confidence and satisfaction in hard-earned victory; above all, of what it meant to love one's ship.

7

Invergordon

IN THE SPRING OF 1931 the *Hood* emerged from a two-year refit and resumed her exalted status as flagship of the Battle Cruiser Squadron, Atlantic Fleet. In May she completed to full complement and a month later sailed from Portsmouth for the usual summer spell at Portland. However, it was quite obvious that matters had changed greatly since she had paid off and passed under dockyard control at Portsmouth two years earlier. For one thing she was now a Pompey ship, having exchanged the outspoken West Country men of her first four commissions with the more stolid crews of the Portsmouth Division. But above all, the world to which she returned seemed very much less stable than it had in the summer of 1929. In October of that year the Wall Street Crash precipitated an economic depression that by the autumn of 1931 had put over 2.5 million out of work and brought the National Government of Ramsay MacDonald to power in Britain. With the economy in crisis, on 31 July of that year the Committee on National Expenditure chaired by Sir George May recommended sweeping wage cuts for civil servants including the armed forces, declaring that 'No officer or man serving His Majesty has any legal claim to a particular rate of pay'. For those sailors who kept abreast of political events, who read *The Fleet* and participated in messdeck discussions about welfare, pay and representation, here was the first inkling of trouble ahead.

Despite these developments, the first few months of the *Hood*'s commission passed off uneventfully as the crew laboured to slough away the dirt and disorder of a prolonged period in dockyard hands. Sea trials off Portland were followed in July by a visit to Torbay where the flag of Rear Admiral Wilfred Tomkinson was hoisted for the first time. Though it had little bearing on subsequent events, his arrival on board was at best inauspicious. Vice Admiral Eric Longley-Cook, then the ship's First Lieutenant and gunnery officer, has left this account of Tomkinson's opening gambit:

> We sailed early one fine morning to take station astern of the Battle Cruiser Squadron. I was on the bridge and wondered what the Admiral's signal would be. 'Glad to see you back'? 'Welcome back to the BCS'? No. A flag signal

'Manoeuvre badly executed'; from tails up to tails nearly down. Next morning, Sunday 0800 in Torbay, we hoisted the flag of ACQ. At 0900 he arrived on board, walked round divisions, then 'clear lower deck, everyone aft'. From the after capstan the Admiral addressed us. Summarily he said 'I was the first Captain of this ship and until you reach something like the standard in which I left her, I shall not be satisfied'. Now, we had worked very hard indeed to get her from dockyard condition to fleet condition, so tails went down even lower. So on we went, not entirely happy.

The crew no doubt recognised this as a particularly gauche example of the ploy often resorted to goad men into action, but Tomkinson remained highly unpopular in this his first and last seagoing command as an admiral. This state of affairs was, however, mitigated by Cdr C R McCrum, an exceptional executive officer and much admired by his men. Years later LS Sam Wheat recalled him thus: 'I'll always say we had the most excellent Commander you could ever have. He's the best admired Commander I've ever known or ever served with, and that was Cdr McCrum. And he was a diplomatic chap.' The months to come would require all of McCrum's powers of diplomacy. Meanwhile there was a lengthy refitting at Portsmouth during which *Hood* was once more the main attraction at Navy Week. Summer leave was taken by watches. Morale was good and the atmosphere calm. It was against this backdrop that the *Hood* sailed from Portsmouth on 8 September to participate in the autumn gunnery cruise of the Atlantic Fleet off Scotland. Though few of her men suspected it, even as she headed north the seeds of disaster were in the wind. The mass disobedience that the Navy had been spared since 1797 was about to return. 'Mutiny' was at hand.

Despite the fears of a generation of senior figures in the Royal Navy, it was not political ideology but the policy and attitudes of the Admiralty itself that constituted the chief source of discontent on the lower deck. The Admiralty not only failed to recognise the extent to which the First World War had altered the British social order, it also took an inordinately long time to accept that the Navy was drawing into its ranks men with aspirations and a level of education unknown in the pre-war fleets. Against the backdrop of social and political change at home and abroad these developments coincided with the growth of the lower-deck societies. In the years before the Great War the lower deck had for the first time found representation by means of a range of semi-unionised societies, most of which confined their membership to a branch or trade such as the Engine Room Artificers' Society. During the war these societies together with *The Fleet*, the influential newspaper edited by Lionel Yexley, successfully lobbied for the improvement in lower-deck pay that culminated in the 1919 settlement which at last provided the British sailor with an adequate compensation for his services. Though it had yielded on this matter the Admiralty was concerned at the increasingly politicised nature of the societies' activities and in 1920 issued a fleet order which effectively destroyed their capacity for organised representation, an action which by the late 1920s left the lower deck in little doubt that its voice had been stifled. Already in 1925 economic considerations had obliged the Admiralty to introduce a lower pay scale for all new entrants to the Service, though assurances were given that the earlier rates would be honoured for all currently in receipt of them. However, the 1925 pay scales were to have serious consequences for the Navy. The two-tier structure was not only resented by those who found themselves receiving less pay for equal work, but did nothing to alleviate the blockage in promotion caused by the mass of men who had achieved higher rating during the Great War. Under these circumstances the closing of official channels of representation hastened the decline of the lower-deck societies and drove men to a more radical expression of their grievances. When in September 1931 the Admiralty tamely acceded to a government proposal that the pay of the entire Navy be reduced to the 1925 levels the stage was therefore set for the Invergordon Mutiny.

The circumstances under which the 1931 pay cuts were decided upon and the catalogue of error, oversight and incompetence that attended their promulgation to the Atlantic Fleet as it gathered in the Cromarty Firth lie beyond the scope of this volume. Suffice to say that confusion following the sudden hospitalisation of Admiral Sir Michael Hodges (Commander-in-Chief Atlantic Fleet) on Monday, 7 September apparently left the ranking officer, Rear Admiral Tomkinson in the *Hood*, unaware of the extent of the cuts until events were already well in train. An Admiralty cipher prepared for this purpose on 3 September Tomkinson either never saw or failed to take in. On Thursday, 10 September, with the fleet still on exercises in the North Sea, the Chancellor of the Exchequer, Philip Snowden, delivered an emergency budget speech to Parliament in which the pruning of government expenditure was finally made public. Despite indications from the BBC later that day, it was not until the day's papers came aboard once the fleet had dropped anchor at Invergordon on Friday 11th that those on the 1919 scale – over 70 per cent of the Navy – learnt that their basic pay was to be reduced by up to 25 per cent. But this was not all. Not only had the Admiralty betrayed its solemn guarantee of 1925, but in sanctioning the government package it had effectively permitted the cuts to be made in inverse relation to rank and seniority. Whereas the basic pay of many able seamen would be cut from four to three shillings a day (25 per cent), that of an admiral of the fleet suffered only by a matter of 17 per cent. Though the proportional cut was in fact rather lower when the allowances earned by most were included, the inequitable division of the reductions, the manner in which they became known, the speed with which they were to be implemented and the likely impact on the men's families and prospects provided the basis for the Invergordon Mutiny.

Although the mutiny owed its impetus to a spontaneous reaction by the fleet at large, it is clear that the seat of the movement, insofar as there was one, lay in ships of the Devonport Division, notably the battleship *Rodney*, the cruiser

Norfolk and the minelayer *Adventure*, together with the battleship *Valiant* of Chatham. Feelings had been running high in Devonport since January when bad leadership in the submarine depot ship *Lucia* prompted thirty-one of her crewmen to barricade themselves below deck, an incident which led to four men being court-martialled and another ejected from the Navy. But above all the mutiny owed its support to the 'staid hands', those leading seamen, able seamen, stokers and Marines on the 1919 pay scales who represented the group worst affected by the cuts. However, the practical difficulties of fomenting a mutiny in a dozen or more ships largely prevented the operation of any central organisation and the degree of participation of individual vessels rested mainly on the morale, convictions and mood of their crews as events unfolded. So it was with the *Hood*, in which the impending cuts were apparently discussed at several illegal meetings before the ship reached Invergordon on Friday, 11 September. With Admiral Tomkinson and his staff still oblivious to the unrest on the messdecks, the *Hood* passed quietly into harbour routine, most of those off watch spending the afternoon of Saturday 12th at the Invergordon Highland Games where the ship's Marine band formed one of the attractions. That night, just as a bundle containing the sixteen-page Admiralty Fleet Order 2339/31 detailing the cuts reached the *Hood*, the naval canteen ashore was alive with men anxiously discussing the measures, details of which had been broadcast in the BBC's evening bulletin. At this meeting it was apparently agreed that a larger gathering should be held the following day and canvassing for action to be taken over the cuts proceeded both in and between ships thereafter.

Early the following day came the first indication that trouble was in store. During Divine Service that Sunday morning the AFO was posted on the *Hood's* noticeboards, so confirming the worst fears of the lower deck. Even before the Rev Archer Turner had issued his benediction, the congregation in the starboard battery could hear threatening voices being raised against the cuts: 'It's the lot! ... And they've bloody well had it!' Shortly before midday Lt Cdr Harry Pursey, one of the handful of officers to have won promotion from the lower deck, and later a distinguished Labour MP, was approached by a trusted member of the lower deck. Shown a copy of one of the Sunday papers with banner headlines of the cuts, he was told, 'The lads won't stand for this'. Within a few minutes Pursey had passed the paper to Cdr McCrum, to whom he offered the following prescient warning: 'If these cuts are not reduced there will be trouble. ... If there is trouble, it will be on Tuesday – at eight o'clock. ... Four capital ships due to sail. ... It's tailor-made for the job.' The capital ships in question were *Nelson*, *Rodney*, *Valiant* and *Hood*, due to sail on the morning of Tuesday 15th for gunnery exercises in the North Sea. McCrum dismissed the suggestion, assuring Pursey that, 'We shall be all right on this ship'. Events were to prove otherwise.

Meanwhile, leaders were emerging from the twelve thousand men gathered in the Cromarty Firth. Out of the fug that filled every flat, caboose and messdeck came the germ of plans that could only be implemented in concert with a significant part of the fleet. These meetings were largely the preserve of stokers and seamen on the 1919 pay scales yet below the rating of petty officer. 'Petty officers made themselves scarce, and the younger ratings were kept out of it, some accused of letting the others down by enlisting on lower pay.' OD Roland Purvis of the battleship *Malaya* lost count of the number of times he was told 'Push off, sonny, this is nothing to do with you'. One of the leaders, AB Len Wincott of the *Norfolk*, had already taken advantage of the Catholic mass celebrated in the *Malaya* that Sunday morning to gauge opinion in the fleet and pass word of the canteen meeting that night. At midday Capt J F C Patterson of the *Hood* received intelligence of this gathering from his counterpart in the *Warspite*, though Tomkinson was apparently not informed and no pre-emptive action was taken. Quite the contrary, leave was given at 1300 as usual and men began to pour ashore. Even in view of the football final being held that afternoon, the number of libertymen heading for Invergordon was unprecedented. Although Patterson and McCrum found nothing untoward during a visit ashore, the men knew different and by late afternoon many were drifting away from the football pitches and into the large canteen overlooking the anchorage. The *Hood's* contingent, whose team had defeated *Norfolk* 2–0, no doubt had something to quell their anger but it could only be a temporary palliative. The men were angry at the cuts and at the breach of faith implied by them; angry above all that the government and the Admiralty thought them stupid enough to take it lying down. LS Sam Wheat:

> Austen Chamberlain [First Lord of the Admiralty] was the bloke – they'd've crucified him if they could've bloody got him, believe you me. […] Because he thought that none of the Navy had any intelligence at all. […] To take a shilling a day from each one was, to put it mildly, bloody silly. […] I mean, they thought that the chaps were unintelligent and this is really what caused it. I think they'd've got away with it if they'd said 'Well, we're going to reduce your pay by five per cent' or whatever it is … But to do that made them look like nincompoops, as though they didn't know anything at all.

Besides, there was the very real issue of whether the men's families could subsist on the new rates. As one of the *Hood's* leaders put it in a letter to *The Daily Herald* a few days later,

> We are fighting for our wives and children. The cuts cannot hit us on board ship. We have not to keep ourselves except in a few essentials, some clothing, soap, shoeblacking and so on. We have cut out the luxuries long ago. We cannot do it on less than 5s a week. Our wives, after the rent is paid, have no more than a pound. How can they stand a cut of 7s 6d?

What began as a sombre occasion gathered steam as the evening wore on and the depth of feeling began to make itself felt. Many, including LS Charles Spinks of the *Hood*, clambered onto tables to deliver speeches and opinions that often owed more to alcohol than common sense. But among them was Wincott, a born orator, who, taking up a theme already mooted, urged the men to remain in their ships and implement a campaign of passive resistance when the order came to put to sea. His words had an electrifying effect on the crowd, now over six hundred strong. One who heard them was Rear Admiral E A Astley-Rushton, commanding the 2nd Cruiser Squadron, who found himself outside the canteen as Wincott was in full flow. Astley-Rushton immediately informed the shore patrol, manned that night by men of the *Warspite*, which promptly called for reinforcements from the *Hood*. By the time these appeared an increasingly rowdy gathering had dispersed and the men were heading back to their ships, many singing *The Frothblower's Anthem* – 'The more we are together the merrier we'll be …' – though some in the *Hood*'s drifter felt the need to shout 'We're not yellowbellies!' to taunts from others. As they did so, the *Nelson*, Hodges' flagship, finally steamed into Invergordon carrying the Admiralty cipher warning of the cuts that had supposedly been in Tomkinson's hands a week earlier, along with AL CW 8284/31 of 10 September, a letter to all flag and commanding officers justifying the measures. Astley-Rushton came aboard *Hood* to discuss the events ashore with Tomkinson, but these were dismissed as being of no consequence and the Admiralty was signalled to this effect the following morning.

Despite the taunts, the *Hood*'s libertymen returned to a ship in which, as LS Sam Wheat put it, the overwhelming sentiment was 'No, we ain't 'avin' this'. Nonetheless, the men settled down for the night and the ship's routine began normally the following morning though Cdr McCrum, sensing the volatile atmosphere, limited work to 'a little General Drill' which was performed in a somewhat perfunctory manner. Shortly after 1000 Tomkinson signalled his captains ordering them to explain the contents of AL CW 8284/31 to the men. He was no doubt astonished to learn that it had been received in only five of the twelve ships in harbour, and it is no surprise that subsequent efforts to interpret the cuts tended to poison the atmosphere still further. So it was in the *Hood*, where the mood of the men was being stoked by copies of the *Daily Worker* which had come aboard that morning. The order to clear lower deck was passed at 1145, but according to Pursey, Capt Patterson's recommendation that the men bring hardship cases to the attention of their divisional officers was greeted with angry calls of 'We're all hardship cases!' His suggestion that they refrain from illegal action and channel their grievances through him can't have cut much ice either. However, daily routine continued and shore leave was granted at 1630, this despite every indication in the *Hood* and elsewhere that a further meeting was planned for the canteen that evening.

Among the many hundreds going ashore that Monday evening was Lt Robert Elkins, in command of the *Valiant*'s naval patrol and charged with arresting anyone suspected of subversive activity. As on the previous night, at least six hundred men gathered in the canteen to hear speeches and settle on the action to be taken. The speeches were mostly of an inflammatory nature and it was while AB 'Ginger' Bond of the *Rodney* was delivering one of these that Elkins reached the canteen at 1815. Gaining entry, he met a hostile reception, being struck by a beer glass and eventually bundled out into the cold, the doors locked behind him. However, he succeeded in being readmitted to the meeting, which broke up to reassemble on a nearby recreation ground. Having called for the *Hood*'s reinforcing patrol, Elkins followed the crowd to a spot where men were speaking from the roof of a wooden hut. Among them was a Marine, apparently from the *Hood*, whose medals denoted him as a veteran of the Great War: 'He talked a good deal about pay and War Service, and again demanded "What are we going to do about it?" This time the crowd called out "Pack up!", and he said "Tonight or tomorrow?" There was a good deal of laughing and someone said "After breakfast – when we've had it!"' At 1930 the meeting adjourned back to the canteen, though many took the opportunity to get off to their ships. By this time the *Hood*'s patrol had made its appearance under Lt Cdr L G E Robinson who marched into the canteen with the intention of closing it for the night. Robinson got up on the bar but was hard put to it to make himself heard over the noise:

> For some minutes I was shouted down, but the majority of the men were shouting 'Give him a fair hearing' – 'Let's hear what he's got to say', and eventually I had silence. I told the men they were going the wrong way about things and would only bring discredit on themselves and the Navy. That they should bring up any complaints in the Service manner and that I would permit of no more speeches.

Robinson's speech impressed Wincott and ended the meeting but it swayed only a minority, who were violently overborne by the rest. As the men headed for the jetty to return to their ships they did so in the certain knowledge that an irrevocable decision had been taken: the Atlantic Fleet would not be sailing on the morrow.

Down on the jetty the libertymen embarked for their ships in what Tomkinson later described as 'a very disorderly manner'. Shouts of 'Don't forget – six o'clock tomorrow' were drifting across the anchorage as searchlights began to play over the pier. Those in the *Hood*'s drifter, the *Horizon*, were belting out stanzas of *The Red Flag*, a court-martial offence. The din interrupted a dinner party being given by Tomkinson for the fleet commanders, the Officer of the Watch, Lt J S Gabbett, ordering the *Horizon* to lay off until the men were silent. However, the singing was a clear indication to the *Hood*'s lower deck that something had been settled ashore. By the time Elkins got away from the pier to report to Tomkinson at around 2100 a crowd of over a hundred cheering men had gathered in the eyes of the ship where a rating was inciting them to refuse work in the morning. Boy Harold Prestage RNVR recorded the scene:

> A stoker spoke, very emotional about keeping wife and two kids on three shillings a day. He said he owed ten pounds, how was he to pay? Several others spoke. They say we on the *Hood* are blacklegs and cowards, our people did not seem to support the crowd on shore much. At last after much haggling they decide to down tools at eight o'clock tomorrow morning.

Once again, the lack of enthusiasm for action noted among the *Hood*'s contingent ashore is significant in the light of subsequent events. Certainly, as a newly commissioned ship with good morale, her men were unlikely to share the militant tendency which characterised *Valiant* and *Rodney*. Whatever the case, her officers were under no illusion as to the gravity of the situation. Gabbett greeted Elkins on the quarterdeck with the information that there had been trouble aboard. On his way to the wardroom he met Lt Cdr Longley-Cook who invited him to dinner aboard the following week, 'if there were still a Navy'. Already at least one messdeck had sent a representative to its divisional officer. Not the least informed was Tomkinson who, as Elkins put it, gave the impression of knowing 'a good deal about it already', though clearly did not think it 'so bad as it sounded'. With this view a majority of the senior commanders were in agreement. How wrong they were.

McCrum had the forecastle cleared by the master-at-arms and one of the regulating petty officers, but a number of men were detailed by the ship's committee to spend the night on deck and send down a warning if any attempt were made to weigh anchor. The size and composition of this committee, how it came into being and the means by which it influenced events in the *Hood* and liaised with those in other ships remains shrouded in mystery. Indeed, virtually nothing of the internal structure and organisation of the *Hood*'s mutiny has survived for posterity. Neither, at eighty years' remove, can the atmosphere prevailing on the *Hood*'s decks and messes, in her passageways and spaces public and private during those six fateful days be reconstructed in any but the vaguest terms. Both then and later the crew closed ranks to protect the identity of the 'spokesmen' who organised the mutiny and those who succoured and lent it their support, often at the cost of their careers in the Navy. But, for the committee as for the ship herself, the moment of truth was drawing near.

That night, in an incident no doubt repeated countless times on the lower deck, R A Feltham was roused by a leading hand and told to lash up and stow in the morning but obey no orders thereafter. On Tuesday, 15 September the crew duly turned to at 0600 but all eyes were on *Valiant* and *Rodney* upon whose action the success or failure of the mutiny depended. Full muster in the *Hood* encouraged her officers to believe that their ship would remain unaffected by what all now sensed was coming, but in this they were soon to be disabused. Making his way down to the boiler rooms, Stoker Walter Hargreaves found his progress barred by a big stoker who told him to 'get back', and left him in no doubt of the result if he didn't. When by 0700 it was obvious that neither *Valiant* nor *Rodney* was being prepared for sea, the forecastles of the eight major vessels in the anchorage began to fill with crowds of cheering men. Stoker Charles Wild shut down the hydraulic pumping engine on which he worked, downed tools and headed forward. At around 0745 Cdr McCrum went forward, climbed onto one of the ship's capstans and implored the men gathered among the shackles to return to work. The request was politely declined and his place taken by a sailor intent on stopping the ship weighing anchor. Four decks below a party of men led by a chief stoker refused to allow the engineer watchkeeper to run the capstan engine. In the cable-locker flat a similar effort to unshackle the bridles by the Torpedo Officer, Lt Cdr (T) J F W Mudford, provides a cameo of the quiet resistance encountered by officers of the Atlantic Fleet that morning:

> With petty officers and a few available hands from the cable party I went on to the forecastle to unshackle the first bridle. No marines were present in the cable-locker flat so that both the naval pipes and cable lockers had to be uncovered by my small party. The demonstrators were standing over both bridles and the hawsepipe cover, which was still in place. I went amongst them to view the cables and was immediately hemmed about by the crowd who stood a yard or two away from me. One man shouted 'What's the use of trying to take the ship to sea like this?' I said 'What about it! If I give order to heave in, are you going to stop me?' They replied 'Yes, Sir, we shall have to'. I felt it would be unwise to use force without instructions to do so from higher authority, and the futility of giving a direct order to so large a number of men, when I knew I could not possibly enforce that order, was too obvious.

Indeed, the strategy couldn't have been simpler. R A Feltham: 'It was made quite clear that we were to keep everything clean and ship-shape, and that the object was to keep the Fleet from going to sea until something was done about our pay.' 'Colours' was carried out with due ceremony on the quarterdeck at 0800, but no sooner had they been hoisted than cheering erupted across the anchorage. Only 30 per cent of the *Hood*'s crew fell in for work at 0830 and the howls of derision directed at them from the *Rodney* settled the matter. The Invergordon Mutiny had broken out.

The sequence of events in the *Hood* over the hour or so that followed remains unclear. There are unsubstantiated reports that Lt Cdr Pursey volunteered to go forward and clear the forecastle with his revolver. If true, the offer was wisely declined by McCrum who had already informed Capt Patterson that 'no good purpose was likely to be served by my also addressing them'. However, it does seem that a large meeting then took place in the foretopmen's mess on the upper deck amidships at which an unnamed able seaman made it perfectly clear to all and sundry that 'We're not going to let this bloody ship sail'. It was also made plain that this was not a mutiny but a strike, and that there was to be no violence. When it was over parties of men returned to the forecastle where a heavy wire hawse was rove through the cables and round the capstan to prevent the anchor being slipped. Shortly after 0900 Tomkinson cancelled the planned exercise and informed the Admiralty of the situation. Much to the officers' surprise, once it became obvious to the crew that the *Hood* would not be putting to sea the ship slipped quietly back into harbour routine. Normal work and divisional drill continued against the background of sporadic cheering between ships, not all of it cordial: it is quite obvious that the *Hood*'s return to work provoked considerable resentment in the *Rodney*. Nonetheless, parties of men kept a permanent watch on the forecastle, from where any developments were communicated to the messdecks below. As AB Fred Copeman of the *Norfolk* later explained, the choice of the forecastle was an obvious one: 'If you're on the forecastle no one else can get there. The hatches from the seamen's mess deck lead directly to the forecastle. If the marines are with you no one can do anything about it. Every ship did the same.' But it wasn't all toil and angst. Many took the opportunity of 'having a good time' in the benign autumn weather. The ship's deck hockey tournament was advanced and rehearsals began for a concert party. On the *Rodney* one of the messdeck pianos was hoisted onto a turret for a stoker to keep the men entertained with the latest music-hall hits. He was flung out of the Navy for his pains.

Communication with neighbouring ships – *Rodney*, *Dorsetshire* and *Warspite* in *Hood*'s case – was carried out in the first instance by means of flags and then by the use of caps, short-arm semaphore and Aldis lights. Wireless was used briefly until cut off in mid-morning. Quite frequently the messages transmitted were no more than 'sticking out okay', for which regular crossing of forearms, lowering of the union flag at the jackstaff or hourly cheering sufficed. In this the mutineers made use of the subtle body language with which sailors always communicated. Len Wincott:

> ... If the crew of a passing motorboat from another striking ship showed crossed forearms, it conveyed to us that the men of that ship were still solid in their strike. This was not a planned signal. The crossed forearms were one of many unofficial signals that had entered Navy life years and years before and actually meant 'Tie up' or 'Finish'. In our particular circumstances at Invergordon it was automatically adopted to mean something more.

The ship's boats were active throughout, used by both mutineers and officers, though manned by petty officers in the latter case. Discipline in the *Valiant* collapsed to such a degree that the *Hood* was obliged to provide a boat for the use of her captain. Officers had difficulty communicating from ship to ship but

Tomkinson was saved by the loyalty of the *Hood*'s telegraphists, thanks to whom he maintained steady contact with London.

Needless to say, the officers of the Atlantic Fleet found themselves in an exceedingly difficult position. Not only had they received no more warning of the cuts than the men, but the erosion of discipline was profoundly disturbing for those accustomed to orders being obeyed without question. Many would have preferred Tomkinson to have taken a firmer line but others, perhaps for the first time in their careers, were completely at a loss as to what to do. The frustration that caused Lt Cdr R H S Rodger of the *Norfolk* to ask 'What do you want?' of Wincott and his companions therefore went hand in hand with a growing anger at the Admiralty that had landed them in this ghastly situation. As one of the *Hood*'s lieutenant commanders told LS Sam Wheat, 'This is the worst bastard thing the Admiralty has ever done to us'. It fell to Tomkinson to bring an initially belligerent Admiralty to a full realisation of the issue facing the Navy. Orders were passed for the investigation of hardship cases to begin and at midday Tomkinson let it be known that he was sending the Chief of Staff, Rear Admiral Reginald Colvin, to London by air to confer with Their Lordships. These measures evidently had their desired effect and the atmosphere in the *Hood* eased as the men decided to await the response of the Admiralty. For many, indeed, it was their first opportunity to reflect on the day's events and the possible consequences. As Stoker Charles Wild put it, 'Everybody was really kind of stunned with what they were doing ... I think everybody was apprehensive of what was going to happen'. That evening the ship's cinema was rigged and the men settled down for a tense night.

The first indication of a response came with the morning papers on Wednesday 16th, in which the Admiralty's optimistic characterisation of the mutiny as 'unrest among a proportion of the lower ratings' provoked considerable anger. During the 1030 Stand Easy Lt Cdr Pursey was again approached by a rating brandishing a newspaper: '"It's all up again, sir", "Why?", "Admiralty statement 'unrest'." ... "What do they want us to do? Chuck the bloody guns overboard?"' The news caught the *Hood* at a particularly delicate moment. Not for the first time the resumption of work after Stand Easy was received with some disgust in the nearby *Rodney*, herself largely at a standstill. Opinions were hardened by the rumours circulating during 'Up spirits' at 1115 that the ship was to be interned at Scapa Flow or placed under close arrest at Portsmouth. For a few hours the *Hood* teetered on the brink of open mutiny and only resolute action by McCrum prevented her joining the most militant ships in the fleet. Capt Patterson:

> The normal work of the ship proceeded throughout the forenoon, though the atmosphere was somewhat strained. It unfortunately happened that the turn of the tide coincided with 'Stand Easy' in the forenoon, with the result that the two ships [*Hood* and *Rodney*] were swung parallel with one another. A mutual

demonstration of cheering between the men assembled on *Rodney*'s forecastle and the men who had gone forward for a smoke during 'Stand Easy' in *Hood* took place. These men returned to their work after 'Stand Easy' but there is little doubt that some signals and signs were exchanged to the effect that *Hood*'s ship's company were not supporting the cause with sufficient enthusiasm. During the dinner hour one or two leading seamen reported to the commander that the feeling on the mess decks was growing strongly in favour of stopping work, and that the life of those against it was being made difficult. It became evident from various sources that the men would probably not 'Turn To' after dinner, and just before the routine time for falling in the hands the Senior Engineer reported to the Commander that the stokers appeared to be not coming down below. In order to avoid an open demonstration, the hands were piped to 'Make and Mend Clothes'. This took them somewhat by surprise and resulted in their proceeding down below to sleep instead of cheering on the forecastle.

For the *Hood* at least this was the high point of the mutiny. However, there was not much longer to wait. Tomkinson had finally succeeded in bringing home to the Admiralty the dire consequences that might ensue from its refusal to make the necessary concession. At 1510 the following signal was received from London:

> The Board of Admiralty is fully alive to the fact that amongst certain classes of ratings special hardship will result from the reduction of pay ordered by HM Government. It is therefore directed that ships of the Atlantic Fleet are to proceed to their home ports forthwith to enable personal investigation by C-in-Cs and representatives of Admiralty with view to necessary alleviation being made. Any further refusals of individuals to carry out orders will be dealt with under the Naval Discipline Act. This signal is to be promulgated to the Fleet forthwith.

Tomkinson allowed the gist of the signal to reach the men in the form of a 'buzz', the eternal currency of the lower deck. The news was received with relief by some but many regarded it with deep suspicion. The directive was interpreted, rightly, as an attempt to end the mutiny and winnow the ringleaders out from the rest. The signal immediately caused a rupture between those for whom a return to home ports meant another spell of leave and those, usually from Scotland and the North of England, who tended to regard it as a potential trap. It was in this atmosphere that Capt Patterson cleared lower deck at 1645 and addressed the ship's company from 'A' turret while Tomkinson looked on from the bridge:

> ... I informed the ship's company of the decision. At the same time I informed them that I could guarantee that any rumours as to this being a ruse to divide

the Fleet were entirely unfounded and that any further refusal on their part would do still further harm to their cause. The information was received in silence, and the men then dispersed.

The speech was certainly not received in silence. In fact, it was punctuated by a stream of ribald comment from his audience: 'All me eye and Betty Martin' ... 'Scapa Flow' ... 'Spithead' ... 'We stay here...'. Worse, during his address Patterson made the mistake of mentioning that 'Of course, we haven't had the Royal Marines up here', a comment that was taken as a veiled threat. For a crew suspicious that the ship might be boarded by Marines off Spithead it met with a predictable response: 'You get the bastards up here!', a reaction which, among other things, shows how difficult had been the position of the *Hood's* Marine detachment.

As was no doubt the intention, the Admiralty signal provoked considerable debate in the fleet and prompted choruses of shouting and cheering across the anchorage. AB Alex Paterson, later a commander and one of the few willing to show his opposition to the mutiny, recalls the aftermath of the captain's speech in the *Hood*:

> Within five minutes a two-badge able seaman convinced nearly everyone the signal to sail was a trick to get the ships to sea and to separate them so they lost mutual support, which would lead to the arrest of the leaders. He claimed the cuts would be made and money never restored. He then called for a vote, with a show of hands. Those in favour of not putting to sea were overwhelming. Only four hands were raised in favour of weighing anchor.

But debate continued and the concerns of the crew eventually boiled down to whether the ship would indeed return to Portsmouth, and what their reputation would be if they allowed her to do so. On the other hand, no ship wished to face the wrath of the Admiralty alone at Invergordon. Lt Cdr Pursey captures the dilemma of a majority of the crew:

> Master-at-Arms reported to Commander: 'Stoker X wishes to see you, sir.' Stoker: 'We've had a meeting on the fo'c'sle and we've decided: if other ships don't go ... we won't go. If other ships go ... we will go. ... We won't stay here alone. ... Can you please tell us whether the other ships will go?' Commander: 'Quite honestly ... I don't know. When I do I will let you know.'

The first sign that a decision had been reached came at 1700 when the full engine room watch turned to for lighting up the boilers. However, cheering and shouting continued from the forecastle where the cable party was prevented from doing its work. AB Paterson:

As we came through the forward screen of the forecastle, we were greeted by loud cheers and laughter from what seemed to be most of the ship's company. Several sailors, who were sitting on the lashed cables, eyed us suspiciously. One glance by us was enough to decide that the anchor couldn't possibly be weighed without a full party. [Lt Cdr] Longley-Cook was politely informed they had no intention of moving without the use of force. Longley-Cook did not argue and withdrew to report to the captain.

Nonetheless, by 2000 the men were preparing for sea and the dire agreement made between Patterson and Capt J B Watson of the *Nelson* that the cables be parted if necessary had never to be implemented. Parties of men began taking their stations, the bridles were unshackled and the hawse rove through the cables the previous morning was removed without difficulty. However, Tomkinson was by no means certain that the rest of his command would follow suit. Indeed, at 1945 he had signalled the Admiralty that 'I am not sure that all ships will leave as ordered but some will go'. In the event, a change of orders allowing ships to proceed independently rather than by squadron extinguished the last embers of resistance. By 2330 the fleet had cleared Invergordon.

No sooner had the last ship passed through the Sutors guarding the entrance to the Cromarty Firth than the aftermath of the Invergordon Mutiny began. On the evening of Thursday 17th the *Hood*'s officers were invited to a SODS opera performed by the ship's company which, as Pursey recalled, 'treated [the] whole affair as one big lark'. But no one could be under any illusion as to the challenges that lay ahead. That morning married men on the 1919 scales had made it plain that they did not wish their hardship statements to be taken by divisional officers with no experience of family affairs. Cdr McCrum obliged with the unprecedented step of himself receiving their statements in his cabin. It was the start of a new era in officer–sailor relations.

Shortly after 0630 on Saturday, 19 September the *Hood* docked at Portsmouth. Leave was given until Monday evening and the pubs of Pompey filled with blabbing sailors, Communist agitators and badly disguised secret-service agents. Hardship statements continued to be taken, but on 21 September the government announced that the pay cuts would be reduced to a maximum of 10 per cent. In the event an order passed on 1 October placed the entire Navy on the 1919 rates *less* 11 per cent. The lower deck could savour a victory of sorts but for the government and the Navy the damage was done. News of the mutiny had been followed by a run on the pound and within days it was announced that Britain had been forced off the Gold Standard. Meanwhile, the Admiralty began to set its house in order through a policy of punitive action and vigorous self-exculpation. On 6 October, Admiral Sir John Kelly, a confidant of King George V and much respected on the lower deck, succeeded Hodges as Commander-in-Chief, Atlantic Fleet. It was a condition of Kelly's acceptance that he be allowed to make a clean sweep of the fleet and sweep he did. He was particularly adamant that the Invergordon ringleaders be rooted out and expelled from the Navy. Despite the amnesty promised by Chamberlain to Parliament after the fleet had left Invergordon, 120 men were confined to barracks before it sailed north in early October, ten of them from the *Hood*. No sooner had the general election of 27 October returned MacDonald's National Government than most of these were discharged, the first of nearly four hundred undesirables to be ejected from the Navy over the next few months.

Nor were these the only casualties. Despite favourable remarks on his conduct, in its zeal to absolve itself of blame the Board of Admiralty began gradually to lay responsibility for the mutiny at Tomkinson's door. There is certainly much in the view that Tomkinson allowed matters to develop by not preventing the meetings being held ashore, but his treatment by the Admiralty represents the final chapter in one of the most discreditable episodes in its history. After a decent amount of time had been allowed to elapse, on 2 February 1932 the Admiralty issued two letters addressed to Tomkinson, the first promoting him Vice Admiral and curtailing his tenure as squadron commander by eight months, and the second censuring him for his handling of the mutiny. Of this Tomkinson received his first inkling by means of a BBC broadcast picked up in the *Hood's* W/T office as she lay off Trinidad on 16 February. Tomkinson fought a bitter rearguard action but it was to no avail and his career in the Navy was broken.

It is a measure of how out of touch was the Admiralty that no official investigation of the causes of the Invergordon Mutiny was ever carried out, a decision which provoked much criticism in the Navy. Months after the event senior officers were still unaware whether their conduct had met with the approval of the Admiralty or if they would eventually join the list of casualties. The gulf-like gap between the views of the Board on the one hand and those of the officers who lived through it on the other is nowhere better demonstrated than in the extracts which follow. First the Admiralty's view, promulgated to the Atlantic Fleet in October:

> The Board of Admiralty has given full consideration to the reports received on the serious refusal of duty which occurred in some of the principal ships of the Atlantic Fleet at Invergordon on the 15th–16th September last. Notwithstanding the decision that, owing to the exceptional circumstances, no disciplinary action should be taken, this insubordinate behaviour was, in Their Lordships' opinion, inexcusable.
>
> Their Lordships note with great satisfaction that, in the whole of the rest of the Navy, the ships' companies acted, at a very critical time, in accordance with the high tradition of the Service. They desire, however, to impress on all Officers and Men that this failure in discipline by a small part of the Fleet has done grave injury to the prestige of the whole Navy and to the country.

They look with confidence to every Officer and Man to do his utmost to restore the proud position the Royal Navy has always had in the eyes of the world.

Against this 'ineffable display of smugness' can be set Capt Patterson's reasoned conclusions as to the cause of the mutiny, in which, like Tomkinson, his sympathy with the men is quite apparent:

I am of the opinion that the primary cause of the intense outburst of feeling on the part of the lower ratings was the sudden shock they received in the announcement of the reductions without any previous preparation. The feeling of unjust treatment was sufficient to unite them and make them very easily influenced to take strong and concerted action on their own lines, rather than await more patiently the orthodox methods which they were convinced would not be effective in the short time available.

The gently chiding tone of Patterson's comments no doubt helped seal his fate as well, and he surrendered his command together with Tomkinson in August 1932. Within a few months, however, the Board that had presided over the Invergordon Mutiny was itself no more, and by year's end the Atlantic Fleet had become the Home Fleet.

Historians will record that the 'quiet mutiny' was in fact less a mutiny than a strike, though it was one which after the frustrations of the Great War and the trials of the 1920s came close to destroying the Navy. Luckily, a new Board of Admiralty proved equal to the task of restoring its fortunes. For the *Hood*, too, a new regime awaited, one that, for a few fleeting years, brought her to the height of her glory. For the lower deck, meanwhile, the Invergordon Mutiny was looked back on as a rubicon in its relations with authority. As LS Sam Wheat put it, 'It did a bit of good. It did make them see that you had intelligent people in the Service, and that they were not going to be trampled on.' How this realisation affected the *Hood* is what concerns us next.

8

A New Broom

THE APPOINTMENT OF Admiral Sir John Kelly as Commander-in-Chief brought a breath of fresh air to the Atlantic Fleet. No sooner had his appointment taken effect in October 1931 than he was moving from ship to ship, addressing the men in their own pungent language, admitting past wrongs and attempting to instil confidence in the future. Anxious no doubt to lay a ghost, within a month of the mutiny Kelly had brought the fleet back to Invergordon for a week of intensive drill where earlier it had lain idle. Despite Kelly's report at the end of November that the fleet was at a high level of efficiency, morale remained low, particularly in the *Hood*, which Tomkinson suggested should be recommissioned with a fresh crew. To have done so would have placed her in the same category as the *Valiant* and the *Adventure*, which were ignominiously paid off before the end of the year. The Admiralty refused and Christmas leave was taken early. In the new year Tomkinson led the *Hood* on a spring cruise to the Caribbean accompanied by *Repulse*, *Norfolk*, *Dorsetshire* and *Delhi*. Under normal circumstances this might have acted as a huge fillip for morale but the cruise was overshadowed first by enormous seas between the Lizard and the Azores and finally by the news that both Tomkinson and Patterson had fallen victim to the attrition of senior officers that followed the mutiny. It is also clear that Tomkinson's personality made for an extremely unhappy wardroom, and by the time he hauled down his flag on 15 August 1932 the Admiralty had reconsidered its earlier decision not to pay off the *Hood*.

The arrival of Rear Admiral William James that same day heralded a new era for the *Hood*, one which was to make a lasting impression on the Navy as a whole. The collective sigh of relief is captured in a stanza by Paymaster Lt J T Shrimpton, a member of Tomkinson's staff, penned two days before James' arrival:

> The summer days are on the wing,
> The bathers' cries are echoing,
> When news of a momentous thing
> Through the warm air goes humming;

We hear the staff now softly sing,
'The King is dead – long live the King!'
The new regime, the new regime,
The new regime is coming.

William James was born into one of those upper-middle-class families from which the Navy has drawn much of its officer corps. His early years were blighted by the portrait of him as a child executed by his grandfather, the artist Sir John Millais, which, as the advertisement for Pear's soap, became one of the first icons of British marketing. From this came an enduring nickname: 'Bubbles'. Despite this stigma, James entered the Navy where he was in the vanguard of officers who embraced the revolution in gunnery led by Admiral Sir Percy Scott at the turn of the twentieth century. He first came to prominence in 1909 as gunnery officer of the cruiser *Natal*, his crews smashing all records for speed and accuracy during the annual firing competitions of the Home Fleet. More even than his technical ability, James had the gift of drawing the best out of his men and when W R Hall, his last captain in the *Natal*, was appointed to the battlecruiser *Queen Mary* in 1913, James followed as executive officer. Between them, Hall and James refined the divisional system and devised a revolutionary watch routine destined to be adopted by all British capital ships on the outbreak of the Great War. This implemented, they turned to amenities aboard, and it was in this ship that a cinema, a chapel, bookstall and electric washing machines made their first appearance afloat in the Royal Navy. Next they saw to improved bathing facilities for stokers and allowed petty officers to rearrange their accommodation in line with their new standing in the Service. James left the *Queen Mary* in January 1916, just months before she was destroyed at Jutland, but the ideas and procedures pioneered in her were enshrined in *New Battleship Organisations*, the influential manual on ship husbandry he completed early that same year.

The *Hood* therefore provided fertile ground for James' particular talents, and rarely can a ship have needed them more. As he later wrote, 'I never met a more unhappy party than when I relieved Tomkinson. He and his Flag Captain Patterson were at daggers drawn, and the Commander, McCrum, had lost all interest through being hunted by Tomkinson whose habit it was to find fault with everything.' As so often, James brought with him as flag captain a companion from earlier days, in this case Thomas Binney, his executive officer in the cruiser *Hawkins*. It was to prove an inspired choice. Judging that the *Hood* had 'a first-rate lot of officers and a fine ship's company', within weeks these two had persuaded the Admiralty to drop its decision to pay her off, judging this 'a confession that it was beyond the powers of naval officers to dispel the gloomy atmosphere and restore vitality and happiness'. But restore them they did. James' overture to the crew on his arrival set the tone for the rest of her peacetime career. Vice Admiral Eric Longley-Cook remembers the occasion:

We sailed to Southend and again on a Sunday forenoon 'clear lower deck, everyone aft'. He addressed us. How differently! 'I am proud to have joined you' and for the first time in my eighteen years at sea I was told what the peacetime job of the Royal Navy was. To train for war in order to keep the peace. To 'show the flag'. In home waters to show the British public what they were paying for and abroad to be good ambassadors for Great Britain. From then on it was 'tails up'.

True to his word, James' tenure began with week-long visits to Southend and then Hartlepool, one of the towns worst affected by the Depression. Children's parties were held aboard and entertainments arranged for the men ashore. At Hartlepool the ship played the town at water polo and hundreds of jobless miners were invited aboard to have tea with the men. As a display of the Admiralty's new sensitivity it could hardly have been bettered. Apart from eliciting some dreadful stanzas of poetry from James, the *Hood*'s visit to Hartlepool left a lasting impact on one small boy who had to content himself with admiring her from afar: Ted Briggs. Thereafter the ship went from strength to strength. Kelly's campaign to restore confidence and morale after Invergordon turned on a relentless programme of drill, exercises, training, discipline, housekeeping and sport, and James did not disappoint. Within the space of a year the *Hood*, showing unaccustomed proficiency in gunnery, had demolished a battle practice target, won the fleet anti-aircraft gunnery competition, and become 'Cock of the Fleet' at the Home Fleet Regatta in May 1933. In October of that year a landing party near Invergordon was performed with such enthusiasm that James had to rebut claims, splashed in banner headlines around the world, that the *Hood* was in the grip of another mutiny.

Apart from the leadership provided by James and Binney, the recovery of the *Hood*'s morale owes much to her executive officer, Cdr C R McCrum, to his right-hand man and Mate of the Upper Deck, the ex-lower deck Lt Cdr Harry Pursey, to the First Lieutenant Lt Cdr Eric Longley-Cook, and to Engineer Cdr A K Dibley. Among the *Hood*'s officers were at least two more who had benefitted from the Mate Scheme, Lt (E) Ernest Mill (later a rear admiral) and Sub-Lt T J G Marchant. Pursey seems to have had a share of unpopularity as 'the Commander's nark' but the fact that three of the ship's officers had begun their careers on the lower deck cannot have been lost on the crew and such evidence as survives suggests an unprecedented entente between officers and men in the months and years after Invergordon. There is evidence, too, that the broader outlook of the engineer officer began to make itself felt in relations with the lower deck; men who, in AB Len Wincott's words, were 'not dependent for prestige on any particular show of aloofness from the mob'. Like so much else in the locust years, the mechanics of this process now seem lost to posterity, but the accomplishment was real enough. Though largely overshadowed by the regime that followed it, there can be no doubt that the successes of the mid-1930s would not have been possible without the qualities of leadership shown after Invergordon. James did not strike his flag until the summer of 1934, but when he recalled his tenure as having been surrounded by 'officers and men who had responded eagerly to everything I had asked of them ... in an atmosphere of happiness and high endeavour', it was to the 1931–3 commission that he was referring above all. Yet it was not all happiness. Morale had improved markedly but problems remained which lay at the heart of the crisis affecting the Navy as a whole. The Invergordon Mutiny exposed many failings in naval organisation, but in shipboard life it did so in three areas above all: in the widespread disillusion over prospects and promotion; in the strained relations that existed between departments; and finally in the failure of the divisional system in which the Admiralty had reposed such confidence. But where the Admiralty proved itself incapable of effective leadership in this matter one officer set himself to influence his peers with a tested paradigm. That officer was Rory O'Conor. The paradigm was HMS *Hood.*

Rory Chambers O'Conor was born into an Anglo-Irish family in Buenos Aires in 1898. In 1911 he entered the Royal Naval College at Osborne and spent much of the Great War in the gunroom of the pre-dreadnought *Prince of Wales* in which he saw action in the Dardanelles. A formidable sportsman, O'Conor represented the Navy at rugby between 1920–4, leading the United Services team during the 1921–2 season. His appointment to the Royal Yacht *Victoria and Albert* on being promoted lieutenant in 1919 was an early sign of favour but it was as a divisional officer in the battleship *Barham* between 1921–2 that he first came to prominence, Capt Robin Dalglish noting his 'exceptionally good command of men'. Specialising in gunnery, he divided most of the next ten years between HMS *Excellent,* the gunnery school in Portsmouth Harbour, and various shore and seagoing appointments including the cruiser *Emerald* and the battleships *Resolution* and *Royal Sovereign.* Promoted commander in 1931, it was while he was on the staff of *Excellent* that O'Conor learnt of his selection as the *Hood*'s executive officer, an appointment which took effect when she recommissioned at Portsmouth in August 1933.

Despite being the subject of an ample biography the reasons for O'Conor's preferment at the age of only thirty-four remain unclear. His zeal and talent apart, the appointment seems to have owed much to Admiral Sir John Kelly under whom he had served in the *Resolution* in the Mediterranean in 1924–5. Whatever the case, O'Conor was one of a generation of younger officers determined to take a hand in restoring the tarnished prestige of the Navy; for whom the surest means to a happy and successful ship lay in a genuine interest in the welfare of her men; for whom the Royal Navy was great enough to afford every man the chance of a fair hearing; for whom punishment existed chiefly to maintain discipline rather than to enforce compliance, and for whom the mere exercise of that discipline could never substitute for engaging the men as befitted their skills and responsibility. Above all, O'Conor and his like brought to their

111

work both a heightened sensitivity to the plight of the ordinary sailor and an enhanced perception of his value as an individual. Among the first of this band was Sir Atwell 'Lou' Lake, Bt, who as executive officer of the *Nelson* had been among the few to emerge with any credit from Invergordon. Although a more formal officer than O'Conor, it was Lake's force of character, love of ship and respect for his men that had made the difference in *Nelson* in September 1931. Another was C R McCrum whose tact and powers of leadership delivered into O'Conor's hands a vessel ripe for the changes he would bring to her life and organisation. Far more than her flag-showing, the *Hood*'s reputation as the greatest ship in the Navy during the 1930s rests on the leading role she played in the introduction of a new dialogue between officers and men, to which first McCrum and then O'Conor made a vital contribution.

The task of executive officer in a capital ship was one of the most challenging the Navy had to offer. Admiral Lord Chatfield, whose two-volume autobiography stands among the finest evocations of life in the Royal Navy ever written, provides these descriptions of a commander's lot:

> There is no greater test of character in the world than to be the executive officer of a big ship. Many shun the responsibility and seek a less exacting duty, such as the command of a small ship; but few captains can efficiently command a great ship's company unless they themselves have been through the mill, can realise the Commander's difficulties day by day and feel the pulse of his men. [...] If the executive officer of a big ship ... wishes to succeed he must, as a first rule, know everything that goes on in the ship. He must be constantly visiting every part of it and be closely in touch with the ship's company's life and thought. He will thus understand his men, rectify just grievances in time and stop abuses before they can spread. His capacity will be accurately appraised by his officers and still more accurately by the ship's company, who will soon take his measure, and the evilly inclined soon know how far they can go in safety.

Equally, the price of failure was very great. Remote as the captain often was from the men, the commander was unquestionably the key figure in the life of a major ship. On him depended the spirit with which his crew approached every endeavour. For him they might either do the least they could get away with or else slog their guts out.

O'Conor's arrival in the *Hood* provided an early indication of how the orchestra of shipboard life was to be tuned for the rest of the commission. Louis Le Bailly, then a midshipman, remembers the occasion in August 1933:

> I suppose the greatest impact was when he tore up the voluminous Standing Orders and substituted his own 'Ten Commandments'. Their introduction to the new ship's company was dramatic. There was ... a magic lantern on the quarterdeck and the ten were put on one by one as he explained their relevance.

Then almost from a puff of smoke, Admiral Sir John Kelly, so beloved by the sailor, appeared from the after hatchway and gave a stirring address.

Cdr Rory O'Conor's 'Ten Commandments', August 1933

SHIP'S STANDING ORDERS

1. – *The Service.* — The Customs of the Service are to be observed at all times.
2. – *The Ship.* — The Good Appearance of the Ship is the concern of everyone in *Hood*, and all share the responsibility for this.
3. – *The Individual.* — Every man is constantly required to bring credit to the Ship by his individual bearing, dress and general conduct, on board and ashore.
4. – *Courtesy to Officers.* — The courtesy of making a gangway, and standing to one side to attention when an officer passes, is to be shown by every man. If an Officer passing through men during stand-easy, meal hours, etc., carries his cap under his arm, it will indicate that no attention, other than clearing a gangway, is required.
5. – *Execution of Orders.* — All orders, including those passed by Bugle and Pipe, are to be obeyed at the Run.
6. – *Punctual Attendance at Place of Duty.* — Every man is personally responsible, on all occasions, for his own punctual attendance at his place of duty.
7. – *Permission to Leave Work.* — A man is always to ask permission before leaving his work.
8. – *Reporting on Completion of Work.* — Any man on finishing the work for which he has been told off, is to report to his immediate superior. Parties of men are to be fallen in and reported.
9. – *Card-playing and Gambling.* — While card-playing is allowed at mess-tables and on the upper deck, any form of gambling is strictly prohibited. Gambling includes all games of chance played for money stakes.
10. – *Requests.* — Any man wishing to see the Commander is to put in a request to his Officer of Division. In urgent cases his request is to pass through the Master-at-Arms and Officer of the Watch.

Implicit in O'Conor's Ten Commandments was the notion that every man who gave of his best could expect fairness, respect and consideration from his superiors; that there were rewards for hard work, and that no one could go very far wrong so long as he kept the interests of the ship at the forefront of his mind;

that no ship could be regarded as successful if she were not happy, and that every officer and rating had a share in this endeavour. Never before had such a contract been laid before the lower deck of the Royal Navy, nor was such a system ever sold to her officer corps in such persuasive terms. The assessment of the 1933–6 commission which follows is based not only on the memoirs and reminiscences of those who lived it, but on *Running a Big Ship on 'Ten Commandments'*, the influential manual on ship organisation O'Conor published within a year of leaving the *Hood*.

The linchpin of the *Hood*'s Ten Commandments was O'Conor himself. What set him apart was his accessibility with respect to the entire crew, of which the outward sign was his celebrated open-door policy.

> In the course of the day's work innumerable people have business to do with the Commander of a big ship, and his ready accessibility is a matter of importance. Even with a properly decentralised organisation, it is inevitable that the Commander should be constantly sought after for consultation, advice, approval, permission, information, and a hundred and one other reasons. [...] The Commander wants to feel free to wander about the ship at will, seeing the hands at work and getting to know them. But there is a time for everything, and there should be at least one hour, both in the forenoon and afternoon, when the whole ship knows that there is *one* place where he can almost certainly be found, and available.

That place was his day cabin. Mindful of Invergordon, here O'Conor acted out the central tenet of his ethos: that it was an officer's duty to make himself a channel for the problems and grievances of those placed under him; that it was his responsibility to ensure that every man could turn to him for a fair hearing:

> In a great ship's company, there must inevitably arise every variety of problem for the individuals composing it – problems of life, love, leave, illness, death, and hardship of all kinds arising from work, pay, food, sleep, to mention only a few. No request must be ignored – all must be considered and given a sympathetic hearing, and the men encouraged to come forward.

The other visible sign of this interest was the length O'Conor went to memorise the names of the *Hood*'s 1,300 crewmen. Although he tacitly admitted being able to hold no more than six hundred in his head at one time, the general impression was and remains that he came to know the name of every man on board. Whatever the reality, the endeavour had a marked impact on the atmosphere aboard: 'Until you know a man's name he has no separate identity for you. Directly you know it, a bridge is slipped across the gap and you very quickly begin to know a lot of other things too – so will he.' An essential part of O'Conor's philosophy was what he called 'consideration for the men' on the part of their officers. This extended from reducing the amount of time liberty-men had to waste waiting for boats and drifters to the introduction of a revised weekend routine which at last gave the crew the complete day of rest prescribed in the King's Regulations. He also saw to it that an off-duty watch was never roused except in the event of an emergency. Many of these innovations were no more than the application of common sense to irksome naval tradition, of which his winter and foul-weather routines are typical examples:

> No good purpose is served by falling men in at 0600 on a wild and wet morning, and possibly also in the dark and cold, to scrub the decks, either at sea or in harbour. [...] In the winter especially it becomes a farce – water is swilled over decks which are neither properly scrubbed nor properly dried ..., and the result is a muddy and sodden deck. [...] It is wiser to wait for daylight, when the elements are better faced by men who have already breakfasted.

O'Conor also took steps to mitigate the constant disruption of work and leisure brought on by the need for men to stand aside and come to attention whenever an officer passed by. Henceforth, an officer carrying his cap needed no special attention other than being given room to pass. If this approach contributed to what he called 'the ideal state of every man knowing what is required of him', then it also had the effect of building a sense of community in the ship. As he put it,

> If these rules are faithfully observed, a man has a chance to feel a sense of peace and security in his leisure time on board, and to think of his ship as his home ... rather than a place of duty only ..., which is all for the good of those leading the abnormal and crowded life of a ship.

That sense of community was assured once a man formed an attachment of pride for his ship. Indeed, a ship's community need not be confined to her crew:

> There is no surer way to increase a man's pride in his ship than for those who are near and dear to him to feel proud of her too. It is impossible to show too much courtesy and consideration in welcoming friends and relations on board on every occasion when it is possible for them to be invited. [...] A strictly legal definition of the term 'Ship's Company' embraces every person borne on her books. But in practice, if it is possible by the warmth of the welcome they are given to make all families feel that they also belong, then the company of a big ship becomes multiplied from one thousand to several thousands. To have so great a community bound together both by family affection and by pride of ship must influence her fortunes decisively.

Evidence of O'Conor's interest in this wider community is provided in the census of the crew and their dependents which he took. It reveals, among other things, that the *Hood*'s 'total family' of crewmen, wives and children numbered 2,562 souls. In his concern for such matters, in the role and impact of a warship in wider society and vice versa, Rory O'Conor was years ahead of his time.

But pride was also bound up with the appearance of the ship and O'Conor laid a great, and indeed excessive, stress on smartness, cleanliness and paintwork:

> It is sometimes lightly assumed that the ship's appearance is the concern only of a small hierarchy which includes the Commander, the Chief Boatswain's Mate, the Captains of the Tops and the Side, and perhaps a few others. No ship was ever kept clean except by the co-operation of all hands, and this needs hammering in, with emphasis on the ways in which every individual can help. [...] Everyone must be jealous of the ship's appearance and must make his contribution, and above all, he must avoid making unnecessary work for others who are striving to keep the ship as she should look.

In this respect O'Conor was found to be the determined enemy not only of the man who skulked off leaving his companions to complete the most disagreeable chores but also of those who spoilt their hard work. Here is O'Conor on the skulker:

> All the world hates a skulker – it must hate him – why should a man slide away and leave his mates to finish off a job, perhaps an unpleasant one and in bad weather? The worst of skulking is that it can easily become infectious – stop it at once. There is only one treatment for deliberate skulking, and that is '14 days No 11.'*

But tiresome as his men often found it, under O'Conor's stewardship the *Hood* brought to a pinnacle the art of ship adornment nurtured by the Navy since the age of Nelson. There was, however, a penalty for this zeal for gleaming paint and that lay in the many tons of it which had to be scraped off her from 1936 onwards.

Many of these measures and devices were not of themselves new. But never had they been brought to bear on the management of a ship's company in such a concentrated and energetic manner. Underpinning O'Conor's style was his notably human and liberal approach to discipline. As in any ship, the barometer of the *Hood*'s morale and discipline lay at the requestmen and defaulter's table, and above all the equanimity with which the commander dealt with the cases that passed before him. First requestmen: 'Every request should be given careful consideration, and requestmen must feel assured of a sympathetic hearing. If a

*Punishment No 11 entailed stoppage of leave.

request has to be refused, the reason should be explained and the man given the option of coming up again if he wants to, or if necessary of seeing the Captain.' Then defaulters, of whom around three thousand came cap in hand to O'Conor's table in the Commander's lobby over the course of the 1933–6 commission:

> The majority of small offences are committed by thoughtlessness or mischance and not by intention, and after one solemn warning most men are careful not to reappear as defaulters. [...] Long-drawn-out punishments are seldom necessary or desirable; the Commander should see all the more serious offenders again on the conclusion of their punishment, when he may be able to give them wise counsel and to urge them to go and sin no more.

Against the yardstick of his Ten Commandments, O'Conor's style of discharging justice appears on the face of it to have yielded good results. Over the three years of his tenure transgressions against the Ship's Standing Orders apparently fell from a typical figure of sixty-three per week at the start of the commission to only seven later on. As Admiral The Earl of Cork and Orrery later reported, despite the many and varied attractions ashore, only one man had gone adrift during the *Hood*'s weeklong visit to Southend in May 1935, and he had been stuck in a traffic jam. But serious offences were also committed and to these O'Conor alludes only indirectly. The 1933–6 commission was plagued by the usual spates of petty theft while the months the *Hood* spent alongside at Gibraltar over the winter of 1935–6 evidently tested his authority to the limit. But by creating a regime in which it was easier to stay on the right side of the law O'Conor moulded a crew that, for a time at least, was more at peace with itself than it had been for many years.

The effect of O'Conor's approach was not only improved morale and discipline but a far greater and wider degree of involvement in the life of the ship among both officers and men. This was reflected above all in the drive for sporting excellence which O'Conor pursued with unrelenting vigour, and for a few years the *Hood* dominated sporting competition in the Home Fleet. Her record in the fleet Pulling Regatta for the coveted Silver Coquerelle could not match the triumphs of the 1920s when the *Hood* was Cock of the Fleet three years running between 1926–8, but the range of trophies won and competed for gives some idea of the enthusiasm O'Conor brought to the ship. Indeed, within fifteen months of recommissioning the ship had won virtually every trophy in the Home Fleet. The *Hood* recovered the Cock from *Nelson* in 1935, won the Arbuthnot Trophy for cross-country running from 1933–5 and the Palmer Trophy for bayonet fighting between 1934 and 1936. These and a dozen others O'Conor proudly displayed in his lobby on the forecastle deck. But not everyone shared O'Conor's devotion for competitive sports. The Pulling Regatta required the active participation of a quarter of the ship's crew, including a good many reluctant volunteers. But O'Conor had no patience for whining: 'Some people grumble about the Regatta; but it does no good to waste time grumbling; it is better to get down to it and go all out. If your luck is in, and even if you don't come out on top, but do well, you will hear no grumbling in your ship.'

For all his obsession with paintwork and zeal for sporting excellence, there were many material compensations for sailing under O'Conor. Among his innovations were the installation of a broadcasting system, introduction of regular film screenings and establishment of a subscription library and mutual aid society. But it was by encouraging training and promotion that O'Conor made one of his most significant contributions. Specialisation was encouraged in all branches; men passed for leading seaman were given appropriate duties to help them develop the power of command; Stoker Jim Haskell, eager to transfer to the Submarine Service, was dissuaded until he had given it more thought and eventually dropped the idea after a sobering visit to HMS/M *Salmon*; thanks to O'Conor's initiative OD Ron Paterson was able to enjoy the rare advantage of qualifying as a seaman gunner during his time aboard, a first step towards an officer's commission. Most of all did O'Conor encourage midshipmen, not only in preparing for their exams but in playing a significant role aboard as officers under training. O'Conor liked the man who 'went all out for his ship' and he found no more willing bodies than in the gunroom: 'Once he realises that he will be treated with the full consideration due to his status as an officer, no one gives a readier response than a Midshipman, in keenness on his job and on his ship, both in her work and in her play.'

Ever the 'revolutionary constitutionalist', O'Conor gave his midshipmen an unprecedented role in the running of HMS *Hood*, though this was one of several points on which O'Conor parted company with his officers. Like all innovators, O'Conor was the subject of jealousy and rumour: that he consulted his midshipman 'doggies' as to the popularity or otherwise of the wardroom officers and that his preference for the best-looking young sailors and snotties said something about his personal inclinations. Be that as it may, there can be little doubt that many of O'Conor's administrative measures came as a rude shock to those used to the traditional way of doing things. O'Conor favoured a highly centralised role for the commander and his men that many would have preferred he did not have and which often undermined the divisional system that lay at the heart of the ship's organisation. Successful as it was, the open-door policy allowed the men to bypass their divisional officers, a cause of some aggravation in the wardroom. The perks granted to sportsmen also raised eyebrows, and not just among the officers. Mid Edmund Poland, selected to represent the Home Fleet in shooting, found himself excused many of his duties so that he could practise his questionable marksmanship on the Tipnor ranges. Meanwhile, the drafting of key players would be delayed for an important fixture. Naturally, this began to have its effect on discipline as the commission wore on. The temptation to take advantage of the Commander's easygoing ways proved irresistible and it was rumoured that captains of sports teams could and did get

The Hood *dominates John Brown's East Yard on 21 August 1918, the day before her launch. The hull is complete except for the armour. Boilers are fitted but not turbines.* National Archives of Scotland, Edinburgh

One of the first shots of Hood *at sea, seen either at Greenock or Rosyth on 9 or 13 January 1920 and with the aloft director yet to be fitted to the spotting top. She is riding high in the water, close to her 1916 design legend but showing greater freeboard than would ever be the case again.* Bruce Taylor collection

The Hood's *officer complement pose beside 'X' turret in the summer of 1920. Capt Wilfred Tomkinson is seated fifth from the left with Rear Admiral Sir Roger Keyes to his right. Sixth from the right is Cdr John Cunningham, later Commander-in-Chief Mediterranean Fleet. Bruce Taylor collection*

Speed and power. The Hood *in full cry, guns and rangefinders trained to port during a gunnery exercise in home waters in June 1927. As a visible symbol of a nation's power the* Hood *can scarcely ever have been matched. Courtesy Craig Twaddle*

(LEFT) *Admiral Sir Frederick Field. Genial commander of the Special Service Squadron in 1923–4 but remembered as a spineless First Sea Lord at the time of the Invergordon Mutiny.* HMS Hood Association

(BELOW) *The crowds disperse after another open day at Melbourne in March 1924, some of the 486,000 people who visited the Special Service Squadron during the eight days it spent in that port.* HMS Hood Association/Mackie Collection

Officers and men on the forecastle as Hood *passes through the Pedro Miguel Locks, Panama Canal, 24 July 1924.*
Illustrated London News

(ABOVE) *A cheery party at work on the* Hood's *boat deck during her stay at Hobart in March or April 1924. This was the last generation of Royal Navy sailors to carry out their duties barefoot as a matter of choice.* Illustrated Tasmanian Mail

(LEFT) *Hard work for a skilled hand: heaving the lead from the starboard chains, c1927. The canvas apron keeps the leadsman's legs from getting wet. One of the tapes indicating the depth of the water in fathoms can be seen just beneath his hand. Starboard No 1, 2 and 3 5.5in guns in the background.* HMS Hood Association/Reinold Collection

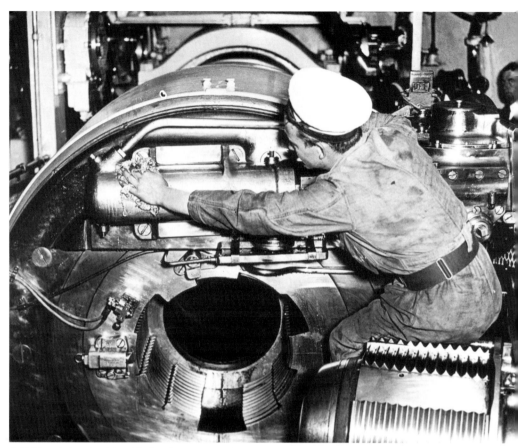

Polishing the breech of the right-hand gun in one of the four 15in turrets. This is the only known photo of the interior of one of Hood's *turrets.* Bruce Taylor collection

'The monstrous anger of the guns.' 'X' and 'Y' turrets engaging in a concentration exercise with another battlecruiser, probably Repulse, *c1925. Double salvoes are being fired, the left-hand gun of 'X' turret recoiling with the concussion while its companion is in the reloading position.* HMS Hood Association/Reinold Collection

Four engine room artificers on the control platform of the After Engine Room, c1931. Two are on the throttles (ahead and astern) controlling the revolutions of the starboard inner shaft. The desk on the left houses the engine-room register, written up hourly. Sellicks

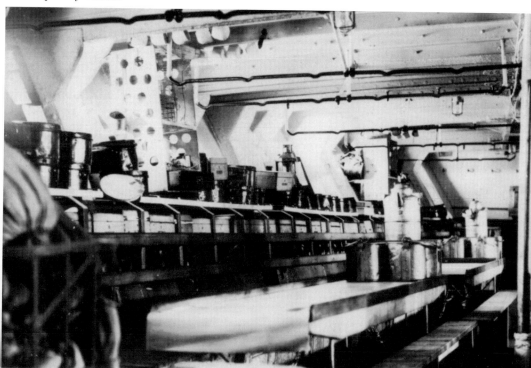

The Sick Bay flat on the port side forward of the upper deck, here taken over for use as a messdeck. This space was home to around thirty seamen whose ditty boxes, cap tins and shoes are ranged outboard. The rack on the left is for stowing hammocks which will later be slung from the kinked bars above. This photo dates from the late 1930s when the Hood*'s complement rose by a hundred or more to accommodate the training needs of an influx of new recruits to the Royal Navy.* Courtesy Brian Withers

The admiral's table laid for dinner in his dining cabin on the forecastle deck aft, c1935. Note the distinctive square ports, the gramophone and particularly the reindeer head on the bulkhead, possibly a memento of the Hood's *Scandinavian cruise in 1920.* Courtesy Mrs Nixie Taverner

A leather-upholstered bench and club fender round a coal fire in the officers' wardroom, 1924. A cosy corner in what was otherwise a surprisingly austere space. Illustrated Tasmanian Mail

'Up spirits!' Leading hands of the messes queue for their rum ration on the Hood's *forecastle deck, c1935. The diluted rum known as grog is being dispensed by a petty officer of the Supply Branch. The smaller barrico on the deck contains neat rum as issued to senior NCOs. Watching the proceedings are one of the sergeants of Marines (second from left), the Master-at-Arms (third from right) and a commissioned warrant officer (extreme right).* Bruce Taylor collection

Role reversal and role playing. Stokers dressed up as women and in uniforms borrowed from their officers. The occasio is no more than a SODS opera in the late 1930s, but there can be no denying the tensions of class and sexuality which, in varying degrees, characterised life afloat. HMS Hood Association/Sait Collection

'Ever the best of friends.' Hood's much loved mascots Ginger and Fishcakes in the late 1930s. Sadly they both went down with her. HMS Hood Association/Mason Collection

(ABOVE) *'Comparisons with other ships are odious.'* HMS Hood *serene in Bighi Bay, Grand Harbour, Malta, c1937. A steam picket boat lies at the port boom while Maltese* dghaisas *ply the harbour. To the left is the Royal Naval Hospital, Bighi.* HMS Hood Association/Mason Collection

(LEFT) *Rear Admiral Wilfred Tomkinson.* Hood*'s first captain in 1920, his career was broken by the Invergordon Mutiny eleven years later.* HMS Hood Association

(RIGHT) *Capt Julian Patterson. Powerless to influence events at Invergordon, like Tomkinson he paid the price for inaction and was replaced in 1932.* HMS Hood Association

(BELOW) *'The quiet mutiny.' Crewmen gathered on the* Hood*'s forecastle during the Invergordon Mutiny, probably Wednesday, 16 September 1931.* Illustrated London News

Hood *sailing from Portsmouth shortly after the Invergordon Mutiny in late 1931 or early 1932. Note the Fairey IIIF seaplane on the quarterdeck.* Bibliothek für Zeitgeschichte, Stuttgart

The new regime.' The charismatic Vice Admiral William James on the boat deck during a round of inspection with the ship's officers in 1933 or '34. Fifth from the right in the main group is Capt F T B Tower and to his right is Cdr Rory O'Conor. It was under James that the Hood *began her recovery from the Invergordon Mutiny.* HMS Hood Association/Willis Collection

Hood's marksmen pose with their trophies and weapons on the quarterdeck at Portsmouth, c1935. With them is Capt F T B Tower, Cdr Rory O'Conor and Judy, O'Conor's West Highland terrier. Note the brass tompions with the ship's chough emblem decorating the muzzles of 'Y' turret. HMS Hood Association/Clark Collection

The Hood's Marine guard and band formed up on the quarterdeck to welcome a dignitary aboard at Madeira in January 1934. Though occasionally overlooked, the Marine detachment not only added lustre and colour to every occasion but manned fully a quarter of the ship's armament, including 'X' 15in turret. Courtesy Mrs Nixie Taverner

Hood alongside the South Mole at Gibraltar in 1937 or '38. Lengthy interludes in Mediterranean waters kept her from the reconstruction she so desperately needed. HMS Hood Association/Percival Collection

Fraternisation with men of the German 'pocket battleship' Deutschland *on Hood's boat deck in the summer of 1937 or the autumn of 1938. Relations were mostly very cordial between the two ships.* HMS Hood Association/Higginson Collection

Part of what Cdr Rory O'Conor referred to as 'Hood's total family' dancing on the forecastle, c1935. O'Conor was the first officer to embrace the wider community represented by the sailors' families and involve it in the life and mora *of his ship.* HMS Hood Association/Willis Collection

Sub-Lt (E) Louis Le Bailly and a party of stokers landed for field training at St Andrew's Barracks, Malta, c1937. The years after Invergordon saw greatly improved relations between officers and the lower deck. Bruce Taylor collection

(LEFT) *And home there's no returning:* Hood *sails from Portsmouth for the very last time as war clouds gather, 13 August 1939.* Bibliothek für Zeitgeschichte, Stuttgart

(BELOW) *The* Hood *seen from the* Dunkerque *while patrolling in mountainous seas off Iceland in November 1939. Gifts (including this photo) were passed between the two ships as gestures of fraternity; eight months later at Mers el-Kebir it was shellfire they exchanged.* HMS Hood Association/Barker Collection

The Hood *in the autumn of 1940 with her degaussing coil prominent along the forecastle deck.* HMS Hood Association/Mason Collection

The Hood *under attack from Italian SM79 bombers in the Western Mediterranean, 9 July 1940. The stern of the battleship* Valiant *can be seen on the left of this photo which was taken from the flight deck of the carrier* Ark Royal. HMS Hood Association/Barker Collection

Swimming races alongside during the Hood*'s balmy interlude at Gibraltar in June or July 1940.* HMS Hood Association/Mason Collection

Hood *being painted at Scapa Flow in October 1940. Note her secondary armament of 4in guns and UP launchers.* Bibliothek für Zeitgeschichte, Stuttgart

The long hard winter of 1940–1. The crew of one of the 4in guns poses with a gunnery officer on the boat deck. They are rigged for Atlantic patrol duty in duffel coats along with a selection of scarves, caps and balaclavas knitted on the home front. HMS Hood Association via Colin Bonner

(BELOW LEFT) *The boat deck seen from the spotting top in the autumn of 1940. It was here, near the base of the mainmast, that the fatal shell or shells landed. Numerous ready-use ammunition lockers are distributed across the boa deck, the contents of which caused a major conflagration in* Hood's *last minutes. The grime of a year of war service is everywhere apparent.* Bibliothek für Zeitgeschichte, Stuttgart

(BELOW RIGHT) *The* Hood's *forward turrets and bridge structure seen from the forecastle in April 1941. The Type-284 gunnery radar fitted at Rosyth a month or so earlier is visible on the aloft director while one of the useless UP launchers is hidden under canvas on 'B' turret. The compass platform from which Briggs and Dundas escaped is the glazed structure above the armoured director. Tilburn sheltered beside Port No 1 UP turret (seen under canvas on the right) and got clear of the ship from the forecastle just forward of it.* Bibliothek für Zeitgeschichte, Stuttgart

Bismarck *seen from* Prinz Eugen *en route to Gdynia (Gotenhafen) in March 1941. She is wearing the Baltic camouflage pattern which was overpainted during Operation* Rheinübung. Bibliothek für Zeitgeschichte, Stuttgart

Hood *steams to her destiny in the Denmark Strait on 22 May 1941.* HMS Hood Association via Barry Roberts

The lesser known of the two images reckoned to be the last of Hood *as an effective unit, taken from* Prince of Wales *during the voyage to the Denmark Strait on the afternoon or evening of 23 May. The relative positions of the two ships are almost identical to those they assumed as battle was joined the following morning.* Bibliothek für Zeitgeschichte, Stuttgart

Bismarck *takes* Hood *under fire in the Denmark Strait on the morning of 24 May 1941. Five salvoes destroyed the pride of the Royal Navy and over 1,400 of her men.* Bibliothek für Zeitgeschichte, Stuttgart

(ABOVE LEFT) *Lancelot Ernest Holland seen in the rank of commodore in 1936 or '37. His flag flew just twelve days in* Hood. HMS Hood Association

(ABOVE RIGHT) *Electrical Lt John Iago* RNVR. *Technical expertise brought him from civilian life straight into the wardroom.* Courtesy Mrs Bee Kenchington

(LEFT) *Boy Bill Crawford: the cost of war at sea.* Courtesy Cdr Jeffrey William Crawford

(ABOVE LEFT) *CPO Supply Geoff Pope, purveyor of 'neaters' in the Victualling Office to a homesick Jon Pertwee.* HMS Hood Association

(ABOVE RIGHT) *To serve her all her days: two key ratings of the Engineering Department pose with an unknown stoker somewhere in the Mediterranean in the late 1930s. In the centre is Chief Stoker Walden Biggenden, master of the* Hood's *oil registers. Seated is Chief Stoker Harry Watson, 'Double Bottom Chief Stoker'. Both died on 24 May 1941, Watson after twenty-one years' service in the ship.* HMS Hood Association

(LEFT) *Ted Briggs as a Yeoman of Signals in the headquarters ship* Hilary, *c1944. He was one of only three men to escape the sinking of the* Hood *and in time became the last surviving member of her final company.* HMS Hood Association

away with murder at the defaulters' table. Warrant Shipwright N C Hill, who joined the *Hood* at Gibraltar in February 1936, was amazed to find himself attending not to her fabric but to the construction of special bathing facilities for the men and the erection of a cinema, stage and boxing ring in a disused coalshed on the South Mole. But despite his efforts to keep the men amused it became increasingly clear that not all were disposed to submit to discipline. Boy Fred Coombes recalls some shenanigans in the renovated coalshed:

> The seating was a bit crude being rough wooden forms knocked together by our Shipwrights. The officers were accommodated at the front on padded and easy chairs brought from the Wardroom by the Duty Watch and returned after the show by men under punishment, though this arrangement was tightened up after a number of easy chairs were found floating in the harbour and even in the Med. [...] It was then realised where the Wardroom chairs were going.

Matters weren't helped by Capt F T B Tower's notorious infidelity at the Rock Hotel during the many months the *Hood* was kept at Gibraltar owing to fuel shortages and the international situation over the winter of 1935–6. Even so, O'Conor appears to have forgotten the critical half of Admiral James' dictum on discipline: that it was an officer's duty 'to help in every way possible the loyal, hard-working men, and come down like a ton of bricks on the lazy and disloyal'. It is a sign of how far discipline had slipped that Tower's successor would find the ship both filthy and restive when he took over in February 1936.

Although the 1933–6 commission came to a climax with the Regatta victory and then the Jubilee Review in 1935, its final year was overshadowed by events of more lasting significance: the collision with the *Renown* in January 1935 and particularly the Abyssinian crisis which came to a head that autumn. If the former broke the morale of the Battle Cruiser Squadron then the latter set the pattern for the rest of the *Hood*'s peacetime career.

By the autumn of 1935 a spell in dry dock at Portsmouth, the Regatta victory at Scapa and the Jubilee Review had restored the *Hood*'s fabric and fortunes, but the international situation for the first time brought the prospect of war onto her horizon. On 3 October, after months of sabre-rattling, Italy invaded Abyssinia. Anticipating a pre-emptive strike on Malta, in August the Admiralty had taken the precaution of ordering the Mediterranean Fleet to Alexandria while elements of the Home Fleet, including *Hood*, were brought south to Gibraltar. The move incensed Mussolini who had massed troops in Libya and feared a blockade of Italian trade and supplies, especially oil, at either end of the Mediterranean. However, he need not have worried for neither Britain nor France had any intention of going to war over Abyssinia, to which the infamous Hoare-Laval Pact of December 1935 bore witness. For the *Hood*, which spent seven months at Gibraltar between September 1935 and June 1936, this translated into an agreeable though, for much of her crew, increasingly unsatisfactory period of enforced idleness. Things got off to a bad start when a disgruntled stoker, angry that the ship was being transferred from her home port, sabotaged one of the turbines with a fistful of razor blades. Then much of the crew was sickened by being fed a meal of corned beef which had been left out in the galley all night. Above all, it encompassed the departure of Capt Tower and his replacement by Francis Pridham whose arrival in February 1936 brought a very different style of leadership to the *Hood*. Whereas Tower had been content to give O'Conor carte blanche to do more or less as he pleased, Pridham was a hands-on captain of the old school and one who immediately found much to criticise in the ship and her commander's style. For one thing she was far below the required standard of cleanliness. As Pridham recalled,

> It took me some time before I could believe my eyes, [but] between decks she was the dirtiest ship I had ever seen. I could find no signs that good 'ship husbandry' was within the knowledge or competence of her officers. [...] The messdecks were disgusting and swarming with cockroaches. These dirty pests are easily eradicated – if you know how; the Commander did not. One of my first orders to him was that I expected to find the Mess Decks free from cockroaches in six weeks' time; and I told him how to set about it. It was so!

The evidence is that the *Hood* was still infested months later, as she could hardly fail to be in the Mediterranean, but Pridham's criticisms of the layers of paint with which O'Conor had coated and recoated every surface proved rather more pertinent:

> It was by no means difficult to point out to the Commander that under all the paint he had plastered on the Quarterdeck were layers of dirt. I had one spot chipped down to bare metal and found a quarter of an inch of layers of paint and dirt on top of rust, indicating two departures from first principles: don't try to cover rust by painting over it, and don't paint over dirt.

There and then Pridham instituted a paint-removal drive that had not been completed by the time the ship was sunk five years later. To his credit, O'Conor noted the gist of Pridham's 'first principles' in *Running a Big Ship*, but by then the *Hood* was loaded down with all too many tons of his paintwork. Nor was this all. The ship was deficient in basic seamanship; the *Hood*'s seaboat drill was 'lacking in any vestige of smart work', and her paravane drill equally laggardly. Pridham set to with a will:

> The sailors soon realised that the 'new Broom' on the Fore Bridge was no silent ornament and quickly adopted a new and enthusiastic demeanour to Seaboat Drill. In any case it presented an opportunity for competition between the two

sides of the ship, just that incentive which can be so valuable when working bodies of men.

Moreover, the *Hood*, thought Pridham, was a ship in which too great a reliance had been placed on machinery at the expense of traditional skills:

> I had first to kill the idea that one must use machinery whenever possible in place of man-power. It was my view that since the days of the passing of 'Coaling Ship', it had been essential to find opportunities for exercising, physically, any Ship's Company; especially is this so in a ship with a very large Seaman complement like the *Hood*'s. This should be backed up by introducing competition whenever possible.

The shortcomings found by Pridham no doubt had something to do with the many months *Hood* had spent tied up at Gibraltar, but there was one respect in which she could definitely be found wanting and that was war readiness – 'our sole purpose and great responsibility'. By early 1936 developments in Germany, the Japanese invasion of Manchuria and the ongoing Abyssinian Crisis had alerted the British political and military establishment to the likelihood of war on a global scale. As O'Conor's priorities indicate, this point had yet to impress itself on the Navy at large. William Harding, Warrant Engineer between 1936–7, recalls the situation:

> The Warrant Shipwright persuaded the Boatswain to convince the Commander to operate again the bower cable holder, which was not used because it spoilt the paintwork. It took two days and a fire around the spindle before the shipwrights freed it. The Torpedo Gunner was also given permission to work the above-water tubes. This entailed spoiling the side paintwork and it took almost a week to get the doors open.

No wonder Admiral Sir Roger Backhouse, Commander-in-Chief of the Home Fleet, dispatched Pridham to the *Hood* with the following brief: 'I want you to get the *Hood* out of cotton wool. Take your time, but as soon as you think you have got the feel of your ship, I want you to bring the *Hood* in here after dark and in foul weather. My ships will most certainly have to do such things in time of war.' It was the commander's principal responsibility to ensure the fighting effectiveness of his ship. Whatever his accomplishment in building a happy and successful community, O'Conor's neglect of the *Hood*'s fundamental *raison d'être* is the one signal failure of his tenure, though here Tower must evidently shoulder much of the blame.

It is not difficult to detect the instinctive clash of personality between the humane and easygoing O'Conor and an opinionated martinet like Pridham. The dissonance between them reflects many of the debates that had exercised the

Navy's officer corps since the end of the Great War: the relative merits of seamanship against technical specialisation, of brawn against machinery; the value of stern discipline against a more tolerant environment; of fitness for war against prowess in sport; ultimately the means by which the Navy's great tradition might be nurtured and perpetuated against the trials that beset it. Though Pridham admitted deliberately 'stirring up my Commander and my Ship's Company', there was no doubt where he stood on these issues, or on O'Conor himself for that matter:

> The Commander was a first-class showman ... He was one of the most upright men I have ever met, and a charming personality. [...] He had been promoted to Commander very young and before he could have had that experience which can only be gleaned in the lower ranks. He knew very little seamanship and nothing about ship husbandry. He was obsessed with the idea of spoiling his Ship's Company by saving them trouble (ie work) and he rarely awarded any punishment. In consequence many of the officers and petty officers were unhappy and felt frustrated in their endeavours to obtain cleanliness and order. The ship was inefficient in her main purpose.

O'Conor's opinion of Pridham is not on record and his premature death deprived him of the luxury of leaving it for posterity. Suffice to add that his commission album contains a single picture of Pridham alongside dozens of his predecessor, including one in bathing trunks.

For all their differences, Pridham and O'Conor had more in common than perhaps either imagined. Both had made their names after the Great War and had had every opportunity to observe the rapid evolution of the Navy and its men at close quarters. Both, too, had lived through the Invergordon Mutiny, O'Conor at HMS *Excellent* and Pridham in the Admiralty itself. Following his appointment to the *Hood* Pridham produced a memorandum, his 'Notes for Newly Joined Officers', by which he expected the ship to be governed. It was never published, but many of his remarks are in the same vein as *Running a Big Ship*:

> Your men must acquire through your manner with them the knowledge that you are available to them and that you expect them to approach you for your advice or help towards their welfare and contentment. Your endeavour should be to inspire in them a feeling of respect for you and confidence in your sympathetic interest and understanding of their problems, as well as your professional ability. This is the basis of discipline and leadership.

However, he took a much firmer line on discipline as something to be earned by example rather than conjured by favour. Leadership came from the top; the 'popularity Jack' soon lost the respect of the hard cases:

Men quickly form a very shrewd opinion of your ability and your capacity for just dealing. On this assessment their readiness to follow your lead and work with a will under you will mostly depend. [...] The amount of strength a body of men will exert is in proportion to the grip of the person in charge and his ability to hearten them. [...] To obtain the essential grip of your men be on the lookout for opportunities to nip slackness in the bud – these will not be rare. Use your voice on these occasions, but don't scream or use much sarcasm. A short sharp hard word is by no means excluded, but it must be justly deserved. [...] Once you have discovered a bad character you must lay for him (by watchfulness not by guile).

But both, though in rather different ways, laid great emphasis on the divisional system:

If you are an officer of a Division encourage your men to come and ask you for your opinion about some facility or privilege, whether for an individual or for the benefit of a mess or section. [...] Learn their names. You must make a sustained effort in this direction. Know their pay, allowances and opportunities for advancement fully. Learn their circumstances, qualities and ambitions. Learn what your men are interested in and their topics of conversation and discussion. [...] Having come across some circumstance in a man's private affairs and perhaps obtained some advice and assisted him, do not let the matter drop and be forgotten. Subsequent enquiry as to how things are going on will sometimes bring to light that fact that a man is still in need of help, but is averse to making a fuss by coming to you a second time.

And where consideration for the men was concerned there was nothing to choose between them:

It is within the competence of any officer to show consideration to his men. Uncertainty as to whether they will be required during non-working hours, a sudden alteration or curtailment of a meal hour, should rarely if ever be necessary. 'Pass the word' as long beforehand as you can. [...] Early infor-mation about long-leave dates, weekends [and] movements of the ship may often enable a man to make private arrangements conveniently. The same remark applies to drafting: a sudden change to another ship may be extremely inconvenient, if not worse.

For all the success of his regime, O'Conor ultimately chose to focus his energies and those of his crew on competition with other ships rather than the fighting efficiency which tradition and circumstance increasingly urged upon him. Pridham shared O'Conor's competitive streak, but it was for the latter failing and all that this implied that he never forgave him. The end of the commission must in these circumstances have come as something of a relief for O'Conor. There was, however, one final junketing to be celebrated, the thousandth day of the commission, which O'Conor laid on during a week of 'holiday routine' at Las Palmas in May 1936. Partly in compensation for their having missed Christmas with their families, O'Conor granted the crew several days' leave by watches. In June the ship returned to Portsmouth where O'Conor saw her pay off with all the pomp and ceremony he could muster. The *Hood*'s greatest commission was over.

Despite his differences with Pridham, O'Conor's performance in the *Hood* earned him swift recognition and on 30 June 1936 he became, at thirty-seven, the youngest captain on the Navy List. Barely pausing for breath, he immediately set about publishing the fruits of his experience in *Hood* for the wider consumption of the Navy. Equally characteristically, Admiral Backhouse sent O'Conor the following admonition when news of it reached his ears: 'I see you have written a book and (I suppose) invented a new routine! Do not, however, be too quick in your reforms, as, once introduced – good, bad, or indifferent – they may be very hard to change!'

But O'Conor pressed on undeterred and the result, *Running a Big Ship on 'Ten Commandments'*, remains one of the most influential naval treatises of the first half of the twentieth century. Although the war would change O'Conor's Navy for ever, the ethos enshrined in *Running a Big Ship*, that every man was entitled to the understanding and consideration of his officers, was to have a lasting impact on shipboard relations in the Navy. That said, *Running a Big Ship* was not beyond reproach. Though written with great verve and skill, its scope was limited by a tendency to over-regulation and by being confined almost exclusively to the executive branch. Neither does it contain a single line on war efficiency, a point Admiral Lord Cork was at pains to qualify in his foreword. However, O'Conor's contribution to the wartime Navy was real enough. The legacy of *Running a Big Ship* rests in the framework it provided for fostering an environment in which a young and diverse crew could withstand the immense strain of war. In this respect it proved of incalculable value for the Navy, and many was the officer who kept a copy by him in the terrible years ahead. Pridham's 'Notes for Newly Joined Officers', by contrast, would enjoy only a limited circulation, but they made the deepest impact on those who read them. In the final analysis, the ability of men of O'Conor and Pridham's stature to give practical expression to their convictions is a measure of how far the Navy had come since Invergordon.

But for those who study HMS *Hood*, *Running a Big Ship* is above all a record of the halcyon years of the greatest warship in the world. It is also, as one of O'Conor's reviewers put it, 'a monument to a very pleasing and capable personality', the more poignant for the cruel fate that awaited him. Rory O'Conor died following the loss of the cruiser *Neptune* in a minefield off Tripoli in December 1941, a disaster which left just one survivor from her 767 men.

9

The Seven Bs

As THE 1930s wore on the Royal Navy began to face the nightmare prospect of war on four fronts: with Italy and Germany in Europe, Africa and the Atlantic, and against Japan in the Far East. Conscious of its weakness, particularly in cruisers and capital ships, the Admiralty was left with no option but to favour the same policy of appeasement and containment pursued by successive British governments over this period. As the ultimate symbol of British sea power it was natural that the *Hood* should feature prominently in this strategy, to which she gave the final years of her peacetime career. Capt Francis Pridham, who commanded her between 1936–8:

> During my two years in the *Hood* 'Up the Straits', as service in the Mediterranean used to be called, I was summoned by the Commander-in-Chief on three separate occasions to receive secret orders about an imminent move of my ship, for which I was to make only such preparations as would not attract attention, particularly of the Press. On the first occasion I was to be prepared to move at speed to the Far East via the Suez Canal. On the second a few months later to the Far East via the Panama Canal. On the third to proceed to Scapa Flow to reinforce the Home Fleet, and I was to pass through the Straits of Gibraltar at night to avoid being sighted. It is true that whenever international relations became strained the question was asked 'Where is the *Hood*?'

Hood's role as the sharp instrument of Britain's foreign policy if push came to shove was not lost on the lower deck, which christened her 'The Seven Bs': Britain's Biggest Bullshitting Bastard Built By Brown. Such is the stuff of legend.

The Abyssinian Crisis of 1935–6 had already provided a first indication of the aggressive expansionism which came to characterise the Italian and German dictatorships. Having renounced the military clause of the Treaty of Versailles, in March 1936 Hitler marched his troops into the demilitarised Rhineland. Four months later the start of the Spanish Civil War provided the backdrop against which the concerns and ambitions of every power in Europe would be played out in a terrible orgy of violence and destruction. The humanitarian effort performed by the Royal Navy from July 1936 had required the transfer of a number of destroyers to French ports and the appointment of a Senior Naval Officer North Spain. In September it also required red, white and blue stripes to be painted on the *Hood*'s 'B' and 'X' turrets to identify her participation in the Non-Intervention Patrol. However, the increasingly aggressive posture of General Franco toward merchantmen supplying Republican ports began to call for a more significant presence in the Bay of Biscay than that provided for by ships of the Non-Intervention Patrol. On 6 April 1937 the attempt by the armed trawler *Galerna* and the 6in cruiser *Almirante Cervera* to deny ss *Thorpehall* entry into Bilbao – foiled only by the intervention of three British destroyers – finally obliged the British government to take action in defence of its prestige and trading interests. The issue was a matter of some embarrassment in London where it was realised that despite Britain's stated policy of non-intervention much war materiel was reaching the Republican cause in ships flying the Red Ensign. However, the decision was made and on 10 April the *Hood*, flagship of Vice Admiral Geoffrey Blake, was hurriedly dispatched from Gibraltar to the Bay of Biscay to lift the supposed blockade of Bilbao. Not for the first time the *Hood*'s symmetry was to stir the emotions of all who laid eyes on her and the Basque population turned out in droves to watch whenever she came inshore. Information provided by Cdr Harry Pursey (late of the *Hood* and by then active in journalism and politics) together with his own observations convinced Blake that the Nationalist blockade was hardly worthy of the name. Blake therefore decided to test the Insurgents' resolve by sending a convoy of three merchant ships into Bilbao protected by the *Hood* and the destroyers *Firedrake* and *Fortune*.

After dark on 22 April the steamers *Macgregor*, *Hamsterley* and *Stanbrook* slipped out of the French port of St-Jean-de-Luz and made their way westwards towards Bilbao at a leisurely 6 knots. Blake's plan was for the merchantmen to fall in with his warships off Bilbao at dawn on the 23rd and then proceed into harbour. Predictably enough, these six were not the only vessels in sight as the mist cleared from the Biscayan coast that morning. There on patrol were the *Galerna* and the *Cervera*. For three hours, efforts by the Nationalists to thwart the entry of the steamers to Bilbao were frustrated by a measured application of power as half-understood signals flashed between the two sides. At one stage *Galerna* fired a shot across *Macgregor*'s bows but the moment of truth was only reached once *Cervera* trained her guns on the merchantmen as they approached the harbour entrance. When Blake brought the *Hood*'s full broadside to bear on the *Cervera* it was obvious to Capitán de navío Manuel Moreu that the game was up, though, as Pridham remarked later, 'we … did feel that we had been "a big bully"'. However, the sight of the *Cervera* hauling away with her guns trained fore and aft was received with particular relief in 'B' turret where the fuse-setting key for the shells had been inadvertently dropped into one of the loading wells. Four days later the *Hood* glided effortlessly into Portsmouth to attend the Coronation Review of King George VI.

By the time the *Hood* returned south, Republican resistance was coming to an end in the Basque Country and with it the need to protect British shipping on the Biscayan coast. However, the position in the Mediterranean remained precarious thanks to the increasingly active involvement of Mussolini on the Nationalist side. At sea this took the form of an offensive against vessels bringing war supplies to the Republic from Soviet ports in the Black Sea. Once again the Royal Navy found itself reluctantly drawn into the conflict. Already on 13 May 1937 the destroyer *Hunter* had lost eight men after striking a Nationalist mine off Almería and on 31 August the *Havock* narrowly escaped a torpedo from the Italian submarine *Iride*, which escaped after a prolonged hunt with Asdic. June therefore found the *Hood* 'up the Straits' where she was once more assigned to the Mediterranean Fleet while Blake was appointed Senior Officer, Western Basin. Sir Geoffrey Blake, however, was not to enjoy his appointment long. On 20 June he was admitted to Bighi Hospital in Valletta after suffering an embolism during his accustomed early-morning pull in a skiff. Five days later he was obliged to strike his flag, a circumstance which brought that most famous of admirals to the *Hood*: Andrew Cunningham.

By turns combative and charming, 'ABC', as he was known in the Navy, was to become the greatest British fighting officer since Nelson. As Pridham discovered during their first encounter, Cunningham liked nothing better than bearding his subordinates:

Among his first remarks to me was that he hated these great elephants of ships, which took so long to get moving. He then boasted to me that he had twenty-four years in destroyers, in which you did not have to wait minutes before the ship gathered way. He liked to feel himself moving at twenty knots a few seconds after giving the order Half Speed Ahead. He claimed that service in destroyers was the only kind fit for a seaman!

Cunningham was full of surprises. One day in May 1938 he returned to the ship minus his trousers after an incident while fishing in Corsica. But no admiral took a more uncompromising attitude to excellence and the *Hood* soon found herself under the sternest of taskmasters as he and Pridham chamfered her to a pitch of fighting efficiency. Boy Fred Coombes:

Lucky for us, 'Cutts' Cunningham, who had clawed his way through a life of des-troyer commands to flag rank, ... was beginning to make his presence felt and bring a bit of reality into our training. [...] The heads of Departments normally ensured picking favourable conditions for our practice shoots in order to show their efficiency. Not Cutts. If the weather was safe enough for the tug to tow the target it was good enough for us. [...] Even the higher ranking officers were not 'excused boots' ...

As Pridham ruefully put it, 'He was an extremely wise and very well educated little man, and though not always "easy" in peace time I found that serving him as his Flag Captain was very pleasant and interesting. [...] With an occasional mild tussle we got on very well.' At least one of these 'mild tussles' centred on the accident while berthing at Gibraltar in March 1937 when the parting of a hawser killed two members of the after capstan party and wounded another. Pridham's refusal to use tugs no doubt had something to do with it, but a board of enquiry found a lieutenant commander guilty of negligence. Months later, examination of the evidence led Cunningham to conclude that the fault in fact lay with those on the bridge and the verdict was overturned. Despite this, Cunningham, who prized seamanship above all else and had no opinion of gunnery officers or their trade, evidently made an exception with Pridham, of whom he tartly noted in his memoirs that 'specialisation in gunnery had not impaired his ability in ship handling'.

Although his abrasive style of leadership ruffled many feathers, the legacy of Cunningham's sojourn in command of the Battle Cruiser Squadron rested in its transformation into a truly effective fighting force. As the Rev Edgar Rea recalled, Cunningham seemed 'hardly ever to have a thought to which he did not immediately give vigorous expression', and this impatience translated into those techniques of bold ship handling and firing at night and in all weathers that would be unleashed onto the Mediterranean theatre a few years later. However, this degree of efficiency came only after many months of arduous practice. Fred Coombes remembers the start of the campaign:

The first 5.5-inch shoot that we did, under roughish conditions with a half gale whipping the spray inboard, would have been postponed by the Gunnery Officer if he had had his way. The Marines, who manned the gun forward on the boat deck and were not protected by the casemate roof as were the others, found that the linoleum-covered deck round their gun was like a skating rink to their leather boots when wet. The loaders running around and clutching an [85]-pound shell soon found it impossible to heave the shell into the breach and still maintain their feet. The loading drill from that one gun suffered and was soon halted – another lesson learned under Cutts. Some special shaped fibre mats and securing eyelets fastened to the decks to hold them in position were later found by the sailmaker hidden away in his store but nobody could remember them ever being used. They were easily rigged for every shoot from then on.

Even so, the first night-firing exercise in battle conditions proved a sobering experience. Capt Pridham:

The first occasion of carrying out a full-calibre night firing produced something of a surprise. The secondary armament of 5.5-inch guns was manned mostly by young seamen, quite inexperienced, who on first being subjected to the blinding flash and blast of the turret guns, were so scared that a few sought shelter well in the rear of their guns, thus slowing down the rate of loading. The only way of dealing with this was for me first to speak some rough words to the assembled guns' crews. I told them that they were not fit for me to take into action against even an Eyetie ship! I then took the ship out the following night to do a repeat shoot. Of course, all went well then, but I had been shown the importance of frequent full-calibre firings.

In all her career the *Hood* was probably never more battleworthy than in 1937–8 and though for various reasons this would not last much beyond Cunningham's tenure it could scarcely have come at a more opportune moment.

In September 1937 the undeclared war against neutral merchantmen and warships by submarines and aircraft of the Italian Navy led to the convening by Britain and France of a conference in the Swiss town of Nyon. The conference was boycotted by the Germans and Italians, both of whom had withdrawn from the naval patrol of the international Non-Intervention Committee in June after losing men to Republican air attacks off the Balearics. Undeterred, the British and French agreed not only to the introduction of declared routes for merchant shipping, but also that these should be patrolled by ships and aircraft with orders to meet force with force. These developments brought Cunningham and the *Hood* into the western basin of the Mediterranean where she was to serve two stints on patrol duty based mostly on Palma de Mallorca between October 1937 and February 1938, though with occasional visits to Valencia and Barcelona. At Caldetas north of Barcelona one of the ship's steam pinnaces would tow a cutter loaded with provisions onto the sands where a group of supply ratings under the protection of a Marine landing party would see them onto trucks bound for the British Consulate. Nor did the boats return empty. A devalued peseta allowed Paymaster Lt A R Jackson (1938–40) to buy three fur coats for his wife, while Cunningham discovered that half a crown would clear a flower stall on the Ramblas of much of its contents.

The Nyon Patrol was not without incident. More than once the *Hood* was buzzed by the Reggia Aeronautica, Cunningham ordering her guns to be manned and trained against the offending aircraft if they did not keep at the requisite altitude. In the event, the transfer of four Italian submarines to the Insurgent navy meant that the Nyon patrols enjoyed only partial success and much of Cunningham's time was spent issuing futile protests to his Nationalist counterpart at Palma, this while the *Hood*'s Intelligence and W/T offices monitored signals between the armoured cruiser *Quarto* and Italian submarines in the Mediterranean. By the time the *Hood* returned for her third stint on 1 April after exercises and a month in dry dock at Malta, the steady advance of Nationalist arms northwards along the Valencian coast had made the evacuation of refugees and British nationals an urgent priority for the Royal Navy. Large parties of civilians were embarked for Marseilles at Valencia and Barcelona and

Hood was never busier in peacetime than she was during April and August 1938. On one of these trips the *Hood*, loaded with over a hundred refugees from Barcelona, was called upon to rescue the crew of the SS *Lake Lugano* after she had been bombed in the Catalan port of Palamós. It was therefore a cause of some relief to the Admiralty when the victory of one party promised an easing of the burden on its ships and men. In November 1938 the Republican defeat at the Battle of the Ebro made it quite certain which party that would be.

Already in April 1938, a month after the German *Anschluss* with Austria, the British had signed their extraordinary rapprochement with Mussolini known as the Anglo-Italian Agreement. As part of this tentative accord it was decided in London that a large squadron of Italian ships should be invited to Malta to renew the traditional friendship between the two navies. No quarterdeck in the Navy lent itself better to such occasions than the *Hood*'s and hers was among those selected to host the entertainments. This was accepted grudgingly by the wardroom and with decided ill grace by Cunningham:

> Most of us in the Mediterranean were sceptical about the results achieved by these same conversations. [...] As our merchant ships were being bombed almost daily by Italian bombers in and outside the Spanish ports it was not easy to work up cordiality. [...] However, orders were orders, and the fleet set out to give the visitors a good time which, in Latin countries, can be interpreted as one official entertainment after another without respite. Sir Dudley Pound, wishing to be particularly cordial, asked the Italian Commander-in-Chief to bring his wife and two daughters. We were to put up one of the two daughters, a tall order in a flat about the size of a large dog kennel.

In the event, the entertainments passed off as well as could be expected:

> I gave a large dinner-party for forty-five in the *Hood* preparatory to a dance in the Commander-in-Chief's flagship, the *Warspite*. Decked out with palms, gladioli and carnations, the quarterdeck looked very fine, and the dinner was a great success. On the whole we liked Admiral Riccardi and the senior officers, who were most courteous and pleasant. The younger officers, however, were ill-mannered and boorish.

Despite the hostility between the two navies and a history of poor relations ashore, fears of unrest proved unfounded. AB Len Williams:

> However, sailors the world over have a knack of conveniently sweeping under the carpet any political rumpus, as having nothing to do with them; and so it was with us. There was time to worry when a war actually started! With their piano accordions and mandolins the Italians spent quite a few happy evenings in the bars of Malta. I know, for I was in their company with a lot more of our

men, singing away with them, and we all thoroughly enjoyed ourselves. On this occasion Hitler and Mussolini were consigned to the dustbin! The visit was a huge success and in due course they left, leaving us with very pleasant memories, international situation or no international situation.

For Cunningham the end of his time in the *Hood* was drawing near. In February he was appointed Deputy Chief of Naval Staff at the Admiralty and struck his flag on 22 August 1938. The news no doubt provoked a sigh of relief in the wardroom since no admiral drove his officers harder. The speech made by Lt James Munn, Cunningham's Flag Lieutenant, at the farewell dinner hosted by wardroom, provides a flavour of his leadership:

'Mr President and gentlemen, you have no idea how lucky I feel to have survived the present régime (prolonged applause). You will understand what I mean by this statement when I tell you that in one of his ships the Admiral had no fewer than seventeen First Lieutenants.' Before the applause had died, the Admiral jumped to his feet and hanging his head as if thoroughly ashamed of himself sadly remarked: 'I'm afraid, gentlemen, it is quite true,' and sat down again to even greater applause.

The ship gave him a fine send-off by sweeping the board at the Mediterranean Fleet sailing regatta at Navarin in July, though duties in the western basin kept her from reproducing the feat for the Cock at Alexandria that autumn. But for Cunningham there would be one lasting memento of the *Hood* and that came in the form of his coxswain LS Percy Watts, who was to accompany him through all his subsequent battles, campaigns and appointments.

The *Hood*'s Nyon Patrol continued under Rear Admiral Geoffrey Layton (1938–9) as the international situation spiralled gradually towards war. Though the damage was slight, the grounding of the ship while leaving Gibraltar on 20 September therefore came at an awkward juncture. Already on the 12th Hitler had delivered a speech at Nuremberg attacking the stance of the Czech government over the Sudetenland, the German-speaking territory claimed by the Reich. This brought to a climax the increasingly fraught diplomacy that had engaged the chancelleries of Europe since February. Despite the craven policy of the Chamberlain and Daladier governments, there seemed every possibility that war might ensue if Czechoslovakia could not be persuaded to accede to her own dismemberment. On 28 September, at the very height of the crisis, the Royal Navy mobilised for war and the *Hood* slipped out of Gibraltar and into the Atlantic. The Rev Edgar Rea describes the atmosphere aboard:

When our men were feverishly fusing shells in preparation for battle, and things were at their critical worst, [Layton] handed me an unsealed envelope with the remark: 'You may find these useful one of these days'. Inside, I found the famous prayers composed respectively by Nelson and Drake before engaging the enemy. Soon afterwards, we started to raise steam. All leave was stopped and men already ashore were recalled by siren blasts. Towards evening we sailed and ordinary mortals like myself were left to guess both our destination and the nature of our mission. In view of all the circumstances most of us were convinced that a formal declaration of war was not far off.

In fact, the *Hood* had sailed to meet the liner *Aquitania*, requisitioned as a troopship, and escort her through the Straits of Gibraltar against the possibility that the German 'pocket battleship' *Deutschland*, then at Tangier, might attempt an interception on the high seas. In the event, the Munich Agreement by which Czechoslovakia was thrown to the wolves brought the *Hood* back to Gibraltar on 1 October where she was joined by the *Deutschland* herself the following day.

Apart from the Coronation Review of 1937 and the Malta junketings already mentioned, the Spanish Civil War had frequently brought ships of the patrolling navies into the same harbour. In December 1936 she visited Tangier where were berthed the German cruisers *Königsberg* and *Nürnberg* and the torpedo boat *Iltis* along with the French destroyer *Milan* and two elderly units of the Italian navy, the armoured cruiser *Quarto* and the destroyer *Aquila*. Despite the differences between their governments, the *Hood*'s men got on famously with their German counterparts, though on this occasion rather less well with those of the French and Italian navies. Boy Fred Coombes:

> The crew chose to chum up with the German [cruisers] when in Tangier, the Non-Intervention port, where the Germans and the British had some battles royal with the French and Italian crew when in port together till it was decided that only one nationality would be allowed ashore at any one time.

AB Len Williams and his friends put this affinity down to the preference of British and German sailors for beer whereas the others favoured wine. Certainly, the beer, which was brewed aboard German ships and then consumed out of glass boots on the messdecks, accounted for part of the attraction, but for others it went deeper. AB Fred White (1937–8): 'We were all very fond of the Germans. [...] A very proud race, and they were clean, smart and a credit to their country.' As AB Joseph Rockey (1938–40) put it, the Germans were 'very efficient, clean, smart, well drilled, well disciplined ... theirs was a harsh discipline, and we were disciplined ...'. In any case, the political complexities of the situation were lost on much of the lower deck: 'Who was fighting who we had not much idea ...'. Relations with the Italians, whom White considered 'slovenly', were to improve at Malta in April 1938, while those with the French remained somewhat distant: the *matelots* 'weren't bad ... but they weren't interested in us'. But it was a different matter with the Germans and the two navies were never closer than when the *Deutschland* put in at Gibraltar after being bombed by Republican aircraft off Ibiza on 26 May 1937. The attack left twenty-three dead and over seventy-five wounded of whom eight would not survive. Many of the injured were hospitalised at Gibraltar where each man received a cap tally from the *Hood* and a total of £5 was voted the ship from canteen funds as a gesture of sympathy; as Fred White recalled, 'That's how much we thought about them'. A German memoir of the visit survives from Matrose Hans Schmid, a young rating of the *Deutschland*. The *Deutschland* had moored alongside the *Hood*, a complicated manoeuvre that the British observed with a professional eye. No sooner had she secured than Vice Admiral Blake was received aboard by Kapitän zur See Paul Wennecker, apparently the first British flag officer to set foot in a commissioned ship of the German navy since 1912. After a tour and refreshments of tea and cakes, Blake was paid the compliment of being rowed back to the *Hood* in a ten-oared cutter manned by German officers. The following day Wennecker received an invitation for the entire off-duty watch of the *Deutschland* to dine in the *Hood*. Matrose Schmid was among them:

> The ship's company was very excited by the prospect. [...] When the German seamen went aboard *Hood* they found her gaily dressed overall. Even the weather gods had joined in the spirit of this unifying festivity. A bright moonlit night and a silver panorama of stars glittering over Gibraltar made a perfect setting. The party in the 'model ship', as the British Admiralty rather conceitedly referred to her, surpassed all expectations. On the long wooden mess tables sat an array of sumptuous dishes which had been visually devoured by the German seamen long before they got a chance to tuck into them. But wine and beer were not served by the English messmen; instead one had to make do with exalted tap water from the springs of Gibraltar. Once the extravagant and princely meal was over the 'Sailors' took us on a journey through this monster of a battleship.*

Despite the curse of Babel, the evening seems to have been a conspicuous success:

> After a 'digestive tour' around this outsized gargantuan of the seas, we assembled at the stern of the ship for a little conversation with our English hosts. Unfortunately, complete mutual understanding was only possible in the rarest of cases, as very few of the British understood German, and the Germans understood almost no English. However, using our hands and feet it was possible to convey all sorts of things in a comprehensible fashion. Both impressed by what we had seen and by now rather tired, my shipmates and I took leave of the British battleship in the early hours in order to snatch a few hours sleep before the night was over.

*Schmid uses the English word 'Sailors'.

133

Though Schmid appears not to have noticed it, the absence of a full armoured deck in the *Hood's* design doubtless made an impression on more than one visitor that night, just as it did an officer of the *Admiral Graf Spee* who came aboard at Tangier three months later.

Much as the *Hood's* crew regarded her as 'good for anybody', and the *Deutschland* in particular, not even the bitterness over Germany's actions in Austria and the Sudetenland could dampen relations between the two ships when the latter edged into Gibraltar just two days after Munich on 2 October 1938. The *Deutschland* was there only to disinter and repatriate her dead from the previous year, but the opportunity was taken to renew acquaintances and drink more beer. The ships' football teams played each other and Capt Harold Walker invited Wennecker to dinner in the *Hood* where they joined in watching the wardroom film. But circumstances prevented any lavish entertainment. Walker had lost an arm at Zeebrugge in 1918 while Rear Admiral Layton, a submarine hero of the Great War, had spent the final months of that conflict as a prisoner of the Germans, whom he despised. Fraternisation was grudgingly approved but there was to be no official entertaining. Besides, a sour note had been introduced by the time the *Deutschland* weighed anchor. The story was still circulating in the *Hood* when Mid Latham Jenson joined her in December 1940:

> After a football game with German officers, *Hood's* officers were entertained aboard the cruiser. When it was time to go, the senior *Hood* officer thanked everyone, and said, 'Come on chaps,' and one by one they dived off the quarter-deck to swim back to their ship. The last officer to go overheard a German scornfully say to another, 'These British officers are just overgrown schoolboys.'

So ended fraternisation in the Mediterranean. But had matters turned out differently the *Hood* might not have been in European waters at all. On 3 January 1938 Admiral Chatfield, the First Sea Lord, met with Rear Admiral Royal E Ingersoll, head of the US Navy's delegation in London, to discuss the size and composition of the force the British would send east in the event of hostilities with Japan. The meeting came three weeks after the bombing of the river gunboat USS *Panay* by Japanese aircraft in the Yangtse had brought the United States to the brink of war. Among the large fleet subsequently promised by the Admiralty was the *Hood*, though how she would have fared against Japanese naval aviation is a matter for conjecture. The fate of British and American units in the Pacific theatre in 1941–2 suggests that the apology and reparation offered by the Japanese government that same month may have been a providential deliverance for both navies.

In May 1938 Capt Pridham ended two successful years in command of the *Hood*. Although not free of the showmanship and favouritism he derided in his first executive officer, Cdr Rory O'Conor, Pridham had accomplished a marked improvement in discipline, seamanship and fighting efficiency. Together with Cdr David Orr-Ewing he had clamped down on the laxity that characterised the last phase of O'Conor's tenure and cultivated a healthier atmosphere on the lower deck. Pridham's own assessment is not inaccurate:

A long uphill task started for me and Orr-Ewing, but under the favourable conditions of the Mediterranean the ship and her company advanced steadily towards the objective to which we aspired. The ship's company seemed keen and not discontented when we drove them hard, as we had to for the first few months. Eventually they became a very happy lot and proud of their ship.

Pridham's *Captain's Memorandum on Discipline*, a copy of which was handed to every officer on arrival, left no one in any doubt where they stood on the matter. Where O'Conor had determined to excel in every sporting competition, Pridham focussed on sailing as the essence of good seamanship, and his zeal was rewarded in 1938 with victory in all five Mediterranean Fleet sailing cups, including the Combined Fleet Sailing Regatta. In this Pridham led by example, and his handling of the *Hood* at Malta and Gibraltar is remembered as one of the great naval spectacles of the late 1930s. But it was in fighting efficiency that Pridham, urged on by Cunningham, made his most significant contribution. On 20 May 1938, the day he turned over command to Capt Harold Walker, Pridham looked back wistfully at the achievements of his tenure:

I told Orr-Ewing about Sir Roger Backhouse's demand when I first joined the ship – to get the *Hood* out of cotton wool – and remarked that together we had succeeded in doing so and a bit more, for we could each be proud of our service in the *Hood* for the rest of our lives. We had made of her not only a ship of faultless appearance but also of her ship's company a truly efficient fighting machine – our main purpose.

Unfortunately, the reality of naval drafting, refit and recommissioning meant that this degree of efficiency could not be maintained and as war clouds gathered the departure of key personnel and constant disruption to training routines began to take effect. Three times between November 1937 and December 1938 the *Hood* spent a month docked at Malta for refitting and improvements to her anti-aircraft armament while drafts of men came and went every week. Add to this the undeniable fact that the 1936–9 commission was more eventful than any which had preceded it. The Spanish Civil War, the abdication of Edward VIII and accession of George VI – the proclamation of which was read by Pridham to an assembly of British and foreign consular officials on the quarterdeck at Tangier in December 1936 – the Coronation Review of 1937 and the Munich Crisis of 1938 were played out against the backdrop of continuous service, training and protocol under the mounting threat of war. This disruption clearly had a marked impact on the atmosphere aboard as the commission wore on. The Rev Edgar Rea:

> The *Hood* never really had an opportunity to settle down. Not only were some eighty per cent of the ship's company relieved in the course of the commission, but the civil war in Spain ... never allowed us to pursue a normal Mediterranean routine. [...] All this, especially the relieving of so many men, had an unsettling effect upon the ship and prevented that harmony of interests and singleness of purpose which are essential to a happy ship.

Even so, perhaps Rea listened too closely to the veterans of the previous commission when he claimed that

> ... *Hood* undoubtedly left much to be desired. There was something lacking in fellowship; in clannishness; in continuity of interest; and in concerted endeavour. *Hood* seemed to be too big; too scattered and divided to have a single soul; a united will; and a common purpose. ...When competing with other ships, either on the field of sport or on board at some service evolution, one never felt that behind the small competing party was concentrated the goodwill and the sympathy of the entire ship.

Perhaps the limited success of his pastoral mission coloured Rea's assessment of the atmosphere aboard, though it is true that the *Hood* was of necessity much less a sporting ship than she had been under O'Conor.

However, Pridham's mission lay in transforming the *Hood* from a ship of peace into a true man-o'-war and in this respect there were several marked successes beyond the improvement of her fabric and fighting capacity. The wardroom was certainly far happier than it had been and a lasting improvement in shipboard relations was accomplished by encouraging comradeship between boy seamen and the increasing number of young stokers joining the ship. Banyan parties ashore at Malta and Greece cooking sausages over open fires and washing them down with bottles of beer and ouzo added greatly to the atmosphere aboard. Evening classes for stokers and artificers gave members of the engineering department an opportunity to relate their work to the operation of the ship. Permission was subsequently given for stokers to be stationed on the bridge structure when the *Hood* left or entered harbour where they could study the finer points of ship handling which governed the orders sent to the engine spaces. Years later Louis Le Bailly, one of the divisional officers involved, recalled the marked effect of these developments both on morale and effectiveness: 'Productivity and efficiency in boiler operation and cleaning increased dramatically. There were even requests, some granted, from boy seamen and young Royal Marines to change over to stoker!' The 1936–9 commission also gave birth to the *Hood*'s Harmony Boys, the harmonica and accordion band which played to appreciative audiences throughout the Mediterranean and on into the war years. Certainly, neither Pridham nor Orr-Ewing had the charisma of an O'Conor, nor was their tenure crowned with the acclaim enjoyed by the preceding regime. But there are many criteria for measuring the success or otherwise of a commission and theirs was of a similar magnitude.

Pridham's successor was H T C Walker, known as 'Hooky' for the brass gaff he wore on the stump of his left arm. Though it encompassed the Munich crisis, Walker's was no more than a stopgap appointment while the ship completed her Mediterranean commission and he did not have time to leave a deep impression on the ship. Instead it was for the brass gaff announcing his presence on the ship's ladders and companionways and brandished vigorously at the defaulters' table that he would be remembered. On New Year's Day 1939 the ship's company posed on the forecastle under the ramparts of St Angelo for the traditional valedictory photo. Nine days later the *Hood* sailed from Malta for the last time. The band of the Royal Marines struck up *Rolling Home* and her paying-off pendant caught the sirocco as she passed St Elmo Point and into the Mediterranean. But the final act remained: the ship's company dance organised by Lt (E) Louis Le Bailly. Few of those attending in Portsmouth in January 1939 can have imagined that she would never celebrate another.

10

S'en va t'en guerre

FOUR DAYS AFTER the loss of the *Hood*, *The Times* published a letter by Admiral Lord Chatfield which remains the most cogent statement ever made on the subject. His closing words were these:

> The *Hood* was destroyed because she had to fight a ship 22 years more modern than herself. This was not the fault of the British seamen. It was the direct responsibility of those who opposed the rebuilding of the British Battle Fleet until 1937, two years before the second great war started. It is fair to her gallant crew that this should be written.

If anyone was in a position to know it was Chatfield, who had occupied the office of First Sea Lord between 1933–8 and served at the heart of naval planning and administration for virtually all of the *Hood*'s career. Delayed first by financial restrictions, disagreement over the future of the capital ship and then by international power politics, as the 1930s wore on circumstances made it impossible to immobilise the most prestigious warship in the world for a lengthy reconstruction. When the long overdue proposals were finally tabled in 1936, diplomatic considerations, the spectre of war and the urgency of refitting older and weaker vessels meant that neither they nor their successors could ever be put into effect. By the time the *Hood* returned from the Mediterranean in January 1939 the opportunity to make her a truly battleworthy unit had thus long since passed and the Admiralty could only offer another refit before she turned her bows towards the enemy. However, as war grew imminent, even the year-long 'reconditioning' envisioned in 1936 had to be reduced to a six-month effort pending a complete reconstruction beginning in 1942. Of the original measures, which included the addition of 4in of plating over the magazines, only the installation of two twin 4in mountings and a magazine on the platform deck could be effected. Though this went some way towards rectifying the *Hood*'s woeful anti-aircraft defence, in adding more topweight the 1939 refit placed further strain on an already overloaded hull and aggravated a series of existing problems. Lt (E) Louis Le Bailly:

Due to extra anti-aircraft armament, ammunition and crew to man it plus the tons of paint applied during *Hood*'s 20 years showing the flag, the ship was a foot further down in the water than her designed draught. In anything but a flat calm, waves now broke over the quarterdeck and salt water penetrated, corroded and immobilised the roller path of 'Y' 15in turret thus reducing the main firepower by 25%.

Moreover, as Le Bailly made clear, there were simply 'not enough skilled maintainers to meet the needs of an aged ship'. By March 1940 salt water contamination of the argolene oil and hydraulic systems was affecting both 'A' and 'Y' turrets, requiring the use of deck tackle if they were to traverse. And with salt water came rust, the mortal enemy of all steel construction. Mid Latham Jenson RCN who joined the *Hood* in December 1940 gives a vivid impression of a ship that had never been allowed to complete the transition from peace to war:

> I don't think there was a great effort to make watertight the various bulkheads at every level, which since 1920 had been penetrated for new electrical leads and so on and were full of holes. In fact, the whole ship was full of little faults that compromised safety and which had accumulated over many years. There were rust holes and patches of endless coats of paint, as well as great lengths of lead-covered electric cable, much of which was redundant and extremely heavy.

So it was that countless layers of paint both above and below decks, amounting in places to several pounds per square foot, not only added to the ship's inflated tonnage but constituted a serious fire hazard in action. To remedy this a major paint-removal drive instituted in 1939 resumed Capt Pridham's assault on the work of a generation of painters and enamellers. Nor was this all. The *Hood*'s boilers and condensers, the basis of her propulsion, were in a desperate condition. They were Lt (E) Louis Le Bailly's particular headache in 1939 and remained an acute problem for the rest of her career:

> The other nightmare affecting the ship's mobility was the feed water's worsening impurity which corroded our boilers. The tubes in the ship's main condensers under the great turbines were aged and rotting. Salt sea water drawn by vacuum into the condensing steam contaminated the water on its way back to the boiler, a constant problem in ships during World War One known as 'condenseritis'. In addition the reserve boiler feed water tanks in the double bottoms were leaking at their seams, causing more contamination. And these two problems fed on each other. When the boiler water became contaminated it was necessary to ditch it and replenish supplies from the evaporators which were sometimes of insufficient capacity to cope with the amount needing

replacement. Then water, probably contaminated, had to be pumped from the reserve tanks.

No wonder Le Bailly spent the last summer of peace immured in the *Hood*'s engine spaces trying to make good the neglect of years:

> Machinery spares, boiler bricks, oaken shores, jointing by the mile, extra hoses ... day and night merged as we strove to make up for a decade's neglect. Disparity widened between what had to be done and the blazing irrelevancies the Admiralty poured on us. Endless hours were spent cajoling officials torn between instincts and orders.

But time had almost run out. Thwarted by the Admiralty in his efforts to have the worst condensers attended to and regarding the ship as neither seaworthy nor battleworthy, the Chief Engineer Cdr (E) Peter Berthon, 'prone on occasion to white-hot shaking rages', refused to pronounce the engineering department 'in all respects ready for war' on being relieved in May 1939. This display of integrity both delayed his promotion and cost him the post of squadron engineer officer, though it was to prove a providential deliverance. Capt (E) S J Herbert who assumed the post in his stead perished with the ship in 1941.

When the *Hood* finally recommissioned on 2 June, Lt Le Bailly found himself the only officer remaining from the previous regime as the ship entered the final stages of her preparation for war:

> Happily, the executive Commander, William Davis, later an admiral of great renown, had joined us some time before. The re-ammunitioning, re-fuelling, speed and gun trials all went far better than might be expected despite the sudden tragic death of the First Lieutenant. Problems there were of course by the hundred. But Davis, [Cdr (E) Terence] Grogan and our new Captain, Irvine Glennie, seemed to brush them off with remarkable phlegm and good humour. And the new wardroom too were full of fun.

But despite the confidence and the effort expended it was still a rather dilapidated ship that left for Scapa Flow on 13 August 1939. Although those who lined the shore of Portsmouth and Southsea could not know it, the Mighty *Hood* was sailing never to return.

In view of the international situation it had been decided to retain most of the key ratings, including much of the engineering department, and only five hundred were drafted to the naval barracks at Portsmouth when the *Hood* docked in January 1939. She recommissioned in June but the mobilisation which followed began to dilute her complement with reservists and eventually Hostilities-Only ratings. By the time the *Hood* sailed after completing engine and compass trials off the Isle of Wight her crew had risen to over 1,400, approximately 15 per cent above peacetime levels. With war imminent and German U-boats known to be abroad, the voyage north was not the autumn cruise of earlier years. Apart from the ceaseless drills, exercises and manoeuvres as the ship worked up to war readiness, the journey provided a first taste of the acute discomfort that was to become routine. Louis Le Bailly:

> We had often practised darkening ship but it had always ended before midnight so that scuttles and hatches could be reopened to admit fresh air. This humid August evening permitted no such relaxation. German submarines were at sea and our departure surely known; a torpedo might strike at any time. Tension and, perhaps, fear added to the stinking heat permeating the ill-ventilated messdecks. We tried to alleviate the fug by drawing air through the ship to the boiler rooms but this involved opening too many watertight doors. For officers the situation was equally unpleasant: what had been the best cabins under the quarterdeck were abandoned and shut off. Those of us with previously less desirable residences behind the armoured belt now had to yield them to our seniors and take to camp beds in passages.

Indeed, the *Hood* was cramped and dulled as never before. Ted Briggs:

> No longer were there great, wide open spaces below decks: the full wartime complement of just over fourteen hundred men were embarked. At night hammocks were slung in every passageway, in every nook and cranny. Sleeping space was guarded jealously, and once a claim had been staked, it was rarely relaxed. At first I slung my hammock in one of the boys' locker spaces. Later I acquired the 'luxury' of hooking up in the warrant officers' cabin flat aft. Black-out curtains were rigged, and 'darken ship' was piped at sunset. Polishing was down to the minimum, and apart from the working parts of the guns, equipment that sparkled was dulled by gallons of grey paint. The once white decks began to take on a greyish tint, and most of the other woodwork was toned down. All the hangings and 'niceties' – including the many mess pianos – were landed. The *Hood* was never to know peace again.

After a week patrolling the Norwegian Sea against the passage of German commerce raiders into the Atlantic, the *Hood* put in at Invergordon to refuel and then made for Scapa Flow on 24 August. Here she lay as the strength of the Home Fleet gathered around her in preparation for war. At dusk on the 31st, the day the Royal Navy mobilised, *Hood* weighed anchor and sailed from Scapa Flow. PO Len Williams remembers the moment:

> On almost the last day of August *Hood* and her destroyer escort of three sailed from Scapa Flow out into the westering sun, and as we watched the low hills

of the Orkneys turn to purple and slowly dip below the horizon we knew in our hearts that when next we saw them we would be a country at war.

So it proved. At 0400 on 1 September the *Hood* went to action stations, the first in a succession of alarms over the next three days. On Sunday, 3 September, while cruising between Iceland and the Faeroes, news was received that Germany had invaded Poland at dawn and that Britain had issued an ultimatum for her withdrawal set to expire at 1100 that morning. Len Williams: 'On receiving this information we realised that it could now only be a matter of hours before the balloon would go up. Our ship's company had taken up cruising stations and our shell was fused. Our torpedoes had their warheads fitted and in all respects we were ready.' At 1100 Ted Briggs made what was at once the first and most momentous operational signal of his career:

> The flag 'E' was hoisted as a preliminary for a general semaphore message, and Chief Yeoman George Thomas ordered: 'Briggs, get a pair of hand-flags and get up to the fifteen-inch director and show up 46.' It was with a strange sort of pride and yet a sinking feeling in my belly that I spelt out to the fleet: 'Commence hostilities against Germany.'

Twenty minutes later came Chamberlain's sombre announcement. It was a beautiful morning as men stood down from their action stations to gather beneath the messdeck tannoys or around private radios tuned to the BBC. The news was received with solemn reflection, with optimism, and, in some quarters, with gung-ho enthusiasm. Lt Stanley Geary:

> A prominent member of the crew thus described the scene, 'I remember passing along the Mess Deck and everyone was crowded round the loudspeakers, waiting for the news which told us we were at war. There was much talk as to how long it would last, and one heard such phrases as 'we shall have them whacked by Christmas' and 'what battlewagons have the Jerries got?'

But for Len Williams, sitting in the autumn sunshine with his companions on 3 September, the riot of thoughts and preoccupations tumbling through his head must have echoed in the minds of many:

> After hearing the declaration of war we sat for a while around the portable radio. We were sitting on ventilators, boat crutches, on anything else available, for we were up on the boat deck. It was a fine morning, with the ship lazily lifting her bows to the long Atlantic swell. [...] It was a day to be at sea. Only one thought marred the peaceful scene and beauty of the morning. Somewhere beneath this heaving ocean, enemy submarines were at their war stations, and we were a prize target. As a single man with no responsibilities, I received the

news with a certain amount of indifference. I was annoyed, of course, because the tenor of my life was now about to be disturbed, which was I suppose a selfish way of looking at it. There was the other side to be considered too. For years we had trained for just such a possibility as this. Now it was up to us to see that the taxpayer got a return for his money. I tried to assess my ability to face up to the new situation. I knew my limits under normal conditions, but how would I react under war conditions, possible action, with all it could mean? I tried to detach myself like a shadow, and study myself from a position outside. 'Will you be afraid,' I asked myself, 'or will you be the stuff of which heroes are made?' I am afraid we all asked ourselves similar questions, and, like myself, received the same answer. 'Wait and see!'

His would ultimately prove the most accurate perception, though to a greater degree than he could possibly imagine. But for now life and routine had to go on. 'We went on talking until the hands were piped to dinner, then, going below, we partook of our first wartime Sunday dinner. At least the news had not affected our appetites.' And indeed, on reflection, there was a certain comfort in knowing that the die was finally cast, that all lingering doubts could be set aside and that it remained only to meet the challenge with all the resolution one could muster:

It was a relief. Now we knew where we were going. However long and difficult the road ahead, we had to get to the end. And so *Hood* and her company went to war.

Within hours of the outbreak of war, the sinking of the liner SS *Athenia* by *U30* served notice that the German navy again intended to prosecute the war at sea through its submarines. In the *Hood*, already zigzagging with her destroyer screen, steps were taken to ensure her watertight integrity in the event of an attack. Len Williams: 'Now the war had started each of us took stock of our situation. From now on we had to be very particular about closing and properly clipping all watertight doors and hatches behind us. There was that little extra alertness and awareness about us as we went about our tasks.' Two weeks later the torpedoing of the aircraft carrier *Courageous* in the Western Approaches brought home the danger posed by submarines to even the largest warships. The *Hood*'s crew had been issued with inflatable lifebelts which were worn night and day, but Williams, who kept watch in the main switchboard, felt he knew enough about the ship's circuitry to take added precautions:

One of the first things I did was to provide myself with an electric torch and a whistle, the latter I tied to my lifebelt. It was obvious to me that if the ship received damage sufficient to sink her, then it was practically certain that all the lights and power would fail, therefore one had to find one's way out of the ship.

Then, once in the water, particularly at night, it was essential to attract attention. Hence the torch and whistle. My job was still at the main switchboard, although my action station was in the engine room attending one of the dynamo supply breakers. It was not a comforting thought to realise that the switchboard was well down in the bowels of the ship, and directly over the forward 15in magazines; and that in order to get out, one had to squeeze through numerous manholes (fitted in the armoured hatch covers) just large enough to pass one's body through.

However, there can be little doubt that, justified or not, such fears gradually yielded to the sheer inconvenience of war stations at sea. The need to keep watertight doors and hatches closed below the main deck confined men to a particular area of the ship and required the installation of makeshift sanitary arrangements, often of questionable efficacy. As Louis Le Bailly recalled, the *Hood*'s damage control regulations placed a particular strain on some of her older ratings:

> Bert Hemmings, the artificer who had presided over the workshop for decades, was a fitter and turner of irreplaceable skill, but also of enormous bulk. Under the new Damage Control rules the only way into the workshop was through a small manhole in the deckhead. To insert Hemmings in the morning, and remove him in the evening, was a major task requiring the help of several pairs of hands; whilst special arrangements had to be made to provide for his wants during the day. But like the great soul he was he made light of the problem; and his gratitude to those who catered for his needs only increased their willingness to help.

By the end of 1939 the *Hood* had settled into a pattern of endless sweeps for enemy raiders and blockade runners in northern waters which, with one or two significant interruptions, would be her lot for the rest of her days. The routine was unwavering. Tanks brimming with fuel, the *Hood* would slip her moorings, gather her destroyer screen and exit the immense anchorage of Scapa Flow through the boom defence guarding the Bring Deeps between Hoy and Orkney. Moving on to 25 knots, the squadron would begin zigzagging through the swept channel in Burra Sound and at length pass into the Atlantic. The departure from Scapa might be enlivened with a practice shoot against a towed battle target at ranges of up to 12,000 yards. But henceforth there was only the strain of maintaining the Navy's lidless eye on the straits through which the German navy had to pass to reach the Atlantic convoys, of remorseless zigzagging in enormous seas and brutal weather, of exhaustion, discomfort and boredom; of being one of the handful of storm-tossed ships that stood between survival and defeat.

The *Hood* preserved the four-hour watch system of the peacetime Navy but circumstances called for a far greater proportion of her crew to be closed up at any given moment. The standard routine for daylight hours at sea was Cruising Stations which required a third of the crew to be on duty. Action Stations at dusk demanded every man in the ship to be closed up for an hour. The hours of darkness were spent at Defence Stations with half the crew at their posts, followed by Action Stations for a further hour around the crack of dawn. Cdr Robin Owen recalls a typical night watch on deck in the North Atlantic:

In these pre-radar days lookout duty was a vitally important but boring and unpopular job for junior ratings, particularly at night when they had to work half-hour tricks scanning a sector of the horizon with binoculars. My Action and Night Cruising Station was Officer-in-Charge of lookouts, of whom there were up to twelve, stationed on each side of the bridge, at the aft end of the open boat deck and in the spotting top. Unlike most watchkeepers who had to remain at their particular station for four hours, I was free to patrol the lookout positions as I saw fit and actually found it quite an interesting job. Also I could occasionally go below for a warm-up, quick smoke or some tea or cocoa from the gunroom pantry. At the start of each watch the lookouts were mustered by a petty officer who detailed them for their positions and tricks. For the rest of the watch he and I between us patrolled the positions to make sure the men were alert, changing tricks every half hour and understood their duties. Men off trick had to remain in the boat deck shelter, a cramped compartment at the base of the forward funnel containing the ship's incinerator. This was quite a popular and convivial place on a cold night where, in the dim red night-adaptation lighting, they could get warm, smoke and gossip, their wet duffel coats creating a damp fug one could have cut with a knife. To begin with, doing the rounds of the lookout positions at night in total darkness was quite an eerie experience but soon I could have done it blindfold, guided by touch, the steady roar of the forced draught fans and the noises and smells from the ventilation openings to machinery, galleys, bakeries, messdecks, heads and bathrooms. On clear nights the slow pitch and roll of the ship made the topmast truck sweep great arcs across the starlit sky, sometimes illuminated by the cold glare of the Aurora Borealis.

Len Williams has a similar tale:

At night the crew went to Defence Stations, and my station in this particular organisation was the searchlight control sight on the starboard wing of the bridge. Two of us shared this duty, and high up on the open sweep of the bridge wings we felt the full blast of the icy wind. Muffled up to the ears in woollies, we braced ourselves against the bitter elements and swept the tumbled horizon with our binoculars. For four hours at a stretch we shared this duty, working in conjunction with each other so that one of us could squeeze under the bridge platform for a cup of hot cocoa and a temporary respite from the freezing wind. Always we had to be in the immediate vicinity of the searchlight control position, and always it was bitterly cold. Far below us, we could hear the swish of the sea as it broke against our huge hull, whilst above us, the heavens spread wide in a black velvety void, on which lay a million brilliant scintillating stars; bigger and brighter than any I had seen before. Those short, star spangled nights in the Denmark Straits will always live in my memory. The sharp, biting, salty wind beating relentlessly against one's face and finding every loophole in one's clothing; and the brilliant display of the Aurora Borealis, weaving across the heavens like a gigantic silvery fan, was an artistic feast to delight one's red rimmed eyes. After four hours in the crisp cold night air one's watch was over and, still wide awake, for the air was like wine, we were relieved by the morning watch, and we tumbled down below to get a cup of thick steaming cocoa before retiring on the mess table for what was left of the night.

Cdr William Davis's memoir of a typical day at sea reveals the burden of his responsibilities:

My own routine as Commander was something like this. I found out first if the Captain [Glennie] who lived pretty well permanently on the bridge or in his bridge sea cabin would like me to take over whilst he relaxed. Normally he asked the Commander (N) [S J P Warrand] to do this as he said I had a whole job keeping the ship running smoothly and efficiently. Then say at 6am we went to action stations and I satisfied myself that the internal repair and damage control organisation was functioning properly. Then about 8am slipped off for a quick wash and breakfast and put the sailors not at action stations to work on routine repair, maintenance and cleaning work. See any men who had requests, discussed the various problems with Heads of Departments, Gunnery and Torpedo Officers etc. Daylight hours were fully occupied and considerable time was devoted to making the rounds of the ship ensuring everything was secured and that the ship's company's living quarters were kept ship shape and hygienic. A session in the Commander's Office was always necessary to ensure appropriate tasks were being tackled and routine for the following day mapped out, as well as making a list of the work to be done on return to harbour which could not be tackled at sea. For instance, touching up the camouflage painting was one thing that always required attention! I usually went the rounds of the ship a couple of times with the Chief Bosun's Mate who was a first-rate seaman and who was of much help in ensuring everything was properly secured. Then again we usually went to 'action stations' soon after 8pm to ensure everything was right before sending half away to 'pipe down'. [...] Pipe down was usually at 9pm but sometimes a little later when we were in areas that could pick up the 9pm BBC news. Then rounds between decks at 10pm with Master at Arms and Sergeant Major. A good stretch as the ship was [nearly] 300 yards long! If the weather was threatening a final round of the upper deck with the Chief Bosun's Mate during which time one not infrequently bathed one's skins! A talk to the Captain and to one's cabin to rest. Then once during the middle watch I did rounds between decks and on the upper deck if the weather was bad.

Evidently, war routine proved more demanding on some officers than others. Louis Le Bailly:

> For engineer officers wartime watchkeeping routine was much as in peacetime, one watch in three. But for our executive messmates who in peacetime had kept a bridge watch of about one in 16 the shock was immense. Much of the main, secondary and anti-aircraft armament had now to be kept ready for action which reduced the executive branch to our sort of routine.

Matters weren't improved by the requirement that all the officers' cabins on the main deck aft be abandoned at sea owing to the danger of torpedo attack, causing many to set up camp beds in passages or lobbies or else doss down in a wardroom that 'quickly became full of sleepy and often crotchety recumbent figures'. Nor were torpedoes the only threat. Arriving off the boom defence of Scapa Flow on the morning of 5 January 1941 the *Hood*'s port paravane was found to have fouled a German mine which came uncomfortably close to the ship before floating away to be sunk or detonated by a fusillade of small-arms fire from the forecastle party.

On arrival at Scapa Flow from a lengthy patrol, the first duty was to secure to a mooring buoy and hook up the telephone and teleprinter cable connection with London. Oiler, drifter, mail boat and ammunition barge if necessary then came alongside to replenish her. Boilers were kept at four hours' notice for steam, giving the engineering department an opportunity to perform essential maintenance before the next call on their exhausted machinery. For most men this might mean the first wash of body and clothing for ten days, the first opportunity to sleep more than three or four hours at a stretch, the first chance of a hot meal, of warmth, comfort, exercise and perhaps even a letter or two from home. But sometimes none of this was possible and within a few hours the *Hood* would be at sea once more. Lt Cdr Roger Batley (1941):

> Glad Portia and Julian are well and fit – I must try to write to them by this mail if we don't push off again as soon as we are refuelled. We did that last time. Most disappointing for everyone. Ten days at sea, eighteen hours in harbour, no leave, and then more days at sea. It does make a difference if both officers and men can land just one afternoon and play golf or football or just have a good leg stretch.

As Lt Cdr Wellings, the US Navy's official observer, noted in one of his reports, this routine was extremely hard on the crews that had to endure it: 'After about four consecutive days of watch and watch with Condition 1 [Action Stations] just before dawn and darkness both officers and men were very tired and their effectiveness reduced considerably. The bad weather conditions undoubtedly had something to do with the ineffectiveness of personnel.'

For much of the *Hood*'s wartime career the scale of the Navy's commitments and the attrition to its fleets made her the most overworked capital ship in the world. The loss of the *Royal Oak* in October 1939, the departure of the *Rodney* for repairs to her steering in November and finally the mining of *Nelson* outside Loch Ewe on 4 December briefly left her as the sole heavy unit at the disposal of Admiral Sir Charles Forbes, Commander-in-Chief Home Fleet. Nor did she escape damage herself. On 22 September HMS/M *Spearfish* was severely depth-charged by German anti-submarine escorts off the Horns Reef. After many hours on the bottom *Spearfish* surfaced and steered for home on one electric motor, unable to dive and with her radio temporarily out of action. When the Admiralty finally learnt of her predicament on the 25th the entire Home Fleet sailed to bring her in. *Spearfish* was met and escorted to Rosyth by the 2nd Cruiser Squadron with six destroyers on 26 September, but the Home Fleet was given its first taste of aerial attack at sea. Louis Le Bailly:

> The bombers struck at *Ark Royal* and, although they scored no hits, vast waterspouts hid her from our sight. The guns' crews on *Hood*'s boatdeck, as well as my damage control party, were watching the attack on *Ark Royal* when a bomb, seemingly the size of a grand piano, fell out of the sun to the south of us towards the boatdeck, a few feet short. A frightening explosion alongside opened up the top of the anti-torpedo bulge and the port lower boom was shredded with splinters. All the hot and cold water pipes in the stokers' bathroom, abreast the explosion, fractured. But more serious was the loss of electrical power to the port eight-barrelled pom-pom. A circuit breaker had been knocked off by the shock. The electrical repair parties were defeated by the *Hood*'s past: brass information plates on the junction boxes detached for polishing had been muddled when replaced. Efforts to run emergency power leads to the pom-pom succeeded only in bringing some warmth to the petty officers' hot locker, not materially adding to our fighting potential.

Moreover, the concussion inflicted severe damage on the condensers which came close to leaving the ship dead in the water. But even if the *Hood* had not been crippled as Lord Haw-Haw proclaimed from Berlin, the attack revealed both the inadequacy of her anti-aircraft armament and the ineffectual drill of their crews, a deficiency shared by the rest of the Home Fleet. Len Williams:

> So sudden had been the attack we had not even been able to fire a shot. Captain Glennie immediately broadcast orders that the guns' crews were in future to open fire without waiting for orders. This had been a lesson to us. We were still

versed in the peacetime practice procedure where one waited for orders before opening fire on the target. We had got off lightly on this occasion but there was to be no further dallying and the skipper made this point quite clear.

Further indignity lay in store on arrival at Scapa the following day, when the ditching of the *Hood*'s petrol tanks during the attack meant that of her flotilla only the two steam picket boats were of any use until fuel was embarked. That afternoon found Boy Signalman Ted Briggs and his pals eagerly digging splinters out of the port lower boom, but notice had again been served. Thus was HMS *Hood* blooded in combat.

Three weeks later the sinking of the *Royal Oak* at Scapa Flow, the principal anchorage of the Home Fleet, further dented the *Hood*'s morale. The *Royal Oak* had also been a Portsmouth ship and her loss while both were still crewed largely by regulars of the peacetime Navy meant that there were few in *Hood* who could not count a friend or relative among the 836 men who died in her. For many the loss of this ship was the first time the war touched them personally, the first infallible indication that they were in it for the long haul against a skilled and determined enemy. Apart from this was the fear that the same fate might be visited on them, and for several months the *Hood* led an uneasy existence in northern waters, her lookouts jumpy and the crew under ever greater strain. The *Hood* had been at Loch Ewe on the night of the disaster and the unthinkable breach of the defences of Scapa Flow meant that she would be seeing rather more of this anchorage than any of her people wanted. Loch Ewe provided a welcome respite from the air raid alarms that had become a feature of life at Scapa, but for all its rugged beauty there was even less to do here than in the Orkneys.

By November 1939 the damage suffered during the *Spearfish* episode and the strain of unremitting service in northern waters had brought the condensers in the *Hood*'s turbine rooms to the brink of collapse. Louis Le Bailly, then a Lieutenant (E), describes the situation and the primitive measures resorted to in the aftermath of the bomb hit on 26 September:

Routine tests then revealed a near-critical contamination of the boiler feed water. Some tubes and tube joints had failed: we were in for a severe dose of condenseritis. Happily our predecessors had discovered a bizarre method of rendering first aid. Valves on the seawater side of the condenser permitted the injection of sawdust from hoppers. The condenser vacuum, which had been drawing in seawater through leaky joints or pinholes in the corroded tubes, also drew in grains of sawdust which temporarily plugged the leaks. None of us had seen this used, but if we were to reach Scapa without irreparable boiler damage we had to try it out speedily.

Once at Scapa, a series of design faults and the need to effect emergency repairs called for extreme measures on the part of the engineering department:

Once at anchor the complex testing of condensers began: although the portside condensers were worst affected, there was trouble in all four. Then we met another snag. The condenser designers had had the prescience to fit sawdust hoppers, but had underestimated the space between condenser tube plates and the outer casing. Sadly the Navy does not recruit midgets so we turned instead to ERA Wigfall, our smallest artificer. Clad in a bathing slip Wigfall crept into the worst condenser to tighten the joints and plug the leaking tubes. We kept him going with drafts of hot Shovril, increasing the proportion of sherry to hot Bovril as his weariness increased. Thanks to his 24-hour slog we were able to report readiness for sea but with restrictions on speed which galled our chief, Terence Grogan. Thenceforward Wigfall was given a high-protein diet so that his dimensions would not increase coupled with light duties when we were not in harbour. I can see him now as we lifted him out of the small manhole, his lips blue, his teeth chattering.

So it was that for some of the most critical weeks of her career the *Hood*'s effectiveness as a fighting unit rested on a slender artificer and quantities of sawdust from the shipwrights' workshop. By November the state of the *Hood*'s condensers, revealed by Cdr (E) Terence Grogan to Churchill during his visit of 31 October, could be ignored no longer. The *Hood*'s best speed was at times down to 25 knots and relentless service in heavy seas was exacerbating other problems. Louis Le Bailly:

> Constant pounding was tiring the old hull even more than the ship's company. Condenser leaks were now a fact of life; the working of the ship's bottom plates worsened the leaks into the reserve feed tanks, as predicted. Boiler cleaning, due to excessive sea time and contaminated water, became never-ending. Machinery maintenance increased daily as [Cdr (E) Peter] Berthon's prophecies came home to roost at the Admiralty.

Besides, the burden on the engineering department was becoming intolerable, with a routine of eight hours on, four hours off at sea followed by constant maintenance in harbour. On 11 November the *Hood* docked at Devonport for an overdue boiler cleaning and a week's leave for her crew, taken a watch at a time. But no sooner had the second watch departed on 20 November than news of the sinking of the armed merchant cruiser *Rawalpindi* caused the *Hood* to recall those on leave and slip her moorings with all despatch. On the 25th, just two weeks after reaching Devonport, the *Hood* sailed from Plymouth Sound in mountainous seas, her refit incomplete and 150 ratings drafted from Devonport barracks to make up numbers. It was to be another four months before her condensers received the thorough overhaul they so desperately needed.

The *Hood* battled on through the winter of 1939–40 but her best speed was now down to 26.5 knots and the long-awaited refit could not be delayed much longer. By mid-February the Admiralty was making preparations for the retubing of her condensers at Malta from 3 March, anticipating that forty-five days would be required for the job to be completed. However, continued patrol, escort and cover duties as well as deteriorating relations with Italy made this impossible and by 29 March the decision had been taken to refit her at Devonport. Two days later the *Hood* reached Plymouth and on 4 April she was docked for repairs. Anxious over Mussolini's increasingly aggressive posture in the Mediterranean, on 12 April Churchill, still First Lord of the Admiralty, urged that 'The most intense efforts should be concentrated upon *Hood*, as we may need all our strength to meet an Italian threat or attack'. When informed next day that what he believed would be a thirty-five-day refit would in fact take over eleven weeks he fairly exploded with rage: 'Pray give me an explanation of this extraordinary change'. It seems that Churchill had leant on the assurances Cdr Grogan had given him during a visit to the ship in October 1939 that the *Hood* could carry on for another six months instead of the rather different picture that would have been presented during his most recent visit of 8–9 March. Whatever the case, Churchill professed himself much disturbed to have been inaccurately informed as to the availability of 'this vital ship' 'at the most critical period in the war'. As it turned out, the *Hood*'s refit kept her from operational duty for a total of seventy-four days, by which time Churchill had become Prime Minister.

Apart from the refitting of her condensers with the latest cupro-nickel tubes the main work of the refit was the replacement of the last ten 5.5in guns with a further three dual-purpose 4in mountings and five UP (Unrifled Projector, or Unrotated Projectile) launchers together with their associated fittings and lockers. Fourteen days' leave was again given by watches, but for those who remained it was to prove an irksome interlude. Len Williams:

> During this refit period at Devonport, life for those left on board was most uncomfortable. The dockyard men were working day and night, getting the old guns out, and putting the new twin mountings in. The clattering of the riveting hammers kept us from getting any sleep, and it was a frequent occurrence to have a shower of red hot fragments and sparks descend on one's dinner when sitting at the mid-day meal, where the white hot giant rivets, holding down the new mountings came through the deck head.

However, for a number of her crew, the *Hood*'s refit was to bring considerably greater excitement.

In the early hours of 9 April 1940, Germany launched her attack on Denmark and Norway. Successful landings were made at Kristiansand, Egersund, Bergen, Trondheim and Narvik on the Norwegian coast and after initial resistance Oslo fell later that day. Even so, the German position remained precarious and though the British had been taken completely by surprise the War Cabinet immediately resolved to send troops to intervene. Among the plans formulated in London was a pincer attack on Trondheim in central Norway following landings at Namsos and Åndalsnes, the latter to be named Operation PRIMROSE. It is a measure of how thinly stretched were Britain's resources that the War Cabinet had to turn to the Navy in order to help man the expedition. In the *Hood*, berthed at Plymouth, the first inkling that something was afoot came on the morning of 13 April when orders codenamed 'Primrose' began reaching the ship. Within a few hours the *Hood*'s ancient 3.7in howitzer, veteran of countless peacetime exercises and the Palestinian revolt at Haifa in 1938, was being swung out onto the quay. By evening an expeditionary force of 250 officers and men had been mustered under Lt Cdr C D Awdry which at midnight boarded a train for Rosyth with a motley assortment of weapons, stores and ammunition. The Royal Marines under Major H Lumley, who formed two-thirds of the force, were equipped with automatic weapons and Lewis guns. In the words of Mid Ian Browne (1939–41) they 'gave the impression of knowing what they were about and regarded the seamen with some tolerance bordering on condescension'. The seamen, on the other hand, drawn mainly from second part of port watch, did not cut a particularly warlike figure. Mid Browne:

> It must however be said that the seamen contingent hardly inspired confidence as a military force. [...] Very few of the sailors had ever fired a rifle or ever handled ammunition. Nor, I fear, were the officers particularly familiar with the .45 revolver. It was discovered on the train that not all the sailors had boots, a fact that they had somehow managed to conceal under their green gaiters. However it was understood that the Gunner's Mate knew something about howitzers which as it turned out was just as well.

After a day's journey the party reached Rosyth where most of it boarded the sloop *Black Swan*, the remainder being distributed with similar contingents from *Nelson* and *Barham* in HM sloops *Bittern*, *Flamingo* and *Auckland*. Originally destined for the port of Ålesund, *Black Swan*'s orders were changed for Åndalsnes after the overloaded flotilla was obliged to put in at Invergordon in heavy seas. The Navy was prepared for opposition, but the Germans had yet to reach Åndalsnes and the subsequent landing on 17 April passed off uneventfully. The nineteen-man howitzer detachment under Sub-Lt D C Salter was immediately sent by rail to Dombås sixty miles away, where on 19 April it scored its only success, assisting in the capture of forty-five German paratroopers, several of whose helmets ended up on the *Hood*'s messdecks. Another party was taken to Ålesund with the task of setting up a number of 4in guns commanding the Indreled (Inner Leads) while a contingent of Marines under Lt E D Stroud RM was charged with defending an airfield improvised on the frozen surface of Lake Lesjeskog. However, once the Germans became aware that the Åndalsnes area was under British occupation the Luftwaffe began to make operations there untenable. From the 20th the main force in Åndalsnes and its various contingents were subjected to constant aerial bombardment which reduced this and the nearby settlements to ashes and wounded nine of the *Hood*'s party, two seriously.

Meanwhile, the breakdown of the Allied offensive as a whole began to make evacuation inevitable and as the days passed the various forces ashore slowly fell into disarray, the men having to fend for themselves in caves and the surrounding forests as the Germans closed in. Spirits generally remained high in the *Hood*'s contingent though some began to wilt under the pressure of constant bombardment and it was with a degree of relief that the order to evacuate came at the end of April. The howitzer detachment was embarked in the sloop *Fleetwood* at Åndalsnes on 29 April followed by the main body in the cruiser *Galatea* on the 30th, the rest being taken off from Afaianes shortly after. Among the very last to leave was a Lewis gun section from the *Hood* which held the final roadblock on the outskirts of Åndalsnes before escaping in the sloop *Auckland* on 1 May. Its Marine crew under Lt Stroud received a DSC and two DSMs. By 6 May, a little over three weeks after they had set out, the *Hood*'s party was back at Plymouth for the loss of four wounded men, including OD George Walker of Aberdeen, destined to spend the rest of the war as a prisoner of the Germans, and AB Harris who escaped into the Norwegian hinterland. Also missing was the howitzer which had been sent over a cliff to deny it to the enemy. Miraculous though this deliverance was, the Norwegian campaign as a whole had been an utter fiasco, the failure of which now brought on the collapse of the Chamberlain government. As Len Williams put it, 'So ended our efforts at playing soldiers'.

11

The Dark of the Sun

THE GREAT ATTRACTION of a lengthy refit was of course the opportunity it afforded for a good spell of leave after many months on active service. To a man the prospect was almost too marvellous to bear thinking about. OD Algernon Foster of Hastings: 'The fellows aboard are all talking about leave, but it is not the custom to believe anything until you are in the train bound for home, but we all hope that it will soon be our turn – perhaps I should of said "their" turn …' However, even when free of the ship, leave was as subject to the vagaries of war as everything else. In November 1939 Len Williams learnt of the curtailment of his in a cinema:

> I was in a Portsmouth cinema when the telegram was received by my mother, who arranged with the manager to have my name and address projected onto the screen. The slide was superimposed on the film being shown, and to my surprise, I saw it appear on the side of a flying boat, which on the film was being launched down a slope. Leaving the cinema, I met my mother at the Box Office and she handed me the recall telegram. I hastily packed my few things and, taking a packet of sandwiches with me, I kissed mother goodbye and took a bus to the station, where I found about two hundred others from *Hood* and a special train laid on to return us to Plymouth.

For many the return from leave, from the comforts of home and the love of family, represented the nadir of misery. Boy Bill Crawford of Edinburgh wrote as much to his mother in March 1941:

> It sure was lousy coming away yesterday, Mother, although it seems years ago. It seems funny that I was walking along Prince's St with you and Nunky just over 24 hours ago. I haven't eaten anything except for a few biscuits since that cup of tea we all had around the fire at 10 o'clock yesterday. [...] I sure wish I hadn't come back yesterday, Mum, and I very nearly changed my mind and came back home again when I reached South Queensferry. I just missed a ferry across the river and had to literally force myself to wait for the next. Even when

I got to Rosyth I walked from there to the dockyard arguing with myself whether I should go back or not. Still, I went on and was charged with being adrift and the ship under sailing orders. I haven't seen the Commander yet, but the Officer of the Watch said it was a pretty serious offence. I am telling you all this just so you won't worry and be worrying how I got on, Mum.

His anguish was not confined to what he had left behind, but to the reality of what awaited his return to the ship:

I thought it would be OK coming back after that long spell in harbour but boy oh boy I sure have found different. Mother, I just feel suffocated, everything here seems to remind me of home, but does not make one feel so comfortable or anywhere near so happy. The wireless, day-old newspapers, and everybody seems to wait until I appear and then they start singing songs which you sung when I was home. I always feel like crying, mum, and there is a permanent lump in my throat.

Beyond the enervating atmosphere was the tyranny of routine and repetition, of a life deprived of physical comfort or mental rest: 'I don't know what's wrong with me, but I feel sick, tired and in every way fed up. I had about five hours' sleep last night as I had a watch to keep from 12am to 4pm. The thought of eating this food again – pooey! – the same things day in, day out.' Certainly, the ship to which Bill Crawford returned was at times barely habitable. Louis Le Bailly remembers conditions aboard off Norway in October 1939:

In October, in the worst weather yet, we were off the Lofoten Islands escorting a precious convoy of iron ore from Narvik. The messdecks grew colder, and the ship's steam heating (never before used) leaked so badly that it had to be shut off as the evaporators could not make up the water lost. Continuous rolling and pitching caused the deck joints between the great armoured conning tower and the upper deck to leak so badly that running water on the messdecks added to the miseries of overcrowding and cold.

Things were little better in the gunroom. Mid Robin Owen spent the winter of 1940–1 in *Hood* while the cruiser *Fiji* was under repair:

As we joined her on a dark cold October evening she looked vast, like a great blacked out city anchored in the Flow but despite her size and reputation we were not at all happy at this change. The Gunroom was overcrowded with 28 midshipmen, most of whom were older and senior to us and, in time-honoured manner did their utmost to treat us like dogs' bodies, and temporary ones at that. Most had formed themselves into small groups, rarely mixing with others, and coming from *Fiji*'s closely knit Gunroom of only six we found this intimidating. The gunroom itself was dilapidated and uncomfortable, we had to take our meals in shifts and the catering was poor. Our hammock slinging space was cramped, cluttered with extra sea chests and noisy fans and with overhead ventilation ducts which leaked water in heavy weather. The bathroom and washplace were damp and smelly and being on a deck below the waterline, often inaccessible due to closure of the watertight hatch above.

But the lower deck had it worst. Among the most hated chores was the 'Energy Party', the detail of men assigned to mop the rivers of water coursing through messdecks and passages at all hours of the day or night when the ship was at sea, while the shipwrights spent their time punching oakum into leaking hatches. Under such circumstances it proved impossible to maintain anything approaching peacetime standards of cleanliness at sea, but nonetheless the failure to do so in comparison with other ships points to a decline in morale and energy as the war dragged on. Visiting her to take an exam shortly before she sailed against the *Bismarck*, Telegraphist James Webster of the new battleship *Prince of Wales* found the *Hood* generally 'shabby' and the torpedo tubes covered in rust. The admiral's barge was so unkempt that Boy James Gordon, also of *Prince of Wales*, got into trouble for ignoring it. Officer morale remained high, but the perspective of the lower deck was rather different. For OD Jon Pertwee, also a veteran of 1940–1, the *Hood*, whose crew had an average age of not more than twenty-three, was 'never a very happy ship'. The grind of sleep deprivation and cold food, of hours without a cigarette in sodden clothing and filthy weather, of seasickness and boredom; peace a distant memory, leave a cherished hope; and ultimately the frustration of an elusive and unwilling enemy. All took their toll as the war entered its second year and men reached a state of profound physical and mental exhaustion. The *Hood* remained a great ship to the end but it is clear that by 1941 life aboard her had become almost intolerable. On May Day another Hostilities-Only rating, OD Philip X, unburdened himself to a friend:

I'm afraid I can give you absolutely no news. This ship is still regarded as *the* crack ship of the Fleet and any suggestion that might lead anyone to think that she is even afloat is immediately snipped out by the censor's scissors. No doubt to you and others who know her from the outside she is magnificent – the Queen of the Seas, one of Neptune's nipples. I sometimes even think that myself when I see her off shore from the background of an open pub, but living inside her and doing her dirty chores day and night I have come to regard her as the biggest, bloodiest and most wanton and unsatiated bitch I have ever known. The work I do could be done far better by an illiterate factory hand – though he would not have to work nearly so hard – and the life is plain hell. I have never been out of my clothes except to wash since I saw you, and sleep only occasionally touches me. If only the enemy would be induced to make less furtive and more frequent appearances in the open it might be almost worth while. The only thing that continually astonishes me is the docile patience with which my Lower Deck mates take everything that comes to them – an attitude of mind that can only come from lack of imagination and one that I find impossible to acquire. [...] It's a very strange life – utterly remote from anything you ever knew about the sea even in your trawler ventures. In fact, even in the heaviest weather, it's strangely remote from the sea, so much so that when I am thoroughly exhausted and embittered by all this ceaseless discipline I only need to look down at the sea to find the most perfect possible refuge. But it's a clean life, and we are fed well. One can't complain of any material defects. I only wonder sometimes if I will ever paint again, or think clearly.

In these conditions it is no wonder men began cracking under the strain. Jon Pertwee:

From what I have written in the last few pages it would seem as if wartime at sea was one endless sky-lark, but this was far from the truth. The combination of lack of privacy, living conditions and the weather with its freezing cold were enough to break the spirit of far stronger men than me.

One whose spirit was broken was Bill Crawford, evidently on the verge of a mental breakdown by the spring of 1941:

But the first chance I get, mum, I am leaving for good as I honestly feel that yesterday something died inside of me and now I don't care much about anything. When the news comes on here I feel a big lump rising in my throat when I know there is no soft chair to sit in and no fire to sit by. Nobody else seems to be as bad as me, mum, but most of them are English and the longer we spent in harbour the more money they spent in going ashore ... even Ian Roy is not upset at all. I guess it is just my nature and the reason I'm telling you this, mum, is so that you won't be too ashamed if I do anything rash in the future. Please believe in me, mum, whatever happens, as I feel I'll go nuts if this carries on much longer. If only I could get off this ship it would not be so bad and there is so many good jobs ashore if one could only get into them. [...] I wonder if it would do any good, mum, if you wrote to the Admiralty and asked them if there is no chance of me getting in at Donnybristle (if that is how you spell it) or a shore job at Rosyth.* You know, lay it on thick, tell them you have two sons away, etc, be sure and tell them my age. I don't suppose it would do any good but it might.

*HMS *Cochrane* II, Donibristle, was a naval barracks near Rosyth.

For Bill, as presumably for Philip X, there was not much longer to wait. On 24 May their torture became their nemesis.

Despite Philip X's remarks on the forbearance of the lower deck, tempers did occasionally reach boiling point. When it was learnt in early December 1940 that the ship would be spending her second Christmas without leave, the mood of the *Hood*'s stokers apparently bordered on mutiny. The incident, which allegedly required the intervention of Capt Irvine Glennie, is related in Bill Crawford's diary:

> *Tuesday 10 December.* There sure is unrest as regards leave. The Captain spoke to us about it today, he said nothing could be done.
> *Wednesday 11 December.* There is open talk about mutiny, especially among the stokers, who have already had one bit of trouble.
> *Thursday 12 December.* Things came to a head today. The stokers practically mutinied, locking up officers and saying they wouldn't work. The captain asked them all to come up into the battery, he told them he could do nothing about leave and asked all the ship's company to stand by him.
> *Friday 13 December.* Things have kind of eased off today. The Captain told us yesterday that he was doing all he could but he did not think we would get leave till next year. He said all he could, also saying he knew some things but he was only a captain and if he was to tell us it might cause unnecessary trouble.

No corroborating evidence has yet been found for this episode nor did it reach the ears of Lt Cdr Wellings USN, then aboard. It may be that Boy Crawford's entries do the stokers living on the adjoining messdecks a grave injustice. But if conditions in the *Hood*'s engine spaces were as they had been a year earlier it is not beyond the bounds of possibility that the stokers, traditionally less inclined to discipline than their seaman colleagues, could have collectively reached the end of their tether. Decades later Vice Admiral Sir Louis Le Bailly had this to say:

> To have to live and work for months on end in the sort of conditions prevailing in *Hood*'s messdecks could never contribute to a Happy Ship. When I was asked by the leaving Mids to come to their farewell party in April 1941 ... I went down to the [Engineers'] Office I knew so well. There I found old [Chief Stoker Walden J] Biggenden slaving over his books as he had always done. He and one or two others he whistled up were tired and the young stokers I had known had grown much older. They were fed up with the war; fed up with trying to keep an old ship going. But there was a certain fatalism in their attitude. They had known good times; now they tried patiently to endure bad ones.

Indeed, for a majority of the crew, increasingly made up of Hostilities-Only officers and ratings, the drudgery was stoically borne. Capt Sir David Tibbits has captured it perfectly:

> The men who took it all in their stride, never complained, and did whatever they had to do satisfactorily and well, were the quiet men, probably married with children, who had worked in a factory, on a farm, or had a milk round. They had always gotten on with their jobs whatever happened, and they just went on doing them, whatever they might be.

Cdr William Davis, *Hood*'s executive officer from 1939–40, left this record of her officer complement:

> It was encouraging to see how the officers stood up to war strain. Most increased materially in stature and the fussers ceased usually to fuss, and the quiet and hesitant frequently blossomed forth. The reserve officers, many of whom had been in the Navy between the wars, fitted into the pattern of ship life instantly. Life in the wardroom was fun.

The end of the war was no more than a dream, but men were sustained by comradeship, love of family, romantic attachments ashore and hope for the future. But above all comradeship. Jon Pertwee:

> Lucky count three was my friendship with the Second in Command of the Royal Marines on board, Lieutenant [Horace] Davies. This was a somewhat dangerous situation for him, as having a lower deck rating as a friend was unheard of, and could've been suspect. But this delightful man found ways of getting me into his cabin that defied any criticism. Running errands, discussing ship's concerts, tuning his guitar, and translating (very roughly) passages of French poetry. Once in, I was made very much at home and over endless cups of tea, laced with some of Geoff's 'neaters', we talked and talked. He was quite besotted by the theatre and the arts, and despairing of finding a kindred spirit among the Officers on board turned to me. Thank God he did! [...] It was my friendship with Lieutenant Davies and [CPO Supply] Geoff Pope that kept me going through some of the most wretched and despairing periods of my young life.

For all their remoteness and isolation, the *Hood*'s men found themselves as subject to the ebb and flow of life on the Home Front as any of their comrades in arms. Before they died on 24 May 1941, Lt John Iago and Paymaster Sub-Lt Robert Browne had respectively announced to their families the affiancing of one relationship and the dissolution of another. Nor could they be spared the harsher realities of life on the Home Front. John Iago:

I expect you have been having some air raid warnings by now. Portsmouth seems to be having a bad time and the majority of the men on board come from around there. The other day one man was punished severely for interfering with some gear that he shouldn't have touched; he lost a good conduct badge which means sixpence a day off his pay for life. However, a message came through that in an air raid a bomb had dropped on his house, killing his wife, mother-in-law and two children. The poor chap's punishment was forgotten.

Where family was concerned, Bill Crawford no doubt spoke for many when he wrote, 'That last leave was the happiest I have ever spent, just because I was in the house more. Sitting round the fire talking, with a good dinner beneath my belt – oh mother, that I did not have to leave all those things behind.' Clearly, it was being deprived of the ordinary things of life and of news from home that were among the hardest things to bear. John Iago: 'Mails have been very bad and tomorrow we shall not have had one for a month, so I don't know what is happening at home. I do hope air raids are not too bad or too near. Your garden must be full of flowers; I wish I could see it.' As Cdr Davis noted, spirits rose immediately the mail came aboard: 'Its prompt arrival did more for a ship's company morale than anything I know, and just the odd senior officer here and there did not always appreciate this.' Then there was the future, almost too distant and too wonderful to contemplate. In one of the last letters he wrote to his wife, AB Algernon Foster laid out his plans for their life after the war that were destined never to come to fruition:

I have not mentioned it to you, but the reason that I wish as much money as possible put away is because I am hoping to save enough to get a start in a Public House. Of course, it will need quite a bit of money, but I will tell you more about it next time I get home. I have been thinking a lot about what I will do at the end of this upheaval. But of course I will want your ideas as well.

Although the Rev Beardmore, the ship's chaplain, accepted that 'a large percentage of British people do not go to church these days', it was equally the case that many found solace in religion as the war broke over their homes and touched them personally. In the few minutes given him at 'Divisions' each morning, Beardmore tried to cater to their needs:

The men appreciate a prayer for their homes. For nearly two years I said the following simple prayer of my own in HMS *Hood*:

We commend unto Thy loving care, O Lord, all those who are joined to us by the ties of kindred, friendship, and love; keep them, we beseech Thee, in all their dangers, their anxieties, and their fears, and enable us by Thy Spirit

THE DARK OF THE SUN

to do our duty by them and the country which we serve; through Jesus
Christ our Lord.

I always noticed that there was an audible 'Amen' to that prayer and the Lord's
Prayer, which seemed to indicate that they understood and appreciated its
meaning. History, no doubt, will one day place on record how these men did
their duty fearlessly to the end.

The Second World War had a profound impact on the structure of British
society, one that was accurately reflected in the Royal Navy. With the onset of
war came tens of thousands of reservist officers and Hostilities-Only ratings
who were destined to transform its outlook and self-perception. The great
influx of volunteers and conscripts did not begin until 1940, but once they
started arriving in numbers the atmosphere in the *Hood* changed perceptibly.
For the regulars of the peacetime Navy it was no doubt an exasperating yet
fascinating spectacle. Here were men, drawn from every walk of life, thrust in
time of war into the unforgiving and largely closed world of the lower deck of
the Royal Navy. Some wilted under the pressure, but curiosity and mutual
respect caused many unlikely friendships to be struck up. OD Philip X, an
urbane conscript struggling to cope with the hardships of war at sea, has left
this testimony of his adjustment: '... since I'm the oldest Ordinary Seaman in
the Squadron, probably in the whole Fleet, I get a few *sub rosa* privileges from
the real old timers in the Lower Deck. They are grand fellows, and a tot of
rum from a Chief PO now is better than a kiss from Garbo in New York.' For
some, like John Iago, their technical expertise in civilian life qualified them for
an immediate commission in the RNVR. Iago, an electrical engineer with
Metropolitan Vickers of Sheffield, volunteered for the Navy on 28 August 1939
and within a month found himself a sub lieutenant in charge of the *Hood*'s high-
power installations as her sole electrical engineer. As technology assumed an
ever greater role in naval operations and attrition thinned the ranks of career
officers, the Navy came increasingly to rely on both the RNVR and the RNR,
which was composed of volunteers from the Merchant Navy. As one regular of
the 'pukka Navy' recalled, 'We began to wonder how we ever got on without
them'. Of course, there were tensions as reservist officers brought their
technical expertise and breezy approach into the conservative environment of
the peacetime Navy. John Iago, on the threshold of promotion to lieutenant,
relates his experience:

There has been a change of officers in our department. Mr Turner, our Commissioned Electrician, has just left because his wife is very seriously ill.
Nominally he and I held the same rank but he had been doing the job for some
20 years, was very well up in service matters, had poor technical knowledge
and, not unnaturally, to begin with he rather resented my intrusion. In the event

we got on very well together but it would have been a bit hard on him should I have gained my second stripe over him.

However, the majority of Hostilities-Only personnel could not expect this degree of adjustment, and the following passage by the Rev Harold Beardmore captures their particular predicament:

In war conditions in the Royal Navy we have to accept the fact that a very large percentage of our parish have never known the meaning of the words 'foreign commission'. They have never been away from their homes for a long period, while only a few ratings on the lower deck attended boarding schools in their youth when they became accustomed to leaving their homes three times a year to go to school. It is, therefore, only natural that so many men feel the strain of being away from their homes.

Conscious of their limitations, most chose to blend in with the herd as best they could. OD B A Carlisle, aboard in 1940–1, describes his strategy when the men were being told off for work: 'In harbour when the ratings fell in to be detailed for duties, I soon learned where to stand in the line to make sure I wasn't given a task with an element of skill such as splicing a rope but rather got detailed to pull on ropes to get the Admiral's barge into the water.'

But it wasn't all misery on the lower deck, not by any means. For those who survived it was not the strain and discomfort that abided in the memory but the camaraderie of hardships shared in an unforgiving environment. Both visitors and veterans testify to the warm and cheery atmosphere that invariably prevailed in harbour. There was intense boredom, of course, but the war brought enough characters into the *Hood* to enliven it with a variety of pranks and entertainments. Cdr Robin Owen:

On one occasion, somewhere north of Iceland, on an unusually calm sunny day at dinner time, the Captain (I G Glennie), making one of his rare addresses over the ship's broadcast, announced that the edge of the Arctic icepack was about fifteen miles away and visible from the spotting top. A few minutes later the rumour went round the ship that we were actually in the ice. Many sailors rushed up from below to see it and there was great excitement and cheering when a smallish block of ice was seen floating down the starboard side amidships. Only later was it revealed that the stoker in charge of the refrigeration machinery had removed it from the icemaking plant, carried it up several decks and pushed it out through a forecastle scuttle, a typical but much appreciated example of Lower Deck humour.

Then there were the SODS operas (Ship's Operatic and Dramatic Society), one of which John Iago described to his family in January 1941:

We had an excellent ship's fancy dress ball a few nights ago with a large number of very good costumes, mostly made on board. The officers all rambled around after dinner, judging the costumes, the most topical, the funniest and so on and then we stayed on for a cabaret afterwards. One of our ordinary seamen, before the war, was Marmeduke Brown of Radio Luxembourg; you may have heard of Marmeduke Brown and Mathilda. He told stories very well.

The 'Marmeduke Brown' in question was in fact OD Jon Pertwee who would make his career in theatre and television. Pertwee was extremely popular and, even allowing for a degree of post-war embellishment, his birthday celebration was clearly an event of some moment:

In my case, on one birthday I was in luck, or in retrospect, perhaps out of luck, for 'Old Marmy' was sufficiently liked to be invited to 'sippers, all round' by two or more mess-decks of a dozen or so ratings. My rum intake therefore was around 36 sippers, which plus my own tot, nine sippers, equalled 45 sippers in all. Within ten minutes I was falling down drunk, and remained so for two days and two nights. Endearingly, I was joshed, picked up, picked up again and finally hidden away to sleep it off, my mates performing my duties and keeping watch for me.

When he awoke it was to find a large cobra tattooed onto his forearm, a lasting memento of the occasion.

However, there were less demanding forms of entertainment. Rugby and football continued informally at Scapa, but the outbreak of war had curtailed most organised sport and the men were obliged to fall back on shipboard recreations. Darts, cribbage, chess and mah-jong were widely played as were whist and bridge under the auspices of the chaplain, prizes being drawn from the war comforts packages. The Rev Beardmore's 'Deep Sea Scouts' and handicraft competitions kept men's minds off the war while demonstrating 'what an abundance of talent there is in the service'. Band Corporal Wally Rees RM of Port Talbot led a six-piece swing outfit with his 'effervescent trumpet'. Films shown on messdecks and in recreation spaces were much appreciated while the wardroom had screenings every Sunday to which the gunroom was usually invited. Charlie Chaplain's *The Great Dictator* premiered to an audience of two hundred at Scapa on 17 November 1940 while *Rembrandt* with Charles Laughton, *The Doctor Takes a Wife* with Loretta Young, Disney's *Pinocchio* and *The Texas Rangers Ride Again* were among the films seen in the wardroom in 1940 and 1941. Under these circumstances the flooding of the ship's cinema equipment during a harsh patrol in the Norwegian Sea in late October 1939 must have seemed something of a calamity; no wonder Sub-Lt John Iago, the ship's electrical engineer, devoted half a day to restoring it. Photography was popular, though film became increasingly hard to come by as the war progressed and for security reasons could not be developed ashore, the crew having to make do with processing aboard. Cdr (E) Terence Grogan went a step further, shooting colour footage of the ship at sea with a 16mm cine camera. The intended result, a film titled *The War from the Hood* with soundtrack, seems never to have been completed but the surviving footage provides a unique and fascinating glimpse of the ship as she passed from peace into war. Above all there was reading. Apart from the ship's bookstall and library there was a wardroom library, together with that set up by the Rev Beardmore 'offering books of the better type, books of travel, music, art, biography, history, and science'. Books and magazines were, however, in very short supply and the consignments donated by *The Times* and the War Comforts Fund eagerly awaited and later exchanged with those of other ships. Then there was smoking, banned between decks (except on Christmas afternoon) but still the support and consolation of many an exhausted or dejected sailor. Cigarettes were cheap and plentiful, but the cartons of American Chesterfields that Lt Cdr Joseph Wellings presented to Vice Admiral Whitworth and Captain Glennie on Christmas morning 1940 were clearly much appreciated. Traditional celebrations were observed as well as circumstances allowed. The first Christmas of the war was spent on the Northern Patrol but festivities went ahead nonetheless. Sub-Lt John Iago:

Christmas Day was the oddest Christmas I have ever had. I managed to go to church two days in succession. After church, all the officers went round the mess decks to inspect the very highly decorated messes. The last was the Warrant Officers' mess where we had a bit to drink and then we went on to the Gun Room and had a drop more, and finally to the Ward Room again to have more! We celebrated mainly on the best champagne at 2/6d a bottle! Christmas Lunch was fun – we all had presents, crackers, paper hats and musical instruments. Afterwards everyone retired to bed to sleep it off and before tea I went on duty in the drifter until midnight.

The *Hood* did not return to harbour until 5 January 1940. Fate also decreed that she would be at sea over Christmas 1940, the orders to sail being piped just as the men were decorating the messes on the afternoon of the 24th. The Beating the Retreat planned by the Marine Band for that evening had to be abandoned as the ship prepared for sea. After what may have been a near-mutiny over leave earlier that month, this must have been a difficult moment but the men made the best of it. Ted Briggs:

It was my second Christmas of the war at sea, but we were all in the same boat and the greyness and knifing coldness of the fringe of the Arctic Circle melted below decks as carols echoed through the messes and as 'sippers' from tots were freely exchanged before the arrival of the turkey and plum pudding. Mess decks were decorated with flags and bunting cadged from the flag deck; the captain carried out a parody of 'rounds', preceded by a boy seaman dressed in a master-at-arms uniform. As far as possible discipline was relaxed below deck, but for those on watch it was 'business as usual'.

However, the New Year was seen in at Scapa and celebrated accordingly. Lt Cdr Wellings has left this description of the wardroom festivities as the *Hood* entered the last year of her life and the Royal Navy the most desperate in her history:

> Just before midnight the officers returned from the CPO party [actually the Warrant Officers' mess]. Paymaster Lt Browne rigged up ship's bell in Anteroom of wardroom. At 24.00 bell was struck 16 times, an old custom. Captain, Admiral, his staff, exec and practically all officers returned to Wardroom. We all drank a toast to 1941 – Peace and Victory. One of the midshipmen from the gunroom [I W V Browne] came in with a bagpipe and played Scotch tunes. Everyone started to dance the various Scotch dances from the Admiral down to the lowest midshipman. The Wardroom tables were cleared away and a regular party was in full swing. It was a very unusual sight to see the Admiral, Captain, staff, Wardroom, gunroom, and Warrant officers dancing. Included in the party but not dancing was the chief Master-at-Arms and Sergeant Major of the Marines. Such a comradeship one would never suspect from the English who are supposed to be so conservative. I was impressed very much. Such spirit is one of the British [*sic*] best assets. This spirit will go far to bring about victory in the end. At 01.45 I left the party in full swing and turned in ...

With their fine food, cases of sherry, frequent parties and Royal Marine attendants, the life of the *Hood*'s officers was rather more comfortable than that suffered on the lower deck. Among the wardroom guests at Greenock in January 1940 was Gracie Fields herself and several officers were able to bring their wives up to Scotland with the prospect of spending time with them when the ship was at Rosyth or in the Clyde. Sub-Lt Iago for one found his lot decidedly less taxing than his peacetime occupation:

> We have great fun on board, especially in the evenings. When we are in harbour we have a proper dinner for which we dress and we have a Royal Marine band in attendance twice a week. At sea it is only a 'running dinner', as then we have to work harder. Breakfast at 8.30am is a bit of a treat after early rising in Sheffield. Lunch at noon, tea 3.30pm (we usually sleep off lunch until teatime) and then, if we are in harbour, we can usually get a run ashore till dinner at 8pm. So you see all the work is done between 9am and 12 o'clock – quite a change after a 47-hour week at Metro Vicks.

Indeed, one of the few concerns Iago expressed during his first months afloat was the provision of sufficient clean collars for the nightly dinners in harbour. On 27 August 1940 Iago wrote to his family that 'It seems extraordinary that tomorrow I shall have been in the service for a year. Time has gone very quickly and it has been very pleasant.' Though his experience was decidedly untypical and was soon to became markedly more onerous, this state of affairs was clearly not lost on the lower deck, which, in war as in peace, preserved its suspicion and resentment of the wardroom. OD Philip X, a Hostilities-Only rating, wrote as much in one of his last letters: 'Except for routine orders one never sees the officers. They are as remote and as inhuman as Chinese Emperors – all except the padre [the Rev Patrick Stewart] who is exceptionally human and intelligent.' Evidently, insofar as conditions in the wartime *Hood* could be recalled with any lasting pleasure it was to the life of her wardroom officers that this memory was owed. But what of the relations between officers and men in the same period? Cdr I W V Browne, a midshipman aboard between 1939 and 1941, puts it in perspective: 'The very high morale retained by the Navy throughout the war ... in unspeakable conditions would not have been possible without genuine respect and cooperation between officers and ratings, helped by tradition and custom.'

There is surely much in this but as in so many other areas insufficient evidence survives to draw any firm conclusions where the *Hood* was concerned. Her life and community were too varied and opinions too polarised for a definitive assessment to be made from available sources. Nor does the coherent study of officer–sailor relations in the Royal Navy exist against which any comparison might be drawn. Unless and until further sources appear this reality seems fated to recede into oblivion.

Early on the morning of 10 May 1940 the German army launched its great offensive in the West. Within two weeks the War Cabinet, its troops outmanoeuvred and its strategy in disarray, was taking the first steps towards the withdrawal of the British Expeditionary Force from the Continent. As these momentous events unfolded across the Channel the *Hood* was quietly completing her refit first at Plymouth and then at the Gladstone Dock in Liverpool where Mussolini's declaration of war was greeted with looting of businesses and boarding of Italian vessels berthed there. A boarding party from the *Hood* was detailed to take over the freighter *Erica* whose crew promptly surrendered. The party returned soon after with the Italian ensign, an autographed portrait of Mussolini for the gunroom, and generally rather the worse for drink, the British matelot's unerring nose for alcohol having taken him directly to the spirit store. When the *Hood* finally emerged from Liverpool on 12 June it was to find the evacuation from Dunkirk past and the Royal Navy girding itself to lift the remnants of the Allied armies from northern and western France. On 17 June, as the *Hood* lay at Greenock with the liners of convoy US3 about her, the French government asked Germany for an armistice.

Five days later the new premier, Marshal Pétain, accepted Hitler's terms, thereby bringing the Battle of France to a close. That night in one of his periodic broadcasts to the ship Capt Glennie asked his crew to remember that, though 'we were likely to have certain dislikes for our previous allies, ... we were to treat them, even now, as our friends and try to realise their terrible fate in the hands of the Nazis'. There was certainly frustration but also relief that another dismal episode was over, that 'On consideration, not having to defend France may be a blessing in disguise'. But, as the *Hood*'s company was shortly to discover, France's agony was not yet over.

With the entry of Italy into the war the Admiralty began taking steps to fill the void created by the collapse of French power in the western Mediterranean with a significant force of British ships. However, once the terms of the Franco-German armistice became known in London, as they had by 25 June, it was plain that this squadron must have a far more urgent remit. Under the terms of the armistice, the French fleet, still largely intact, was to be 'demobilised and disarmed under German or Italian control'. This clause did not satisfy the British government which was already moving to prevent scattered units and squadrons of the French navy falling into the hands of the Axis. The officer chosen to enforce this policy in the western Mediterranean was Vice Admiral Sir James Somerville who assumed command of Force H on 27 June. First constituted as a hunting group during the search for the raider *Admiral Graf Spee* in October 1939, Force H was now transformed into an independent command based on Gibraltar but directly responsible to the Admiralty in London. Over the next eighteen months Somerville's 'detached squadron' asserted a control over the western Mediterranean which would not be relinquished while the war lasted. This accomplishment, together with the many famous actions in which it was involved, gives Force H a special place in the history of the Royal Navy. It was to join this squadron as flagship that the *Hood* was ordered south from Greenock on 18 June, reaching Gibraltar five days later with the carrier *Ark Royal*.

The first task to which Force H was committed was the neutralisation of the French Atlantic Fleet at Mers el-Kebir near Oran in Algeria. After two days of earnest deliberation in Somerville's cabin, Force H sailed from Gibraltar on 2 July stiffened by units of Admiral Sir Dudley North's North Atlantic Command. There can be no doubt that Somerville's task was among the most unenviable ever assigned to a British commander. His brief from the War Cabinet was to lay before his French counterpart, Amiral Marcel Gensoul, the following options for the disposal of his fleet, which consisted of two modern battlecruisers, two elderly battleships, a seaplane carrier and six large destroyers: that he (a) put to sea and continue the fight against Germany; (b) sail with reduced crews to a British port; (c) do likewise to a port in the French West Indies, or (d) scuttle his ships at their berths. Should these prove unacceptable a fifth was to be offered, namely that Gensoul demilitarise his force at Mers el-

Kebir. Any measure resorted to would have to be enacted within six hours, a proviso which greatly hindered both admirals' freedom of manoeuvre. In the event of these proposals being rejected Somerville was to present Gensoul with the ultimatum of having his fleet destroyed at the hands of Force H.

Shortly after 0800 on the morning of 3 July Force H appeared off Mers el-Kebir. Somerville had already sent the destroyer *Foxhound* ahead with his emissary Capt Cedric Holland, but it was not until 1615 that the latter gained direct access to Gensoul. The story of the protracted and ultimately fruitless negotiations between the British and Gensoul, the stirring of the French navy across the western Mediterranean and the mounting pressure from London all lie beyond the scope of this volume. Suffice to say that by 1730, some three hours after the expiry of his original ultimatum, Somerville found himself with no alternative but to open fire. Within a few minutes Boy Signalman Ted Briggs was hoisting the order for instant action to the starboard signal yard. A little before 1800 it was the order to open fire that he bent on to the halyard:

> The response was immediate. Just as I turned round to watch, the guns of the *Resolution* and *Valiant* roared in murderous hair-trigger reaction. Then came the ting-ting of our firing bell. Seconds later my ears felt as if they had been sandwiched between two manhole covers. The concussion of the *Hood*'s eight fifteen-inch guns, screaming in horrendous harmony, shook the flag deck violently.

Moments later the harbour at Mers el-Kebir was being crucified by the first salvoes of British 15in ordnance. Within three minutes the battleship *Bretagne* had blown up with huge loss of life. Her sister *Provence* and the battlecruiser *Dunkerque* had to be beached after sustaining repeated hits, the latter mainly under *Hood*'s fire. The destroyer *Mogador* lost her stern to a direct hit which left her a smouldering wreck in waters turned black with oil and writhing bodies. With the harbour shrouded in a dense pall of smoke, at 1804, nine minutes after the action had commenced, Somerville gave the order to cease fire. A few minutes later increasingly accurate salvoes from the shore battery at Fort Santon obliged the *Hood* to return a withering fire while the squadron sailed out of range under a smokescreen. This might have been the end of the affair except that at 1818 reports began reaching *Hood* that a battlecruiser was emerging from the harbour. Initially dismissed by Somerville and his staff, by 1830 it was apparent that the *Strasbourg*, unscathed by the holocaust enveloping her companions, had negotiated the mine barrage laid by aircraft from *Ark Royal* and was making for Toulon with five destroyers. *Hood* turned to give chase, working up to over 28 knots at the cost of a stripped turbine, while *Ark Royal* prepared to launch an air strike in the fading light. The *Hood* again came under attack as the pursuit developed, first from a salvo of torpedoes fired by the light cruiser *Rigauld de Genouilly* and then by a flight of bombers from Algeria.

However, attacks by Swordfish aircraft failed to slow the *Strasbourg* and at 2020 a dispirited Somerville called off the chase. A second Swordfish strike at 2055 reported two torpedo hits but the *Strasbourg*'s speed remained unimpaired and she reached Toulon without damage the following day. Three days later an announcement by Amiral Jean-Pierre Estéva at Bizerta, that 'The damage to the *Dunkerque* is minimal and the ship will soon be repaired', brought Force H back to Mers el-Kebir where Swordfish from *Ark Royal* put paid to her operational career.

So ended one of the most regrettable episodes in the history of the Royal Navy. As Somerville put it in a letter to his wife,

> We all feel thoroughly dirty and ashamed that the first time we should have been in action was an affair like this. [...] I feel sure that I shall be blamed for bungling the job and I think I did. But to you I don't mind confessing I was half-hearted and you can't win an action that way.

It was, he added, 'the biggest political blunder of modern times and I imagine will rouse the world against us'. Those who expressed an opinion did so largely in the same vein. Writing to his family on 6 July, Sub-Lt Iago echoed Somerville's fears for the wider implications of the engagement:

> I think that the events in Oran were a great pity – they solved the problem of the French fleet but I hope we shall not look back on it as too much of a mistake. Lord Haw-Haw has evidently been rendered speechless with anger – or perhaps it is that we just can't pick him up on the wireless.

In fact, Lord Haw-Haw, like the rest of the German propaganda machine, made enormous capital out of the incident, christening Force H 'Somerville's assassins' in one particular broadcast. There was grim amusement to be had from this but also anger; anger at the Axis for precipitating the disaster, and anger at Gensoul for not continuing the war alongside the British. Above all there was chagrin and astonishment that matters should have come to such a pass. But for all that there was no shortage of pragmatic opinion in the *Hood*. Mid Buckett's was one: 'Coming back past the harbour we could still see large columns of smoke and small fires coming from the ships and the town behind. We realised, too, how unpleasant the action had been. Nevertheless it had been our duty and we had done it successfully.' There were other voices too, overheard by Somerville and related with some disgust to his wife: 'It doesn't seem to worry the sailors at all as "they never 'ad no use for them French bastards".' Though they certainly existed, surviving accounts suggest that such opinions were neither widely held nor deeply felt. It was a vile episode from which no one could derive any lasting pride or satisfaction. Years later Mid Ross Warden recalled the atmosphere aboard as the *Hood* made for Gibraltar: 'There was no elation aboard our ship that night. The gunroom was for once subdued, and from the Admiral down to the youngest seaman there were heavy hearts.'

The *Hood* emerged largely unscathed from her second action. Towards the end of the engagement she was straddled by a salvo from *Dunkerque* which blinded AB Patsy Ogan in one eye, wounded Lt G E M Owens in the arm and caused splinter damage to the funnels and starboard side. But that was all and again it seemed that she had got off lightly. For the crew, however, it was a different matter. The engagement off Mers el-Kebir was the *Hood*'s first prolonged experience of battle and it left an impression on all who endured it. From the time the *Hood* cleared Gibraltar at 1700 on 2 July to her return at 1900 on the 4th there was barely a moment's rest for any of the crew. The hands, changed into clean underwear, were piped to the usual dawn action stations at 0445 on the 3rd and then again at 0830 as Force H closed Mers el-Kebir. Then the waiting began. Grog was issued followed by a lunch of soup and bully beef sandwiches for the men and stew and rock cakes for officers in brutal heat, but, as Mid Buckett wrote in his journal, 'the anxiety of waiting for the French admiral's decision began to have its effect on us in the afternoon'. At 1600 the ship briefly went down to Defence Stations, giving the Rev Beardmore an opportunity to hand out cigarettes and offer what encouragement he could as the men waited at their posts:

> ... I remember we had been closed up at action stations since dawn, having had meals at our action stations, but the ship did not open fire until 6pm; thus, the canteen having been shut and the men confined in one space, cigarettes were hard to come by as the evening approached, so that when I went round during a lull in the action and handed out cigarettes, they were as welcome as another meal.

By 1630 he was back at his post as broadcaster on the bridge, after which the ship was in action almost continuously until 2100. The intervening period gave the *Hood* her first taste of heavy-calibre gunfire as the *Dunkerque* and then the *Strasbourg* began to range on her. Ted Briggs:

> Suddenly pinpoints of amber light punctuated the blackness. Above the roar of our guns came the high-pitched, blood-curdling, crescendoing, low whine of being under fire ourselves by warships for the first time. There were vivid red flashes as a salvo fell just short of the starboard side. Within seconds came a series of blue flashes.

Peering through the periscope of 'B' turret, OA Bert Pitman watched the French salvoes burst in towering geysers of red and blue water, ingeniously coloured to assist the *officiers de tir* in spotting their fall of shot. Meanwhile, battened down under armoured hatches in a damage-control party on the lower deck, AB Len Williams struggled to conquer his fear:

It was not a pleasant experience to be fired on, particularly when it is known that the projectiles coming your way weighed almost a ton. I, and most everyone else, was scared stiff. To begin with, my action station was three decks below, in an electrical repair party, and although we could hear the shells passing over us like express trains, we could not see what was going on. We did see our two wounded men being helped down to the dressing station below us, and their blood-stained appearance did not help us any. I had often searched my soul to try and analyse my feelings should I ever be faced with this sort of situation. How would I react? Would I show my feelings? Could I take it? Yes, fear was present without a doubt, but I was consoled by the fact that none of the others looked very happy either! And this made me realise that it was only a question of mastering it, and not breaking down under the strain. Had we been given something to do, it would have helped. We just had to wait for a shell to come through the deck and if it did not either kill or wound us, we could then proceed to repair the damage. We talked when we did not feel like talking and we walked up and down in the limited space at our disposal, and in this way we tried to forget what was going on above us. We were all very thankful when the gunfire ceased and we were told that the action was over. Our highly strung nerves relaxed and we began to live again. It was some time before the memory of Oran faded from our minds.

In the torpedomen's mess, meanwhile, AB Joseph Rockey and his companions were distracted by one of the ventilation fans, which began to disintegrate in clouds of rust once the *Hood*'s main armament opened fire.

After it was over came the exhaustion that only battle can bring. Ted Briggs describes the crew's first rest in perhaps sixty hours of exertion, tension and combat:

When I finally got below at 22.00 [on 4 July] the messdecks were quiet. Everyone was dog tired, and off-duty watches were collapsed all over the ship. Many, like myself, were too exhausted to sling their hammocks. I joined a bunch of friends dozing on top of the hammock stowage. They were still fully dressed, with anti-flash gear on.

It had been, Mid Buckett concluded, 'a very terrifying experience for all of us, but a very necessary one'.

Seventy years on, the events of 3 July 1940 continue to resist judgement, a mark of the immensely complex situation from which they evolved. In retrospect, the tragedy of Mers el-Kebir accurately reflects the scale of the disaster that had befallen Britain and France in the space of less than two months. It also foreshadowed the dark night of war that lay ahead for both countries. For the *Hood* there was the lingering sadness that her guns had received their baptism of fire against not only an ally but, in the case of *Dunkerque*, a companion in arms. The return by the *Dunkerque's* officers of souvenirs presented to them by members of the *Hood's* wardroom in happier times made this all the more poignant and unpropitious. With them came this bitter note:

> The captain and officers of the *Dunkerque* inform you of the death for the honour of their colours on 3 and 6 July 1940 of nine officers and 200 men of their ship. They return to you herewith the souvenirs they had of their comrades in arms of the British Royal Navy, in whom they had placed all their trust. And they express to you on this occasion all their bitter sadness and their disgust at seeing these comrades having no hesitation in soiling the glorious flag of St George with an ineffaceable stain – that of an assassin.

Worse still, a number of civilians, some of them pushing prams, had been seen on the harbour mole just before the squadron opened fire. When Mid Latham Jenson joined the *Hood* at Rosyth five months later it was to find veterans of the action still reticent on the subject:

> When I joined, *Hood* had just arrived from the Mediterranean, where she had taken part in the destruction of the Vichy French naval ships at Mers el Kabir, Oran, Algeria. This was sad and no one wanted to talk about this terrible affair. Some of the midshipmen who were junior to me were envious of people who had seen action and said they hoped that soon we would see some real action. [...] Our '[snotties'] nurse' overheard the conversation and interjected, 'My young friends. You have no idea of what you are talking about. Action means seeing your friends lying dead and wounded in pools of blood. Who would ever wish to see such a thing?' The worst of this exchange was that almost all of them, including the 'nurse' himself, would suffer a fate far worse than he had described.

There was one souvenir, however, that the French did not return. To this day an unexploded shell from the *Hood* rests in a glass case outside the officers' mess of the naval barracks at Toulon.

For a month after the Mers el-Kebir affair the *Hood* continued in the van of Force H as Somerville took the battle to the Italians in the Western Mediterranean. On 8 July Force H sailed from Gibraltar to mount a diversionary attack on the airfield at Cagliari, Sardinia to cover the passage of two convoys between Malta and Alexandria. Just before 1600 on the 9th the squadron began coming under unexpectedly heavy air attack from Italian SM79 bombers. There were no hits but sticks of bombs came uncomfortably close, one of which flung Boy Signalman Ted Briggs into a heap under the flag-deck ladder. Len Williams describes the experience of aerial bombardment at sea:

One gets a tingling sensation down one's spine when being deliberately bombed, which is not relieved until you see the splash of the missile striking water; then one heaves a sigh of relief, relaxes one's taut nerves and hopes that there won't be any more like that. It is one thing to be bombed in a city, where you are not the prime target, but in a ship, particularly a much sought after ship like *Hood*, it is not so funny, especially when you know it is your vessel they are after. We were glad when darkness descended and we were left in peace.

Indeed, no sooner had dusk fallen than Somerville decided that the risk of damage was hardly worth the objective and promptly cancelled the operation, ordering his force to return to Gibraltar.

Recent events evidently convinced Somerville that his crews were raw and the *Hood*'s anti-aircraft defence still inadequate. However, Force H was now able to spend three weeks at Gibraltar being welded into a cohesive force under the admiral's genial personality, the major units taking their turn as anti-aircraft guard ship against the daily incursions of Italian aircraft. There were constant exercises, of searchlights against aircraft and motorboat attack, against the possibility of torpedo hits or gas bombs. In many of these the *Hood*'s crew was found wanting in drill and organisation, focusing too many beams on one target or proving laggardly in taking basic precautions. Practice shoots with the main armament were characterised by ineffectual drill, control failures and poor accuracy, though by early August it was obvious that the inner lining of the port gun of 'A' turret was in need of replacement. Even so, efficiency in this area remained poor for some time. Matters were not helped by the anti-flash garb of asbestos hood and gauntlets that all gun crews and exposed personnel were required to wear, though, as OA Bert Pitman admitted, 'if we were doing anything we used to take it off'. Worse still was the burden of ineffectual equipment. The UP launchers installed in the spring refit misfired during the attacks off Cagliari and again at Gibraltar on 27 July when the forward mounting discharged an impromptu barrage over the harbour leaving three ratings severely burnt. The launchers, of which five were installed, were designed to fire a salvo of twenty rockets or 'unrotated projectiles' at attacking aircraft. Once aloft the rockets would release an explosive charge dangling from a small parachute by a series of wires which, it was confidently expected, would be snagged with dire consequences for the aircraft in question. Not only did this improbable scenario fail to eventuate, but the charges had an alarming tendency to drift boomerang-like back towards the firing vessel and ultimately proved of considerably greater danger to the ship than to the enemy.

On the other hand, it is clear that the *Hood* was quietly absorbing the lessons of war, though it required the absurdities of peacetime naval structure to be overcome for a truly effective organisation to emerge. Damage control was a case in point. Louis Le Bailly:

Damage control, a new phrase to us, spawned a more comprehensive organisation than the old 'Fire and repair parties' ever did. Essentially technical, it should have been under the direction of an engineer or shipwright officer, but in those days no (E) officer could give orders to shipwrights or sailors and no artificer, mechanician or stoker would take them from a chippie. So the first lieutenant whose knowledge of pumping, flooding, shoring, the cross connecting of damaged fire and hydraulic mains and the running of emergency electrical leads could have been written on a postage stamp, had perforce to become the damage control supremo, all orders being issued over his name.

Len Williams gives a flavour of some of the work undertaken as time passed and experience accumulated:

As one would expect, the first few months of the war revealed loopholes in our fighting efficiency. Reports were received by the Admiralty from various ships who had received damage in action. This information was thoroughly gone into by experts and various remedies were produced, which were put out in fleet orders. For instance, it was found that a 'close by' underwater explosion caused messdeck steel ladders to jolt out of their housings, thereby crashing to the deck and preventing escape to the upper deck. To overcome this, we fitted all such ladders with wire strops, shackled to the ship's structure, so that if the ladder lifted out of its housing, the strop prevented it falling to the deck. Other ships had reported that 'near miss' explosions caused the dynamo supply switches to be automatically thrown off due to shock, thereby plunging the entire ship into darkness, and bringing all ventilation and auxiliary machinery to a standstill. This meant that should it become necessary for the crew to abandon the ship, they would have extreme difficulty in finding the ladders and escape routes, apart from the additional hazards of falling kit lockers, loose equipment, and the possible acute angle of the listing ship. We adopted two cures for this trouble. First we drilled the covers of all the dynamo switches and fitted a bolt into the hole, which penetrated the insulated part of the switch arm, thereby locking the switch in the 'On' position. This, of course, upset the overload safety arrangement, but the risk had to be accepted. Secondly, we fitted automatic electric batten lanterns, which, when the mains failed, the battery took over and automatically lit the lamp. These were placed in strategic positions throughout the ship, such as near ladders, hatchways and corridors.

But it wasn't all work. Between whiles the *Hood*'s crew was able to savour the pleasures of the Mediterranean at the very moment that Hitler was turning his attention to the metropolis. For officers there were regular visits to the beach at Sandy Bay on the opposite side of the Rock. John Iago wrote home of idyllic days in the sun:

We wondered last week what sort of a war you would be imagining us to be fighting, as we spent the afternoon bathing on a beach! The sun was hot and my shoulders were badly sunburned. This particular beach is very fine and is reserved for Officers and nurses. There are heaps of fish in the water and they sometimes catch small octopuses and basking sharks – not dangerous ones!

As in earlier years there were Carley-float and swimming races between the ship and the South Mole along with the more traditional recreations. For most it was a chance to unwind and for the 'Jack-my-Hearties' among the crew the moment to strut about like battle-hardened veterans, picking fights with the Black Watch garrison. A three-week drought of beer was broken towards the end of July by the arrival of a convoy from Britain. OD Howard Spence of Portsmouth recalls the atmosphere.

We had shore leave and the main street in Gibraltar was a seething mass of sailors, soldiers, airmen and refugees. I remember having a few drinks in a bar and moving with mates to the main street and it was a mass of sailors and soldiers fighting each other. The next that I knew was being dumped in a picket boat and eventually it was dark and I fell asleep aboard the *Hood*.

But the war was never very far away. Fears of attack from Spain kept the ship ready to slip her moorings at a moment's notice. Then there was 'George', the Italian reconnaissance aircraft which appeared daily at 1800 but occasionally proved the harbinger of something worse. OD Spence:

Eventually being awoken by crashes, explosions and gunfire, I staggered to the upper deck to my position as loader in the 4in AA gun's crew and my mates warned me of trouble because there was an Italian air raid going on. CPO Sheppard listened to my excuses and I explained that my promotion board was coming up and that it would be a disaster if I went on Commander's Report. He relented and told me not to be so stupid in future and that kindness saved my life.

There remained just one more sortie, a second diversionary attack on Cagliari while the carrier *Argus* flew off a dozen Hurricanes for Malta, before the *Hood* turned her bows northward on 4 August. Her coveted position as Flagship Force H was to pass to the *Renown*. It was with regret that the *Hood*'s company watched Somerville haul down his flag at Scapa Flow, to be replaced by the uncharismatic regime of Vice Admiral William Whitworth. Nor was this all. The meridian sun that had kissed the *Hood*'s decks and men for a generation had shed its last beam on her.

12

Nemesis

ON MONDAY, 11 November 1940 HMS *Hood* gratefully entered Scapa Flow from a six-day patrol in the Bay of Biscay, her tired crew observing Armistice Day with red poppies fastened to their uniforms. A year later they and their ship would form part of that remembrance, another 1,400 flowers in the harvest of war. This chapter, which covers that year from the bleak winter of 1940–1 to the holocaust of the Denmark Strait, attempts to provide the structural, operational and psychological context of one of the greatest tragedies to befall the Royal Navy during the Second World War.

The autumn of 1940 was among the bleakest periods in the *Hood*'s career. In December, news that she would pass a second Christmas without leave apparently brought part of her stoker complement to the brink of mutiny. The threat of invasion was past but the Luftwaffe had now turned its resources to the bombing of British cities, placing an added strain on any whose family was on the receiving end. It was a depressing period that not even the raid on Taranto and the collapse of Italian arms in North Africa could lighten. Constant patrolling in terrible weather had left many exhausted and for the first time the strain of war began to take its toll on the *Hood*'s company. On 21 December Lt (E) Tristram Spence wrote a letter which captures the frustration and despair of the moment:

Dear Uncle Frank and Aunt May,

Herewith card to wish you, shall we say, a happier new year, for I doubt if there will be much to crow about in 1941. But we hope that we may emerge next year from this winter of our discontent a little more prosperously. [...] The ship is a little restless for leave having been at sea on and off since May and never having been in touch with wine, women and song for the entire nine months. We find our minds get a little diseased in this acrid bachelor atmosphere. It is rather refreshing to find that everybody manages to live in comparative harmony, boxed up as we are together, day in and day out.

Hard as the circumstances were, the spirit of comradeship never faltered in *Hood*, and the remarkable coming-together of branches and ranks which characterised the Navy at war was echoed in this ship as much as any other. On Christmas morning the midshipmen hosted the sergeants of Marines together with the chiefs and petty officers to drinks in the gunroom before lunch. On New Year's Eve it was the turn of the warrant officers, the master-at-arms and the Marine colour sergeant to celebrate Hogmanay in the wardroom with every officer in the ship from Vice Admiral Whitworth to the most junior midshipman. Two short patrols later and the *Hood* found herself at Rosyth for what would be her final refit, her crew dispersed by watches on their first leave in six months.

Drained of oil and emptied of ammunition, on 16 January the ship was hauled by tugs through the outer lock from the Forth and over to the flooded dry dock. Hawsers were then secured to her fairleads and she was drawn by electric capstans bow-first into No 1 dock, one of the few capable of accommodating her 860 feet. Once her bows had filled the niche at the head of the structure, the caisson was closed and the water pumped out until the ship had come to rest on an arrangement of carefully laid baulks of timber chained to the bottom of the graving dock. Immediately, parties of dockyard maties began coming aboard, welders, caulkers and shipwrights to replace fittings and equipment and effect repairs on her tired hull and structure. Particular attention was paid to the deck seams on the forecastle through which water poured into the ship at sea. Planking was renewed and pneumatic caulking tools put to work on the overlapping plates to staunch the leaks that were making life unbearable on the lower deck. The hull itself was inspected and scraped clean before a squad of formidable ladies with brushes on lengthy poles began applying a new layer of red lead paint. In earlier years prolonged spells in harbour and in temperate waters would have revealed a layer of marine growth encrusted on the ship's bottom. This time inspection showed it to be largely stripped of paint by the severity of her wartime service, fresh coats being applied over bare metal. Also at Rosyth was a team of engineers from John Brown & Co which spent a week dismantling her Clyde-built Brown-Curtis geared turbines and repairing damaged nozzles and misaligned wheels. Blades were renewed in the starboard inner turbine, stripped in the pursuit of the *Strasbourg* after the bombardment of Mers el-Kebir. However, the main work centred on the installation of radar in the shape of a Type-284 gunnery set on the spotting top and Type-279M air-warning equipment on the mainmast. Meanwhile, over in the fitting-out basin the new battleship *Prince of Wales* was in the final stages of completion.

There had been another change also. On 15 February, Capt Irvine Glennie, recently promoted Rear Admiral, was succeeded by Ralph Kerr who had made his name in destroyers. Kerr's new command had still to work up after her refit but as so often these plans were disrupted by news that German raiders had broken out into the Atlantic. On the afternoon of 18 March the *Hood* passed under the Forth Bridge for the very last time and hastened in search of the enemy. There was further disappointment for, despite hopes of an interception on 20 March, Admiral Günther Lütjens, the German squadron commander, slipped through the net and reached Brest with *Scharnhorst* and *Gneisenau* on the 22nd. Low on fuel, dawn on the 23rd found the *Hood* back at Scapa Flow.

It was at this time that news reached the *Hood* of a new German battleship and the name *Bismarck* was first uttered in her messdecks. Two years earlier on 14 February 1939 the Kriegsmarine had launched its first battleship since the Great War at the Blohm & Voss shipyard in Hamburg. The *Bismarck* mounted eight 38cm guns on a standard displacement of 41,800 tons, nearly 40 per cent of which was devoted to armour protection (as against 33.5 per cent in *Hood*). She was 823 feet long and capable of 30 knots. Commissioned in August 1940, she underwent extensive trials and exercises in the Baltic before being deemed ready for service in April 1941. The appearance of the *Bismarck* for the first time presented the *Hood* with an opponent armed and powered to the same standard as she. Until that moment much of the *Hood*'s crew had been glad to regard her as largely invulnerable to German surface vessels. As Sub-Lt (E) Brian Scott-Garrett (1940–1) later recalled, 'There was always a feeling of superiority about the *Hood*, that she was a magnificent ship, that nothing would ever go wrong with her'. The fate of the *Courageous* and *Royal Oak* soon demonstrated U-boat attack to be a major threat but the danger of air power seems to have been taken less seriously, despite the known weakness in *Hood*'s horizontal protection. Two weeks after *Hood* was bombed by a Ju88 in the North Sea, Sub-Lt John Iago advised his family to 'Console yourself about air attack on us; we think it would be quite impossible for aeroplanes to sink us – you should see our armour plate!' Nor, by all appearances, did Italian high-level bombing in the Mediterranean the following year shake his confidence: 'The more I have to do with it, the more faith I have in this ship. Bomb splinters only spoil the paintwork and aircraft are finding out that it is better to keep clear of us.' Admittedly such letters may owe more to a desire to calm family nerves than any firm conviction on the subject; Paymaster Lt Cdr A R Jackson (1938–40) can't very well have been serious when he penned the following to his wife on 20 September 1939, three days after the loss of the *Courageous*: 'I shouldn't be too worried in relation to me when you think of the *Courageous*. *Hood* is a very different kind of ship, and also is constructed quite differently, and so the chances of our being sunk, even if we are hit, can be considered negligible.' But the *Bismarck* was a very different proposition. AB Len Williams remembers the tenor of messdeck discussions during his last months in the ship in 1941:

As an ex-member of *Hood*'s crew I can recall numerous discussions we had in our mess about a possible meeting with either *Bismarck* or her sister *Tirpitz*. We were not at all happy about such a prospect. We knew our weakness and the risks of not having an armoured deck. We had the speed, yes, and we had the gun power; but we did not have our armour in the right place!

By the end of April few in the *Hood* can have had much doubt as to the vulnerability of their ship in the event of a confrontation with the *Bismarck*. On the 19th, following reports that *Bismarck* had sailed from Kiel towards the North Sea, Vice Admiral William Whitworth issued his battle orders should contact be made. Sub-Lt R G Robertson RNVR, who had joined the ship at Devonport in May 1940, recalls Whitworth's instructions:

> Next day Admiral Whitworth made known his plans if an enemy report was received; our escorts, the cruiser *Kenya* and three destroyers, would act as a searching force, and if the *Bismarck* were encountered we would close on the enemy at speed in order to bring the guns of the *Hood* within effective range. If possible, we would make the approach end-on so as to present the minimum target.

For the first time, too, a fatalistic note emerges in surviving correspondence from the *Hood*. On 1 May Lt Cdr Roger Batley wrote this to his sister Mary: 'I am sorry Uncle Roger has gone. But quite agree, suddenly – like he & Charlie – is by far the best way to go, & I hope when my time comes that I shall go that way also.' Even Boy Bill Crawford sensed that something was up: 'We haven't been away very long, but have had some tense hours since I left. And now that Germany has started sending her warships out there looks as if there will be <u>action</u> for the Fleet soon. Anyway, the sooner we get them the better.' That day was not far off. Nine years earlier, a walk on the shores of the Cromarty Firth in May 1932 had left Mid Louis Le Bailly with a terrible premonition of the fate that awaited his ship:

> We trained so hard that one day in the Cromarty Firth the chaplain gave us an afternoon off to play the wardroom at golf on the lovely course at Nigg (alas no longer in use). Later we were also to be the wardroom's guests in the pub (still there). Thus it was, at peace with ourselves, and pleasantly tipsy from a modest, but, for us, unusual quantity of McEwans Scotch Ale, that we walked back to the jetty through the heather-scented twilight to the sorrowful questing note of the curlew. I remember shivering, as if drenched in ice, and putting it down to the McEwans I had imbibed. But it was late in May, possibly the 24th, the day HMS *Hood* blew up in action with the *Bismarck* and all but three of her 1500 crew lost.

For Le Bailly, now Senior Engineer in the cruiser *Naiad*, there was to be one last visit:

Seventeen months [after leaving her], in April 1941, HMS *Naiad* anchored close to *Hood* in Scapa Flow. The midshipmen for whose engineering instruction I had been responsible, had just passed for sub-lieutenant and were celebrating their success and departure and requested my assistance. Hearing that I had accepted, [Lt Cdr (E) J G M] Erskine invited me to supper after the gunroom had finished with me. When leaving I found a couple of dozen or so of the ship's company, not all from the engine department, waiting to say goodbye and to wish me luck. Who arranged this, I shall never know. In less than six weeks they all were dead.

Death in battle has an arbitrary quality impossible for any survivor to explain or grasp. To be spared the fate of one's comrades, to find oneself preserved when they have lost everything, is beyond the pale of reason; for some, indeed, physical survival proved to be beyond mental endurance. The fate of the *Hood*, annihilated in a matter of seconds, affords this reality a starkness which sets her loss apart from most others. Submarine crews were routinely wiped out but ships' companies much less often: the destroyer *Exmouth*, the corvette *Gladiolus* and the cruiser *Sydney* are among the relatively few examples of the Second World War. Others suffered a slow and terrible attrition by fire and water: the cruisers *Dunedin*, *Neptune* and *Indianapolis*, the *Scharnhorst* and *Bismarck* herself. But one needs to return to the First World War to find precedent for large ships being destroyed with all but a handful of men: the vanquished of Coronel and the Falklands; above all the disasters at Jutland which prefigured that of *Hood* herself. The experience of those who survived the loss of the *Hood* will be dealt with in due course. But what of those who were spared death yet had to live the experience vicariously in the sufferings of those who replaced them, who escaped through an inscrutable turn of fate? Some like PO Len Williams, drafted on promotion in February 1941 after five years in the ship, had reached the end of a particular phase in their career. The time had come to move on. Others like OA Bert Pitman got an unexpected 'pierhead jump' to another ship, in his case the battleship *Barham* whose sinking he survived later that year. In April Latham Jenson was one of the last party of midshipmen to take their sub lieutenants' exams in *Hood*. The stakes couldn't have been higher: '... those of us facing our examinations for acting sub-lieutenant those lovely Scapa days in April had lots to reflect upon, more than we knew. Failure, and consequently remaining on board for another run, in this case would actually mean death!' Others survived by being selected for officer training. After a statutory three months as Ordinary Seamen on the lower deck, those who wished to receive a commission or who had otherwise been identified as being of officer material were tested and, if successful, drafted for further training ashore. One such was B A Carlisle:

Despite the fact that I was a clumsy Ordinary Seaman it fortunately did not stop me from being chosen to go for a Commission. About every three months the Captain of the ship (Glennie at the time) presided over a Board to decide who was potential Officer material, and my Board must have been in January 1941. Having had the privilege of public school education and having been a prefect and an officer in the school OTC, I fortunately did satisfy the Board that I was Officer material, although very sadly some of my friends from a similar background failed the Board, and as there was no further Board until May, went down with the ship ...

Another was Jon Pertwee, unwittingly passed as a CW (Commissions and Warrants) candidate after half an hour explaining the finer points of broadcast radio to Capt Kerr. He and OD Howard Spence were part of the last draft to leave the *Hood* on or about 21 May, the eve of her sailing against the *Bismarck*. But as Spence's memoir reveals, there were other ways of escaping the *Hood*:

Some 13 of our crew, myself and Jon Pertwee included, had draft chits to go south. Another was a matelot who had hit a PO with a rifle. On route to Pompey I stopped at a pub near Victoria station in London (Waterloo had been bombed) and at the end of the bar was a stocky chap in nondescript clothes – he was a deserter from the *Hood* – neither of us spoke, but went our separate ways.

Lucky as they were, there were men who enjoyed even greater good fortune. A day or two before she left Scapa for the last time Sub-Lt R G Robertson was taken ill with a perforated duodenal ulcer and transported across the Flow to the hospital ship *Amarapoora*. Another, Mid Harold Carnell, given compassionate leave from the *Hood*, was recalled by telegram but failed to reach Scapa thanks to a protracted wartime rail journey.

Then there were those for whom Fortuna's wheel turned in the contrary direction. As Lt Cdr Roger Batley, a member of Vice Admiral Whitworth's staff, informed his sister on 12 May, his remaining in the ship depended on whether the new admiral, Lancelot Holland, liked the cut of his jib. The admiral evidently did. Two days later another staff officer, Paymaster Lt Robert Browne, wrote telling his parents that 'I am staying on here for about 5 weeks with the new Admiral until they are all settled in, then I will be relieved. As to what follows once again I cannot say.' Others went to their deaths with an eagerness that haunted those who remembered them. Surgeon Lt Cdr R Ransome-Wallis RNVR was principal medical officer of the cruiser *London*:

I also recollected sadly a very young midshipman who had spent a couple of days in *London*'s Sick Bay. He had recently been sunk in another ship and had only survived after a bit of an ordeal. He said to me rather bravely 'But I shall be all right now sir, I am going to the *Hood*.'

For those who were spared there was no doubt enormous relief, but also a measure of guilt: guilt that they had not been there with their friends, guilt that someone had died in their place. So it is when a great ship and her company are destroyed. Short of nuclear war, only in naval combat is it possible for a unit to be annihilated in battalion or double battalion strength in the twinkling of an eye. On this awful reality rests much of its depth and fascination. For HMS *Hood* that dread moment had come.

By the spring of 1941 the Admiralty was girding itself for an onslaught of German commerce-raiding sorties against convoys in the Atlantic. On 14 February the heavy cruiser *Hipper* returned to Brest having sunk over 30,000 tons of merchant shipping. At the end of March the armoured cruiser *Admiral Scheer* reached Norway after a prolonged sortie during which sixteen merchantmen and the armed merchant cruiser *Jervis Bay* had been destroyed for a total of nearly 115,000 tons. All the while the battlecruisers *Scharnhorst* and *Gneisenau* were abroad in the Atlantic, making Brest on 22 March after a two-month operation during which twenty-two ships had been sunk or captured and the entire Atlantic convoy system disrupted. Then on 19 April came reports that the new battleship *Bismarck* had sailed from Kiel, steering northwest towards the North Sea. These proved false, but apart from drawing the *Hood* into the Norwegian Sea on another wild goose chase they decided Admiral Sir John Tovey, Commander-in-Chief Home Fleet, to maintain a permanent vigil on the northern exits leading to the Atlantic. Meanwhile a concerted campaign of minelaying and above all aerial bombardment greatly reduced the options open to the German High Command. In early April it seemed as if the *Scharnhorst* and the *Gneisenau* might be unleashed with *Bismarck* and the heavy cruiser *Prinz Eugen* in a catastrophic breakout into the Atlantic. In the event, boiler repairs to the *Scharnhorst* made her unavailable before June, while the *Gneisenau* was heavily damaged in repeated attacks on Brest by RAF Bomber and Coastal Command. To the north, extensive minelaying in the Denmark Strait and the Iceland–Faeroes gap narrowed the already constricted waterways through which any German force had to pass in order to reach the Atlantic shipping lanes.

By early May persistent German aerial reconnaissance between Greenland and Jan Mayen Island in the Arctic Sea had made it increasingly plain to the Admiralty that the long-awaited appearance of the *Bismarck* was nigh. Already on 28 April the *Hood* had sailed from the dismal anchorage of Hvalfjord in southern Iceland as distant cover for two eastbound convoys against surface attack. For a time it was thought that an attack on Iceland or Jan Mayen might be afoot, but by 18 May Tovey and his staff had concluded that a naval breakout was the more likely outcome and on that day the heavy cruiser *Suffolk*, then on patrol in the Denmark Strait, was warned to be on her guard for the appearance of German warships. These fears were confirmed on 21 May with news that a German squadron was refuelling near Bergen in Norway. This was the *Bismarck* and the *Prinz Eugen* which had sailed under Admiral Lütjens from the Baltic port of Gdynia (Gotenhafen) on either side of midnight on the 18th. Their departure had been delayed almost a month by the mining of *Prinz Eugen* in the Fehmarn Belt off Kiel; Lütjens would have had it delayed until the *Scharnhorst* or *Tirpitz* were ready to join him, but he was overruled by Grössadmiral Erich Raeder, the head of the German navy. The aim was to enter the Atlantic on a commerce-raiding sortie via the Denmark Strait, but 'Rhine Exercise' (*Rheinübung*) as it was called was compromised from the outset. Even before it had cleared the Kattegat, the body of water separating Denmark and Sweden, the German squadron was sighted by the Swedish cruiser *Gotland* which promptly reported the matter to the naval authorities ashore. Lütjens' foreboding was to be realised for by the end of that day, 20 May, the report had reached the Admiralty in London. On the morning of the 21st the *Bismarck* reached Grimstadfjorden near Bergen and it was here that an RAF Spitfire photographed Lütjens' force from an altitude of 25,000 feet. That evening, just as *Bismarck* and *Prinz Eugen* put to sea once more, Admiral Tovey ordered the Battle Cruiser Squadron to sail from Scapa to Hvalfjord. At 2356 *Hood* and *Prince of Wales* and six destroyers weighed anchor and exited the Flow shortly after midnight under a veil of rain and mist. By 0100 on the 22nd they were through the Hoxa Boom and out into the Atlantic. The chase from which the *Hood* would not return had begun.

Two weeks earlier Vice Admiral William Whitworth had struck his flag, being succeeded on 12 May by Lancelot Holland, Vice Admiral Battle Cruiser Squadron and Second-in-Command, Home Fleet. Relatively little is known about Holland who was born at Eydon in Oxfordshire in 1887 and specialised in gunnery before the First World War. He first comes to prominence as Assistant Chief of Naval Staff at the Admiralty in 1937–8 and then as Rear Admiral 2nd Battle Squadron in 1938–9. In 1939 he was briefly appointed as the naval representative to the joint Air Ministry-Admiralty staff advising on enemy attacks on shipping, before assuming command of the 18th Cruiser Squadron the following year. In November 1940 this force took part in Operation COLLAR, one of the early defended convoys in the Mediterranean which resulted in the inconclusive Battle of Cape Spartivento off Sardinia. Days before he joined *Hood* Holland had led his cruiser squadron north to Jan Mayen to capture the German weather trawler *München*. On the 7th she was surprised and boarded by the destroyer *Somali* which managed to recover cipher material of great importance to the breaking of the Enigma code. 'Len' Holland as he was known to his friends was part of a clique of officers, eventually headed by Dudley Pound, which monopolised many of the senior posts in the Navy from the early 1930s. The Battle Cruiser Squadron was to have been his last seagoing command before he returned to the Admiralty as Pound's Vice Chief of Naval Staff in succession to Rear Admiral Sir Tom Phillips in late 1941. He had hopes of one day becoming First Sea Lord. It was not to be.

Holland had, of course, little opportunity to make an impression on the ship's company. A more reserved man than Whitworth, one of the very few opinions on him to have survived is that of Lt Cdr Roger Batley to his sister on 19 May, three days before *Hood* sailed on her last voyage: 'Last night I dined with the new Admiral. I like him. We had gulls' eggs, soup, lobster & pheasant.' Equally, little survives to record the atmosphere in the *Hood* as she sailed to her fate. The only source of note is Ordinary Signalman Ted Briggs's memoir of the bridge and boys' mess deck, but it is possible to imagine the preparations and emotions throughout the ship as she girded her loins for the coming battle. Initially, however, there was nothing to indicate that this sortie would not end as inconclusively as the many that had preceded it. The squadron had been ordered to refuel at Hvalfjord on 22 May before joining the heavy cruisers *Norfolk* and *Suffolk* on patrol in the Denmark Strait. Routine gunnery exercises were performed during the forenoon and then the afternoon watches of the 22nd. Meanwhile, the crew viewed the chances of encountering the enemy on this their fifteenth war patrol since returning from Gibraltar the previous summer with some scepticism. The *Hood*, after all, had not laid eyes on an Axis man-o'-war since 1938. However, all this changed at around 2030 when the Battle Cruiser Squadron was ordered to abandon its passage into Hvalfjord and make directly for its patrol line in the Denmark Strait. An RAF reconnaissance flight over Grimstadfjorden that afternoon had found the anchorage empty. Though Tovey and his staff did not know it, *Bismarck* and *Prinz Eugen* had been racing north for twenty-four hours. The news evidently came as something of a shock in the *Hood*. Ted Briggs:

> As soon as the *Hood* had altered course in accordance with the [2030] signal of the C-in-C, Commander [W K R] Cross updated the ship's company of the situation, and for the first time the nervous feeling of an approach to battle began to build up. 'Perhaps this is it,' I wondered. 'Perhaps this is the big one.' The feeling that I was hungry, yet did not want to eat, nagged at my stomach. Looking around me, I could see my mates yawning nervously and trying to appear unconcerned. We all knew it was an act, yet we did not discuss the possibilities of action seriously.

For all this, the morning of the 23rd brought a familiar sense of anticlimax. The night had passed off uneventfully; the sun rose to the usual routine of action stations and endless vigil, of frigid watches staring into the grey unity of sea and sky. AB Robert Tilburn, manning a 4in gun on the boat deck, was clad in long johns, a vest, sweater, overalls, trousers, overcoat, duffle coat, oilskins, anti-flash gear, tin helmet, gas mask and gloves. Another gunnery exercise was held in the afternoon watch as the weather began to deteriorate. Those off duty played cards, read and wrote letters destined never to be sent as Vera Lynn echoed across the mess decks, the last woman's voice many of them would ever hear.

At 1930 that evening this reverie was abruptly and definitively broken. Ten minutes earlier the *Suffolk*, patrolling a hundred miles northwest of Iceland, had sighted *Bismarck* and *Prinz Eugen* as they began the southward leg of their passage through the Denmark Strait. From the mists enveloping him Capt R M Ellis signalled 'From *Suffolk*: Enemy in sight'. A few minutes later the *Norfolk*, wearing the flag of Rear Admiral W F Wake-Walker, strayed too close to the edge of the fog bank shrouding her and was immediately given a taste of the *Bismarck*'s gunnery, straddled before she could regain cover. Three hundred miles due south Holland left his admiral's bridge and installed himself on the compass platform with Capt Kerr and his staff. At 1939 he ordered the Battle Cruiser Squadron to work up to full speed and shape an intercepting course of 295 degrees. A little after 2000 a signal from *Suffolk*, now shadowing by radar, confirmed that it was the *Bismarck* and her consort towards which he was heading at an aggregate speed of some 50 knots. After a day of routine, the revelation that battle was again a distinct possibility had a sobering effect in the *Hood*. Nothing, not even Mers el-Kebir, had prepared them for this impending collision. Ted Briggs: 'With this sudden diversion the ship's company were alive again to the realization that deadly action could be just ten hours away. The back of my neck began to prickle with excitement, and I found myself stuttering slightly, a nervous habit which until then I had managed to conquer since the age of ten.' Within an hour of the alteration of course, Holland's squadron was crashing into a full gale at 27 knots, wind and water forcing *Hood* and *Prince of Wales* to train their forward turrets to port. The *Hood*, battered and riven by war, was as beautiful as ever as she steamed into her last battle. The sight offered her consorts in the hours left to her cannot have differed greatly from that recalled by the Rev Gordon Taylor from the destroyer *Arrow* off Iceland on Easter Sunday, 13 April 1941:

> I took no services that Easter Day, for the sea was too rough and the closest attention had to be paid to the *Hood* as she made flag signals to her escorts – but I watched her for hours on the *Arrow*'s bridge. As she was only about two cables (or 1200 feet) abeam away from me she was truly a magnificent sight as she drove along, zig-zagging to foil U-boats, in the green and gold sea whenever the sun came out upon her. [...] I felt unbelievably privileged to be watching her and [...] had already decided the whole experience of seeing the *Hood* that morning would be completely imperishable, and so it has proved to be for 60 years.

Before long the buffeting endured by the four destroyers left in the squadron had obliged them to reduce speed to avoid structural damage. At 2200, as the destroyer screen fell astern, a broadcast by Cdr William Cross informed the men that contact with the enemy was expected at 0200 on the 24th and that they had two hours to change into clean underwear and ready themselves before the ship went to action stations. Ted Briggs:

> Apprehension was heavy in the air. I think that most of my mates, like myself, were fearing not instant oblivion but the horror of being fearfully wounded or mutilated and screaming out in painful insanity. I had the depressing dread of being afraid of fear and showing it. Yet I was not feeling afraid – just wound up. I wanted the action to be hurried on, and yet at the same time I did not want it to happen. Wouldn't I wake up tomorrow in my hammock and find it was all a mistake?

His sentiments are echoed by Bob Tilburn: 'Everyone was prepared as far as they could be. Everyone knew that there would be casualties, but it would be someone else, not you. No one thought that the *Hood* would be sunk. No one gave it a thought. But there would be casualties, which were to be expected.' And so the last preparations were made. The last shells fused and torpedo warheads inspected, the fire and damage-control parties mustered, the galley fires extinguished and instruments laid out in the Medical Distributing Stations. Words exchanged, bladders emptied. At midnight the bugle sounded its galvanising call over the tannoy and the men hastened to the positions from which their minds had not strayed in many hours.

Shortly after midnight Holland ordered the *Hood*'s immense battle ensign hoisted but, even as it unfurled in the wind, events 120 miles to the north were eroding his tactical advantage. By 0030 it was obvious that the *Suffolk*, the only vessel in Wake-Walker's force equipped with effective search radar, had lost contact with the enemy in a blizzard. At this Holland informed his squadron that if contact were not regained by 0210 he would alter course to the south until such time as it had been re-established. In the event, Holland decided not to wait that long and at 0203 he hauled *Hood* and *Prince of Wales* round onto a course of 200 degrees, the last reported heading of the German squadron. Having now caught up with the heavy ships his destroyers were ordered to continue their search to the north and played no further part in the interception. The men went down to the second degree of readiness.

Until then Holland had intended to close the *Bismarck* at speed from her port bow, a tactic which would not only shorten the range between the two squadrons in quick time but minimise the number of guns that could be brought to bear against him as he did so. By the time *Suffolk* had reported regaining contact at 0247 and the *Hood*'s relative bearing on the enemy been determined, the *Bismarck* was 35 miles distant and steering a diverging course at 28 knots. This meant that Holland had not only 'lost bearing' on the enemy but had no prospect of regaining it either. Rather than the end-on attack for which he had planned, any approach had now to be made on the *Bismarck*'s port beam and in the teeth of her main armament. As at Trafalgar, the Battle Cruiser Squadron would have to endure a prolonged exposure to the full weight of enemy fire before being able to bring its own broadsides to bear. Aware of the *Hood's* vulnerability to plunging fire, on 19 May Holland had endorsed the tactics laid down by Whitworth a month earlier in the event of an encounter with the *Bismarck* and from these he seems never to have strayed. Holland's adherence to this plan despite the adverse tactical situation that now presented itself has been the subject of trenchant criticism. The outcome of the Battle of the Denmark Strait leaves no doubt how disastrous it proved to be. However, like most a posteriori judgements of this sort, these generally fail to embrace the wider context of Holland's decision-making. For an officer who had served during the First World War, who recalled the unbearable frustration of an unwilling and elusive enemy and the chagrin of tainted victory, there could only be one tactic against the principal unit of the new German navy. Despite Jellicoe's caution at Jutland and the vague caveats of the Fighting Instructions as they applied to battlecruisers, the tradition of the Royal Navy was to bring the enemy to battle no matter what the risk or tactical disadvantage implied by it. On this her matchless fighting record was built. On this, too, one of her greatest ships was to be sacrificed.

At 0340 Holland ordered revolutions for 28 knots and brought *Hood* and *Prince of Wales* onto a course of 240 degrees to force the enemy to battle. By 0430 visibility had improved and dozens of pairs of eyes were scanning the northwestern horizon where, 30 miles off, *Bismarck* and *Prinz Eugen* were steaming towards their unexpected encounter. Shortly after 0500 Holland passed the order to 'Prepare for instant action', the men rousing themselves to the first degree of readiness. On the compass platform actors took their places for the final drama. Ted Briggs:

In the dimness of the binnacle and chart-table lights I could make out a stage-like setting. On the starboard, facing forward, stood the robust figure of Commander E H G 'Tiny' Gregson, the squadron gunnery officer, and Lieutenant-Commander G E M Owens, the admiral's secretary. Alongside, centre of stage, in the captain's chair was Admiral Holland, with Captain Kerr on his right. Then on the port side were [Lt Cdr H D] Wyldbore-Smith, Commander S J P Warrand, the squadron navigating officer, eighteen-year-old Bill Dundas, action midshipman of the watch, Chief Yeoman [George Carn], who was attending the captain, Yeoman [George] Wright, who looked after the demands of the officer of the watch at the binnacle, and myself, who was required to attend the flag lieutenant and answer voice-pipes. All the officers, except Holland and Kerr, were huddled in duffle coats, over which was anti-flash gear, topped off by steel helmets. Some had their gas-masks slung on their chests. [...] The short, slim admiral preferred to emphasize his rank by wearing his 'bum-freezer' type of greatcoat. He sat bolt upright, with his binoculars' strap around his neck, his fingers somewhat nervously tapping the glasses themselves.

Then they were upon the enemy. At 0535 lookouts in *Hood* and *Prince of Wales* sighted the German squadron at a range of approximately 38,000 yards:

> The sighting was reported by voice-pipe from the spotting-top as 'Alarm starboard green 40.' I did not have any binoculars, so I could not see the top-masts, which everyone else was focusing on, but the maximum visibility from our perch was seventeen miles at this time. Almost in a whisper Captain Kerr commanded: 'Pilot, make the enemy report.'

Holland's force was sighted almost simultaneously by the German ships but its presence was already suspected. At 0515 hydrophone operators in *Prinz Eugen* had detected the sound of high-performance turbines to the southeast and it was on this horizon that two columns of smoke were spotted in the cold light of morning. At 0537 Holland ordered a 40-degree turn to starboard which placed Lütjens' force broadside on and fine on his port bow. And so the *Hood* screamed into battle at almost 29 knots. Twenty degrees off her starboard quarter lay *Prince of Wales* at a distance of four cables (800 yards). To Kapitänleutnant Burkard von Müllenheim-Rechberg, surveying the spectacle from *Bismarck*'s after gunnery control position, the squadron looked like 'an enraged bull charging without knowing what he's up against'.

Waiting to be hoisted from the *Hood*'s flag deck was Flag 5, the order to *Prince of Wales* to open fire. Shortly after leaving Scapa on the 22nd, Holland signalled Capt John Leach of the *Prince of Wales* what his gunnery tactics would be: 'If the enemy is encountered and concentration of fire required, the policy will be G.I.C. (individual ship control); if ships are spread when enemy is met they are to be prepared to flank mark as described in HWCO 26.' Translated, these instructions called for *Hood* and *Prince of Wales* to concentrate their fire on *Bismarck* while the now-absent escorts positioned themselves to provide corrections for gunnery range and deflection. This decision was confirmed in a second signal at 0030 on the 24th which also stated Holland's intention that *Norfolk* and *Suffolk* should engage *Prinz Eugen*. In the event, neither aspect of Holland's plan came to fruition. Radio silence prevented the orders being transmitted to *Norfolk* and *Suffolk*, which consequently took no part in the action. Moreover, in requiring *Prince of Wales* to maintain such close order Holland not only denied Leach the freedom to manoeuvre his ship but made it possible for the Germans to find his range with a minimum of targeting adjustment after *Hood* was lost. The first circumstance was probably inevitable; the second rather less so.

But this lay in the future. At 0549 Holland ordered a further turn of 20 degrees to starboard to close the range once more. A minute later he ordered concentration on the leading ship in the German squadron. This was not *Bismarck* but *Prinz Eugen* which Lütjens had ordered into the van after his flagship's radar had broken down while engaging *Norfolk* the previous evening.

The error was immediately spotted in *Prince of Wales* and fire redistributed accordingly, but it was against *Prinz Eugen* that *Hood*'s forward guns now trained with an awe-inspiring rumble. None would survive from the *Hood*'s turrets but the following passage by Admiral of the Fleet Sir Henry Leach, turret officer in *Duke of York* at the Battle of North Cape, gives an impression of the atmosphere as their crews went into action:

> Then came the long-awaited order 'All positions stand to!' In an instant, tiredness, cold and seasickness were shed and all hands became poised for their individual tasks. 'Follow Director', and the huge turret swung round in line with the Director Control Tower. 'All guns load with armour-piercing and full-charge – load, load, *load*!'; the clatter of hoists as they brought the shells and cordite charges from the magazines, the rattle of rammers as they drove them into the chambers of the guns and the slam of the breeches as they closed were music to all. Then a great stillness for seemingly endless minutes, disturbed only by the squelch of hydraulics as layers and trainers followed the pointers in the receivers from the Director. 'Broadsides!', and the interceptors, connecting the firing circuits right up to the Director Layer's trigger, were closed; a glance at the range receiver whose counters were steadily, inexorably, ticking down …

Then the ticking stopped. At 0552 *Hood* fired her opening salvo against *Prinz Eugen* at a range of 25,000 yards. *Prince of Wales* followed against *Bismarck* a few seconds later.

Elsewhere in the ship the moment of firing doubtless came as an intense, almost exquisite release of nervous tension. Years later, Ted Briggs recalled casting his mind over the ship and her crew as she went into action:

> I could visualize how the mates I knew in other departments would be preparing. Ron Bell was on the flag deck at the other end of the voice-pipe I was manning. His voice did not betray any signs of funk, as I was sure mine did. Near him would be [Frank] Tuxworth, helping to handle the halyards and still joking, no doubt. Alongside in charge of the flags I guessed that Yeoman Bill Nevett would be as outwardly calm as ever, despite the pallor of his face. On the boat deck I knew another mate, Petty Officer Stan Boardman, would be readying the crew of [Sammy], the starboard multiple pom-pom. Would he be thinking of his adored wife and his newly born baby or would he be questioning what on earth he could do with his anti-aircraft guns against the *Bismarck*'s fifteen-inchers? And what of the sick-bay, where I had spent the first few days of my life in the ship? There the 'tiffies' under Surgeon Commander [Henry] Hurst and Sick-Bay Petty Officer [George] Stannard would be sterilizing operating instruments, laying out blankets, making sure bandages were handy.

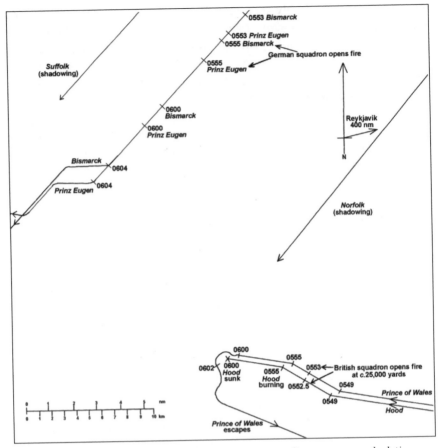

Sketch map of the Battle of the Denmark Strait, 24 May 1941. Courses, ranges and relative positions approximate.

In the damage-control centre the First Lieutenant Lt Cdr John Machin awaited the first call on his organisation. Standing by to repair damaged circuitry or perhaps on duty in the high-power switchboard room for which he was responsible was the ship's electrical engineer, Lt John Iago. Not far away the Marine bandsmen chased pointers and wound wheels in the transmitting station as the *Hood*'s guns struggled to find the range. There was ERA Bert Hemmings, immured perhaps in his workshop, and OD Philip X and Boy Bill Crawford in ammo supply somewhere, listening as the Rev Patrick Stewart broadcast what Briggs remembered as a 'very calm, matter-of-fact running commentary' of events over the tannoy. Further below, in spaces Stewart's voice would never penetrate, Sub-Lt (E) John Cambridge, late of the Yarrow Co, Glasgow, tended one of the ship's boiler rooms in an inferno of heat and hell of noise. Then there was the 'Chief' himself, Cdr (E) Terence Grogan, performing a miracle of naval engineering from the control platform of the forward engine room. To this miracle the speed of his ship and the efforts of her consort to keep pace bear witness. Vice Admiral Sir Louis Le Bailly (1932–3, 1937–9): 'I shall always hope that, just as he died, he became aware that the brand-new HMS *Prince of Wales* was having difficulty in keeping up with her twenty-year-old flagship as Grogan drove *Hood* into her last battle.' Like much else during her last minutes, the number and placing of the *Hood*'s salvoes is a matter for conjecture. AB Bob Tilburn recalled six salvoes from the forward turrets and Ted Briggs at least one from 'X' turret but the actual numbers may never be established. It seems likely that she did indeed redirect her fire from *Prinz Eugen* to *Bismarck* but at what stage and to what effect is not known for certain. Holland had prohibited the use of radar during the approach to battle but it must be supposed that *Hood*'s Type-284 gunnery set was in action by the time she opened fire. What is certain is that none of her shells registered on their targets. The reasons for this are not far to seek. Not only had her firepower been reduced by half by the angle of approach, but the turret rangefinders were being drenched in spray as she thundered into a head sea at 29 knots, the speed at which vibration in the spotting top became 'excessive'. Gunnery conditions that morning closely matched those recorded by Capt Pridham in the spring of 1938 and the pneumatic cleaning apparatus attached to the rangefinder windows is unlikely to have coped with the deluge. Accuracy must therefore have rested on the 30-foot rangefinder in the armoured director, such information as may have been provided by radar and the *Hood*'s inadequate Mk-V Dreyer Table. In view of the conditions, the probable need to shift target and the high rate of change of range as *Hood* closed the enemy, her failure to land a hit is not to be wondered at.

No such difficulty faced *Bismarck* and *Prinz Eugen*, and the Battle of the Denmark Strait would provide a further demonstration of the lethal accuracy of German naval gunnery. After a brief delay the German squadron took *Hood* under fire against the morning horizon. Soon their shells were screaming in 'like an express train going through a tunnel'. *Bismarck*'s first salvo, unleashed at 0555, fell just wide. Her second straddled, the *Hood* pressing on between towering geysers of water. But it was *Prinz Eugen* which drew first blood. A shell from her second salvo struck *Hood* on the boat deck, the Rev Stewart calmly informing the crew that 'That sound you heard was *Hood* being hit at the base of the mainmast'. As Briggs recalled, the blast sent those on the compass platform sprawling over the deck:

Then I was flung off my feet. My ears were ringing as if I had been in the striking-chamber of Big Ben. I picked myself up, thinking I had made a complete fool of myself, but everyone else on the compass platform was also scrambling to his feet. [Cdr (G) E H G] 'Tiny' Gregson walked almost sedately out to the starboard wing of the platform to find out what had happened.

When he returned it was to inform Holland that 'She has hit us on the boat deck and there is a fire in the ready-use lockers'. Etched on Briggs's memory was the grin on Gregson's face as he uttered these words, the grim satisfaction of the fighting officer whose ship was at last to win her spurs. If so, the sensation was a fleeting one because *Hood*'s agony had already begun. *Prinz Eugen*'s shell had started an uncontrollable fire among dozens of ready-use lockers for 4in and UP ammunition which soon began to take a terrible toll of the boat-deck personnel. Mindful of Mers el-Kebir, orders had been passed for the gun crews to take cover in the lobby beneath the bridge structure when action commenced and it was here, between the reading room and the dental surgery, that many gathered. One of those who stayed behind was AB Bob Tilburn, a member of the crew serving Port No 1 gun abreast the after funnel. As the ammunition began detonating, PO Edward Bishop came aft and ordered Tilburn and two others to help put it out, to which they wisely told him, 'When it stops exploding, we will'. However, others were spotted from *Prince of Wales* making futile efforts to control the blaze with deck hoses. The same wind that was dousing the *Hood*'s rangefinders with spray fanned this fire into an enormous conflagration that swept back over the roof of 'X' turret, pulsating in a lurid pinkish flame as ammunition went off like fire crackers. Rear Admiral Wake-Walker describes the scene from *Norfolk*, 30,000 yards off:

> I can describe it best as a brilliant rose colour with no yellow or white in it. [...]
> This was at the time the fire first appeared in the *Hood*. [...] I watched this fire
> and it then spread forward until its length was greater than its height and after
> a time it died down, particularly at the forward end. I thought that they may be
> able to get this fire under control. Previous to this I had been so impressed by
> the fire that [I thought] the ship would not continue as a fighting unit.

But much worse was to come. No sooner had Bishop returned to the bridge structure to report the matter to an officer than a shell landed inside making a terrible execution of the two hundred men sheltering there, a massacre only Tilburn lived to relate. On the compass platform this carnage unfolded not in the eyes but in the ears of those present. Ted Briggs:

> Then came a crazy cacophony of wild cries of 'Fire' through the voice-pipes
> and telephones. On the amidships boat deck a fierce blaze flared. This was
> punctuated by loud explosions. The torpedo officer [Lt Cdr Anthony Pares]
> reported by phone: 'The four-inch ready-use ammunition is exploding.' I could
> hear the UP rockets going up, just as they had roared off accidentally in
> Gibraltar a year earlier. Fear gripped my intestines again as agonized screams
> of the wounded and dying emitted from the voice-pipes. The screeching turned
> my blood almost to ice. [...] But the bursting projectiles were making a
> charnel-house of positions above the upper deck. The screams of the maimed

kept up a strident chorus through the voice-pipes and from the flag deck. I was certain I heard my 'oppo' Ron Bell shouting for help.

Echoing the assessment of Tilburn and his companions, Holland ordered the fire on the boat deck to be left to burn until the ammunition had been expended. He had, in any case, far more pressing concerns than this. The *Hood* was being hammered and the moment when the squadron's full weight of fire was brought to bear could not be delayed much longer. At about 0555 Holland passed the order for a 20-degree turn to port to open the 'A' arcs of 'X' and 'Y' turrets. Ted Briggs:

> 'Turn twenty degrees to port together,' he commanded. Chief Yeoman [George Carn] passed the word on to the flag deck, where surprisingly someone still seemed to be capable of obeying orders. Two blue – flag 2, a blue pendant – went up the yard-arm. I remember musing: 'Not everyone on the flag deck is dead then.'

On came the *Hood*, shells raining down as her after turrets strained against the stops to find bearing on the enemy. His approach completed, at approximately 0600 Holland ordered another 20-degree turn to port. It was just seven or eight minutes since she had opened fire. Until now Holland and his officers had followed the progress of the battle with the steely composure of their forebears, outwardly unperturbed by the havoc being wreaked on their ship. But this detachment was not to last. Even as the *Hood* began to execute her turn, a shell from *Bismarck*'s fifth salvo was hurtling in from about 16,000 yards. With it came the mortal hit. Capt John Leach of *Prince of Wales*:

> I happened to be looking at *Hood* at the moment when a salvo arrived and it appeared to be across the ship somewhere about the mainmast. In that salvo there were, I think, two shots short and one over, but it may have been the other way round. But I formed the impression at the time that something had arrived on board *Hood* in a position just before the mainmast and slightly to starboard. It was not a very definite impression that I had, but it was sufficiently definite to make me look at *Hood* for a further period. I in fact wondered what the result was going to be, and between one and two seconds after I formed that impression an explosion took place in the *Hood* which appeared to me to come from very much the same position in the ship. There was a very fierce upward rush of flame the shape of a funnel, rather a thin funnel, and almost instantaneously the ship was enveloped in smoke from one end to the other.

For Ted Briggs, time, which had been passing with agonising slowness, seemed now to stop altogether:

As the *Hood* turned, X turret roared in approval, but its Y twin stayed silent. And then a blinding flash swept around the outside of the compass platform. Again I found myself being lifted off my feet and dumped head first on the deck. This time, when I got up with the others, the scene was different. Everything was cold and unreal. The ship which had been a haven for me for the last two years was suddenly hostile.

Bob Tilburn and his companions were face down in the lee of the port forward UP launcher when *Hood* received her death blow: 'The next shell came aft and the ship shook like mad. I was next to the gun shield, so I was protected from the blast, but one of my mates was killed and the other had his side cut open by a splinter. It opened him up like a butcher and all his innards were coming out.' This shell, or another from the same salvo, seems to have passed through the spotting top because the boat deck was now showered with debris and body parts from the upper reaches of the bridge structure. Tilburn, struck on his legs by a torso, turned to vomit excruciatingly over the side.

Back on the bridge there was a fleeting air of normality before the enormity of what had taken place set in:

After the initial jarring she listed slowly, almost hesitatingly, to starboard. She stopped after about ten degrees, when I heard the helmsman's voice shouting up the voice-pipe to the officer of the watch: 'Steering's gone, sir.' The reply of 'Very good' showed no signs of animation or agitation. Immediately Kerr ordered: 'Change over to emergency steering.' Although the *Hood* had angled to starboard, there was still no concern on the compass platform. Holland was back in his chair. He looked aft towards the *Prince of Wales* and then re-trained his binoculars on the *Bismarck*. Slowly the *Hood* righted herself. 'Thank heaven for that,' I murmured to myself, only to be terrorized by her sudden, horrifying cant to port. On and on she rolled, until she reached an angle of forty-five degrees.

Realising the ship was finished, those on the compass platform began to file noiselessly out of the starboard door. Only Holland and Kerr remained, the admiral broken in his chair and beside him his flag captain, struggling to keep his footing as the *Hood* capsized. Neither made the slightest effort to escape. By the time Briggs emerged from the compass platform and began to move towards the admiral's bridge, the *Hood* was almost on her beam ends. Halfway down he was washed off the ladder and into the sea. For Mid William Dundas, who had spent the battle manning phones and voice pipes on the compass platform, the pitch of the deck prevented him reaching this exit and he was forced to kick his way through a window as the platform met the water. Though these two cannot have been more than a few yards apart their subsequent experiences differed in several important respects. As Briggs recalled from their discussions later, Dundas struck out to put distance between himself and the ship but was soon dragged under by suction as the *Hood* left the surface. Almost as quickly he was caught in a burst of escaping air and shot to the surface far enough away to make good his escape. Briggs, on the other hand, had a much more prolonged ordeal:

> This was it, I realized. But I wasn't going to give in easily. I knew that the deckhead of the compass platform was above me and that I must try to swim away from it. I managed to avoid being knocked out by the steel stanchions, but I was not making any progress. The suction was dragging me down. The pressure on my ears was increasing each second, and panic returned in its worse intensity. I was going to die. I struggled madly to try to heave myself up to the surface. I got nowhere. Although it seemed an eternity, I was under water for barely a minute. My lungs were bursting. I knew that I just had to breathe. I opened my lips and gulped in a mouthful of water. My tongue was forced to the back of my throat. I was not going to reach the surface. I was going to die. I was going to die. As I weakened, my resolve left me. What was the use of struggling? Panic subsided. I had heard it was nice to drown. I stopped trying to swim upwards. The water was a peaceful cradle. I was being rocked off to sleep. There was nothing I could do about it – good night, mum. Now I lay me down … I was ready to meet God. My blissful acceptance of death ended in a sudden surge beneath me, which shot me to the surface like a decanted cork in a champagne bottle. I wasn't going to die. I wasn't going to die. I trod water as I panted in great gulps of air. I was alive.

On the boat deck Tilburn looked up from his retching to see the bows rising out of the water. Knowing the end had come, he immediately abandoned the UP launcher whose splinter shield had served him so well and dropped down onto the forecastle abreast the compass platform from which Briggs and Dundas were making their escape. There was not a moment to lose. The first waves were lapping onto the decking as the *Hood* began to heel over. He barely had time to strip off his battle helmet and many layers of clothing before being swept into the sea. Tilburn did his best to get clear of the ship but everywhere the speed of her destruction was outpacing the efforts of the crew to separate their destiny from hers:

> I had my sea boots on and a very tight belt. I paddled around in the water and took my knife and cut my belt so I could breathe properly. Then I looked around and saw the ship was rolling over on top of me. It wasn't a shadow, it was a big mast coming over on top of me. It caught me across the back of the legs and the radio aerial wrapped around the back of my legs and started pulling me down. I still had my knife in my hands so I cut my sea boots off and shot to the surface. I looked up to see the *Hood* with her bows in the air. Then she slid under.

In each of these cases the time elapsed between the fatal hit and the moment of abandoning ship seems to have been little more than a minute. Tilburn was clearly the only man in the vicinity capable of getting away, testament to the attrition of her boat-deck personnel once the *Hood* came under fire. But at least three others were seen trying to escape from the compass platform, an unnamed officer of the watch, Cdr Gregson and Cdr John Warrand, the squadron navigating officer, who graciously gestured Briggs to pass ahead of him as they made their exit. Distinct as their experiences were, there is one aspect of their ordeal that unites the three survivors: the release of air from collapsing boilers and bulkheads which propelled them to the surface. As a result Dundas, Tilburn and Briggs all emerged on what had been the port side of the ship, some distance from her towering wreck and from each other. So it was that, a little after 0600 on the morning of 24 May, the pitiful remnants of the *Hood*'s crew found themselves adrift among the sparse wreckage of their ship in a fifteen to twenty foot swell. The battle raged on under leaden skies. Beneath them the pride of the Royal Navy and 1,415 of her company were sinking to the bottom of the Atlantic.

Having reached the surface Dundas, Tilburn and Briggs each swam away from the wreck and at length selected one of the numerous three-foot-square biscuit floats with which the *Hood* had been equipped during her final refit. Dundas was able to manoeuvre himself into a seated position on his float but the others couldn't perform the feat of balance necessary and lay belly-down on theirs. In this way they paddled towards each other, dodging patches of oil and wreckage and looking in vain for any other survivors. Overhead an RAF Sunderland of 201 Squadron spotted 'one large red raft and a considerable amount of wreckage amidst a huge patch of oil'. Briggs and Tilburn were exhausted from their ordeal and only Dundas's encouragement prevented them succumbing to the sleep from which they might never have awoken. The first hour or so was spent singing and recounting the stories of their escape, but they had drifted apart by the time *Electra*, a destroyer of Holland's escort, appeared on the scene at about 0800. Ted Briggs recalls the moment of rescue:

Slowly the *Electra* approached my raft, on which I was prostrate. Then a rope sailed into the air in my direction. Although I could not feel my fingers, somehow I managed to cling on to it. A man yelled unnecessarily at me from the scrambling net: 'Don't let go of it.' I even had the heart to retort: 'You bet your bloody life I won't.' Yet I was too exhausted to haul myself in and climb the net. After nearly four hours [*sic*] in the sea my emotions were a mess. Tears of frustration rolled down my oil-caked cheeks again, for rescue was so close and I could not help myself. I need not have worried. Several seamen dropped into the water, and with one hand on the nets they got me alongside and manhandled me up to the bent guard-rail, which had been battered by the storm, and into the waist of the *Electra*.

No bodies were to be seen. Among the few items recovered was a Marine's cap inscribed RMB/X 738, indicating that it belonged to Musician William Pike, who no doubt met his death in the transmitting station. After a forlorn search through the wreckage the *Electra*, desperately low on fuel, turned for Reykjavik where she arrived that evening, discharging the survivors to hospital.

The destruction of the *Hood* was an awesome spectacle which brought a brief lull in the Battle of the Denmark Strait. In the *Bismarck*, astonishment turned swiftly to unbridled exultation. Kapitänleutnant von Müllenheim-Rechberg:

> They just stared at one another in disbelief. Then the shock passed and the jubilation knew no bounds. Overwhelmed with joy and pride in the victory, they slapped one another on the back and shook hands. Their superiors had a hard time getting them back to work and convincing them that the battle wasn't over and that every man must continue to do his duty.

In *Prince of Wales*, by contrast, the sight was met with stunned silence. 'Not a word was said.' There was, in any case, precious little opportunity for reflection. No sooner had the Germans regained their composure than a storm of shellfire began to burst round *Prince of Wales* which was struck seven times in as many minutes by both *Bismarck* and *Prinz Eugen*. Among the hits was a 15in shell which passed through the compass platform killing or wounding everyone on it save Capt Leach and the chief yeoman of signals. However, the *Bismarck* was not to emerge from her moment of triumph unscathed. Despite problems with her turrets that eventually reduced her to only three operational guns, *Prince of Wales* was able to score three hits on the *Bismarck*, one putting a boiler room out of action and the other contaminating two of her oil tanks. With this the Battle of the Denmark Strait ended, *Prince of Wales* retiring under a smokescreen while Lütjens turned for Brest. 'Rhine Exercise' was effectively over, but the Royal Navy was to have its revenge. A wrathful Admiralty summoned every unit at its disposal to prevent *Bismarck* reaching harbour. Force H was brought up from Gibraltar and convoys ruthlessly stripped of their escort. Three days later the *Bismarck* suffered her own Calvary under the withering fire of the battleships *Rodney* and *King George V*. After a savage two-hour engagement *Bismarck* disappeared with 2,100 of her crew.

13

The End of Glory

'IF EVER A SHIP died in action, the *Hood* did.' How was the greatest ship in the British Navy transformed from an effective fighting unit to a shattered wreck in a matter of seconds? How could she disappear from the face of the water within three minutes? For seventy years these questions have exercised an increasingly broad spectrum of writers and readers. The opinions generated have frequently owed less to fact than to imagination, but the raw material on which the more rational conclusions have been drawn rests principally in the transactions of the two boards of enquiry held in 1941, together with an increasing fund of structural and operational data and personal memoirs from both sides. To these can be added the preliminary findings of the expedition which discovered the wreck in 2001.

None of the survivors formed any great impression of the event which destroyed the ship beyond that she had been wrecked by a major explosion aft. The main visual evidence for that explosion comes from *Prince of Wales*, steaming 800 yards off the *Hood*'s starboard quarter. As the battle unfolded, most of those on her disengaged port side had little to do but watch the flagship trading salvoes with the enemy. Their first impressions of note centre on the boat-deck fire resulting from the hit by *Prinz Eugen* in the early stages of the action. However, the dominant memory is of the events following *Bismarck*'s fifth salvo. The result of this salvo is not in any doubt. It ignited the 112 tons of cordite stowed in *Hood*'s after magazines. After a brief pause an immense pillar of orange flame towered 600 feet over the ship in a roiling cloud of grey smoke. A few seconds later it was seen to collapse outwards into a funnel-like shape leaving her wreathed in a shroud of smoke. The explosion was first seen in the vicinity of the mainmast, its strength venting through the engine-room exhaust housings on the boat deck and then among the after turrets themselves, which were tossed bodily into the sea. When the smoke began to clear those in *Prince of Wales* beheld a desolate sight: some 300 feet of the after section of the *Hood* had been ravaged by the explosion. The inferno raging inside permitted Lt Cdr A H Terry to distinguish the frames on her starboard side as the ship capsized, the bottom plating blown out between 'X' turret and the mainmast.

198

Waves lapped against the shattered hull. The remnants of the stern stood up briefly before breaking off together with over 200 feet of wreckage. On *Prince of Wales*'s bridge Boy James Gordon found himself staring into a severed section of the ship. What had been whole and intact moments earlier now lay tortured and eviscerated. On both sides the sight was more than many could bear to look at.

Hood's agony was not prolonged. As Capt Leach related, once the quarterdeck had gone the remains of the ship settled quickly by the stern: 'I formed the impression that the gunwale of the *Hood* was just showing outside the cloud of smoke and quite a short distance above the water, I should say about two to three feet.' By the time AB Bob Tilburn got clear of the ship the funnels were completely awash. Having heeled seven or eight degrees to starboard with the concussion of the explosion, the *Hood* righted herself before assuming the movement to port from which she never recovered. Soon her bows began to rise in response to the flooding aft, the dual motion causing her to pivot round on her axis as she subsided into the depths. The final plunge brought her bows up almost perpendicular, some 250 feet of the ship standing clear of the water. Then the end came, her bows pointing heavenward 'like the spire of a great cathedral', the barrels of 'B' turret slumped hard over and the waves creaming over her hull one last time.

The speed with which the *Hood* sank – under three minutes – can be accounted for by the enormous damage inflicted on her hull and internal structures and the flooding of her engine spaces. The extent of this damage was revealed when the upturned midsection of the ship was found in 2001. With this discovery the full magnitude of the disaster that had befallen her became apparent. What, though, was the cause and process of that event? This the boards of enquiry which followed the loss of the *Hood* were above all concerned to establish. Not only was the matter of the gravest importance to the Navy but there were lessons to be drawn for the design and fitting out of its heavy ships; lessons, it was felt, that should have been learnt after Jutland. The sense of dismay is captured in the letter the First Sea Lord, Admiral of the Fleet Sir Dudley Pound, sent to the Controller of the Navy, Vice Admiral Bruce Fraser, on 28 May:

> Now, after the lapse of 25 years, we have the first close action between one of our capital ships and that of the Germans since the Battle of Jutland and the *Hood* has been destroyed in what appears to the onlooker to be exactly the same manner as the *Queen Mary*, *Indefatigable* and *Invincible*, in spite of the action which was taken subsequent to Jutland to prevent further ships being destroyed as a result of 'flash'.

No one who witnessed the loss of the *Hood* could have had any doubt that it was the detonation of her after magazines that destroyed her. The question, both then and now, was quite how this had occurred. The first board convened on 30 May under the presidency of Vice Admiral Sir Geoffrey Blake (who had flown his flag in *Hood* from 1936–7) and submitted its report just three days later. It determined that one or more shells from *Bismarck* had landed in the vicinity of the mainmast and reached the *Hood*'s 4in magazines, which had been doubled in size in 1939–40. The explosion of these had in turn brought on the detonation of the 15in magazines. Though this finding was subsequently endorsed, the enquiry had taken no technical advice, left no minutes, and limited its interviews to a handful of officers; of *Hood*'s survivors only Mid Dundas had been called. Above all, it had summarily dismissed what many influential commentators regarded as a likely cause of the explosion: the detonation of the upper-deck torpedoes. A second board had therefore to be convened under the presidency of the *Hood*'s last peacetime captain, Rear Admiral H T C Walker. This began by taking evidence from 176 witnesses to the sinking while advice was solicited from a range of former officers and technical experts. The first interviews were held in the cruiser *Devonshire* on 12 August, continuing the following day in the *Suffolk*. The sessions were completed at Dorland House in London between 27 August and 5 September, to which both Tilburn and Briggs were summoned. Dundas was not able to attend but evidence gathered from survivors of the *Bismarck* was taken into consideration. Throughout the proceedings the board took pains to establish whether or not the boat deck fire and the ship's torpedo armament had any bearing on her loss. Its conclusions, submitted on 12 September 1941, were little removed from those of the first board. They read as follows:

1. That the sinking of *Hood* was due to a hit from *Bismarck*'s 15-inch shell in or adjacent to *Hood*'s 4-inch or 15-inch magazines, causing them all to explode and wreck the after part of the ship. The probability is that the 4-inch magazines exploded first.
2. There is no conclusive evidence that one or two torpedo warheads detonated or exploded simultaneously with the magazines, or at any other time, but the possibility cannot be entirely excluded. We consider that if they had done so their effect would not have been so disastrous as to cause the immediate destruction of the ship, and on the whole, we are of the opinion that they did not.
3. That the fire that was seen on *Hood*'s Boat Deck, and in which UP and/or 4-inch ammunition was certainly involved, was not the cause of her loss.

Though there continue to be dissenting voices, with these conclusions a majority of expert opinion is now in essential agreement. However, although the boards established with some certainty that a shell from the *Bismarck* had brought on the detonation of the *Hood*'s after magazines, it was not possible for any determination to be made as to the trajectory of the projectile. The question, of course, turned on whether the *Hood* had been struck on the boat deck or whether penetration had occurred below the waterline – essentially, whether it was horizontal or vertical armour that had been defeated. Both of these possibilities are consistent with the geometry of the ship, and credence was lent to the latter by the 15in shell which penetrated *Prince of Wales* below the waterline during the same action. However, in view of the highly uncertain trajectory of a shell under water this seems the less likely of the two scenarios. But, as W J Jurens wrote in 1987, 'The exact origin of the explosion is now, and shall probably always remain, somewhat in doubt', destined ever to remain in the limbo of conjecture.

This view was borne out in the summer of 2001 when the wreck of the *Hood* was filmed at a depth of around 9,000 feet. Lying amidst three vast debris fields were the bow and stern sections (approximately 165 and 125 feet respectively) and, at some remove, an upturned section of the hull some 350 feet long. Missing were approximately 225 feet, corresponding to the area between 'Y' turret and the middle engine room inclusive. The stern section had been seen to break away at the surface, but the real surprise of the expedition was the severed bow section, lying on its port side wrapped in anchor cable. It seems probable that the break was owed first to structural weakening when the bow rose out of the water and then to implosion damage once the ship left the surface, though arguments have been made for a major explosion in the vicinity. The other revelation was the unprecedented degree of implosion damage inflicted on the hull as the *Hood* sank. This field of desolation stretching across a mile of the ocean floor yielded few reminders of the ship as a living entity. One item, however, could hardly have been more poignant: the ship's bell on which the new year had been tolled in on 31 December 1940.

Where the process of the explosion is concerned, one can do no better than cite the conclusion reached by Jurens in 1987. His hypothesis is based on the detonation of a 15in shell in or near the 4in magazines aft:

If this occurred, and ignition of the propellant in the magazines followed from it, then a large part of the rapidly expanding gas bubble would have taken the path of least resistance and vented into the engineering spaces immediately forward of this area. For a time the sheer inertia of *Hood*'s structure would have slowed expansion in any other direction. Once the expanding gases had reached the engine rooms, the quickest exits to the outside would have been the series of massive exhaust vents located on the centreline immediately forward of and aft of the mainmast. These huge ducts, changing in size and shape as they rose through the ship, ended in roughly square vents 1.8 meters [each] side on the boat deck. It was as spectacular, near-vertical columns of flame from these vents near the mainmast, foreshortened to observers on surrounding ships, that the explosion first became visible. Shortly thereafter, the entire stern of the ship exploded. At the time of the blast, the Boards of inquiry calculated the 'X' 15-

in magazine contained about 49 tons of cordite, 'Y' magazine contained 45 tons, and the 4-in magazines contained about 18.5 tons. The uncontrolled burning of this quantity of propellant in the after magazines might have slowed briefly as the volume of the engineering spaces served as a space into which the gases could expand, and as the vents directed much of the combustion products outboard. But although this expansion and venting could temporarily relieve the pressure, it could never be enough to prevent an explosion from eventually tearing the ship apart.

But it takes a former crewman to convey the enormity of this event as it engulfed his friends and smashed through passageways and mess decks long frequented and fondly remembered. Leonard Williams (1936–41):

> In a tremendous flash, a split second of searing time, *Hood* was gone, rendering all our efforts null and void. After serving for four and a half years in the ship I knew every compartment, nut and bolt in her. I can almost picture the terrible scene between decks when that fatal shell struck. The gigantic sheets of golden cordite flame sweeping through the narrow corridors and passages, incinerating everything in its path. The terrific hot blast, the bursting open of the armoured hull under the colossal pressure; and, finally, the merciful avalanche of the cold sea, cleansing the charred and riven wreck, and bringing peace to those gallant souls I knew so well. On more than one occasion I have dreamed this scene and have returned to consciousness with the thought that 'There, but for the grace of God went I.'

The lack of survivors was due not only to the enormity of the explosion but the speed with which it brought on the sinking of the ship. Except for a few unfortunates, sealed in compartments as yet untouched by the unfolding catastrophe, the end must have come very quickly in fire, water and displaced equipment. Only those in exposed positions had any hope of survival but the hit on the spotting top and the terrible attrition on the boat deck and in the bridge shelter had accounted for most of these when the end came. Fewer than a dozen men can have got into the water where layers of protective clothing worn over uninflated lifejackets will not have improved their chances. Those who survived to be rescued did so by the greatest providence.

Those who see warships as pieces in an elaborate board game abstracted from the reality of combat would do well to remember the hell of destruction brought down on their crews at the hour of their death, their vessel become a storm of fire and metal, burning oil and escaping steam, of collapsing bulkheads and walls of water. As much as any ship, the *Hood* was destroyed with the energy of her creation. One can put it no simpler.

The first indication of disaster in the Denmark Strait came in a terse signal in code from Rear Admiral Wake-Walker in *Norfolk* to the Admiralty and Tovey, then at sea in *King George V*: '*Hood* blown up in position 63° 20' N, 31° 50' W.' This signal, made at 0615 and classified as 'Secret' by Wake-Walker, took some time to reach its intended recipients. However, the '*Hood* sunk' signal made en clair by *Prince of Wales* shortly after was picked up across the Atlantic and beyond. Capt Philip Vian was commanding the escort of convoy WS8B west of Ireland when the news reached him in the destroyer *Cossack*: 'I believe I felt no stronger emotion at any time in the war than at the moment when I read this signal.' So it was throughout the Navy. In the cruiser *Hawkins* lying at Durban Paymaster Lt Keith Evans (1938–9) was one of many veterans unable to control his emotions:

On that fateful day, after visiting Capetown and the Seychelles, we were coming alongside Mayden Wharf in Durban when on the tannoy of another ship (I think *Dorsetshire*) we heard the announcement 'We regret to announce that in action with the German Battleship *Bismarck* in the Denmark Strait off Greenland, HMS *Hood* has been sunk, it is feared with considerable loss of life'. All hands on deck seemed to stop what they were doing for about a minute (in fact more likely several seconds). As a former shipmate I just could not comprehend that the Mighty *Hood* had gone and am not a bit ashamed to say that I began to cry.

For others, grief for lost friends was tinged with a desire for revenge. Lt Cdr George Blundell, a midshipman in the *Hood* between 1922 and 1924, was First Lieutenant of the *Nelson* off Freetown:

... the captain came on to the bridge and said 'The *Hood*'s been sunk by the *Bismarck*.' I thought for a moment he was fooling. [...] I felt terrible thinking of Tony [Lieut Commander Anthony] Pares ... I can hardly believe that lovely ship is gone nor that one 15-inch shell can do such a horror. [...] All I hope and pray for is that we get the *Bismarck* in revenge. It would be terrible for her to get away. Those poor fellows in *Hood* – Tony, Tiny Gregson, dear old Grogan, Tubby [Crosse]. [...] It is a rotten war. What is the point of it?

At the same moment the Navy was being crucified in the withdrawal from Crete. Lt Cdr (E) Louis Le Bailly was senior engineer of the cruiser *Naiad*:

... when I went aft ... the commander broke the near unbelievable news that *Hood* had blown up. That there was another world outside the conflict in which we were engaged was difficult enough to comprehend; that the navy should be fighting two such great sea battles, so many thousand miles apart, was almost beyond understanding; but that the ship in which I had been weaned and had come to love should have disappeared in seconds was a kick in the stomach.

In the *Rodney*, escorting the troopship *Britannic* westwards across the Atlantic, news of the death of her 'chummy ship' came as a numbing blow. Her chaplain, the Rev Kenneth Thompson, describes the atmosphere in a ship which, days hence, would exact the Navy's revenge:

> We have taken some hard knocks this war, and there were others still to come, and many, for all we know, still in store. But it is doubtful if anything could equal the Captain's tragic broadcast that the *Hood* had been sunk with very few survivors, and that the *Prince of Wales* had been hit and forced to break off the engagement. It is difficult adequately to describe the gloom that existed; food went untouched in most messes, and many men, especially those who had served in the *Hood*, went about their work in a daze. For a time one of the chiefs cheered his mess with the suggestion that perhaps the signal had been misread, but that consolation was very quickly removed. The *Hood* had indeed been lost, together with most of her ship's company.

Others knew of the action before they learnt its outcome. Two hundred and fifty miles to the southeast firemen in the steamer *Zouave*, sailing in convoy SC31, picked up the reverberations of a distant battle. On the bridge Capt William Cambridge was losing his son John in one of *Hood*'s boiler rooms.

In Berlin Goebbels crowed triumphantly at the news. At the Admiralty, meanwhile, it was received with a mixture of shock and stoicism. Civil Service telegraphist Gladys Wilkin was on duty in the Admiralty Signals Department on what had been a heavy night of bombing:

> The Signals Department was situated beneath Admiralty Arch; roughly beneath the left hand pillar looking down the Mall. [...] On the night of 24th May 1941 there was a particularly bad air raid on London and a direct hit struck the above mentioned pillar, killing a dispatch rider standing beside his motor-cycle at that spot and damaging a portion of the Signals Department below. Now, it just so happened that at that particular time several members of the Signals staff were either at rest, supper, off sick or just not on duty. There was not terribly much 'traffic' that night and I was working two positions. On one position I received the signal that HMS *Hood* had been sunk; this was marked 'MOST SECRET' and needed to be handed immediately to the Officer in Charge. I was shocked, stunned and unhappy. For another reason also. One of the telegraphists with whom I was particularly friendly at this time was a girl we all called 'Len' because her surname was Leonard. [...] Her fiancé was a member of the crew of the *Hood* and when she came back from supper I was unable to tell her of the signal because of its classification. Naturally, she learned eventually when lists of the casualties began coming in.

Though no less of a shock, for anyone aware of the *Hood*'s design the news came as no particular surprise. Capt William Davis, a deputy director of operations at the Admiralty, had been *Hood's* executive officer until September 1940:

> The loss of the *Hood* was a tremendous shock to all of us, and especially to me as her last Commander, but I certainly knew of her extreme vulnerability to 15 inch fire with only 3 inches of mild steel armour protection over her magazines. [...] The *Hood's* destruction was unlucky, but to me not unexpected for she was not fit to take on modern 15 inch gunfire.

Luck was one of the themes of the communiqué released by the Admiralty later that day. At 9pm on the 24th the country at large was made aware of the disaster in a BBC radio broadcast:

> British naval forces intercepted early this morning, off the coast of Greenland, German naval forces, including the battleship *Bismarck*. The enemy were attacked, and during the ensuing action HMS *Hood* (Captain R Kerr, CBE, RN), wearing the flag of Vice Admiral L E Holland, CB, received an unlucky hit in a magazine and blew up. The *Bismarck* has received damage, and the pursuit of the enemy continues. It is feared there will be few survivors from HMS *Hood*.

The news was received with utter disbelief. OD James Edwards (1933–4):

> I was in a pub and had just ordered a pint of beer when the news came over the radio and the pub went totally quiet. I looked at my pint and could no longer face it, so I walked out, leaving it untouched on the bar. I had lost friends and companions but above all I had lost the beautiful ship which gave me my first real sea-going experience and I felt shattered.

OD Howard Spence, part of the last draft to leave the ship before she sailed against the *Bismarck*, got home just as the news was breaking:

> I arrived home at Portsmouth by 24th May 1941 and heard a radio announcement that HMS somethingorother had been sunk – we could not catch a name, but I had a presentiment that it was the *Hood*, and this was confirmed the next day. A telegram arrived for my parents and I took it from the telegraph boy: 'Regret your son missing, presumed killed.' A further telegram arrived dated 29th May 1941: 'Your son not on board, regret anxiety caused.'

But most relatives had no such reprieve and for them life would never be the same again. Some, indeed, suffered a double tragedy. At least four pairs of brothers were lost in the *Hood*, including George and Arthur Brewer of Newfoundland. For Portsmouth, heavily blitzed since 1940, the loss of its greatest ship together with virtually her entire crew was almost beyond endurance. Sheila Harris, just five at the time, recalls the atmosphere:

> HMS *Hood* and its loss became the topic of conversation that permeated everything. I can only describe the atmosphere now when I look back as that of a pall of shock and misery descending on the city and its environs. Every conversation wherever people gathered was constantly punctuated by the word '*Hood*'.

Nor was Portsmouth the only city to grieve. In their undemonstrative way the people of Glasgow also mourned the loss of 'oor ship'. On 30 May, Sir Stephen Pigott, Managing Director of John Brown & Co, submitted the following in his report to the Board of Directors:

> The loss of this great Clydebank-built ship has caused genuine depression and regrets with all at Clydebank, and through the medium of the shop stewards we are endeavouring to exhort the workers to give expression to their feeling by increased effort on the work in progress ... A letter expressing sympathy and regret at the loss of HMS *Hood* has been sent to the Controller of the Navy.

Before the 24th was over one of the ladies entrusted with the task of maintaining the Admiralty's warship index made a final entry on the *Hood*'s card: 'At 0635 today blew up and sank in action in the Denmark Strait.'* That evening Churchill descended to the parlour at 10 Downing Street in a sombre mood. The *Hood* had been destroyed and the *Bismarck* was at large in the Atlantic:

> [Vic Oliver, his son-in-law] wrote of an evening in 1941 when Churchill came down from his study 'looking inexpressibly grim'. Scenting there had been a disaster but knowing he would not reveal it, Mrs Churchill quietly poured him a glass of port. Oliver went to the piano and, on reflection, began Beethoven's *Appassionata* sonata. Churchill rose to his feet and thundered: 'Stop! Don't play that!' 'What's the matter?' asked Oliver. 'Don't you like it?' 'Nobody plays the *Dead March* [*sic*] in my house,' said Churchill. Knowing that Churchill was notoriously unmusical, the company laughed. Oliver turned back to the piano. 'But surely, sir, you can tell the difference between this ...' – and he struck a few chords of *Appassionata* – 'and ...' Before he could finish Churchill thundered again: 'Stop it! Stop it! I want no dead march, I tell you.'

The outlook, indeed, could hardly have been more grim. As Churchill recalled,

> The House of Commons ... might be in no good temper when we met on Tuesday. [...] How would they like to be told ... that the *Hood* was unavenged,

*The actual time was of course 0600.

that several of our convoys had been cut up or even massacred, and that the *Bismarck* had got home to Germany or to a French-occupied port, that Crete was lost, and evacuation without heavy casualties doubtful?

On the morning of the 27th Churchill was able to announce the sinking of the *Bismarck* to Parliament but nothing could efface the destruction of the *Hood* on, of all days, Empire Day – 24 May. From a material standpoint Germany's loss had been much the greater. Her only commissioned battleship had been sunk with huge loss of life including that of the Kriegsmarine's most distinguished seagoing commander. But the *Hood* had a symbolic power out of all proportion to her value as a fighting unit and her annihilation had an effect on morale exceeded only by the fall of Singapore in February 1942. Both events raised in the minds of ordinary Britons the spectre of total defeat. And both in their different ways had far-reaching consequences for the prestige of the British Empire. But that lay in the future. For now the gleaming sword of the Navy had been unmade, never to be reforged.

So to the aftermath. In Yorkshire, Applegarth School transferred its affiliation to *King George V*, the battleship that had led the final attack on the *Bismarck*. From Bubulu, Uganda, a young Jeremy Woods sent Churchill his accumulated savings of two shillings towards the construction of a replacement. Lt Cdr Wellings had a letter to his friend Warrand returned to the US embassy in London as hundreds must have found their way back to families and friends struggling to cope with their loss. In March of 1942, Canon Thomas Browne of Newmarket received from the Navy the sum of £18 7s 2d, the balance of his son Robert's pay. The final reckoning came to 1,415 men including four Polish midshipmen and four Free French ratings; representing the Empire were men from the Canadian (three), Australian (two), Indian and New Zealand navies (one each), and several ratings from Newfoundland.

The loss of the *Hood* was very much present as the conflict drew to a close. There are many descriptions of Sunset, the ceremony which closed the naval day, but none more moving than Louis Le Bailly's memory of evening on 2 September 1945, the day the Second World War ended. The ship was *Duke of York* and the place Tokyo Bay:

When Admiral Fraser arrived the Quartermaster reported 'Sunset, sir'. The 'Still' sounded. The Royal Marine Guard presented arms and the band played *The day Thou gavest Lord is ended*, interspersed with the Sunset call as only Royal Marine buglers know how. For the first time in six bitter years the White Ensign came down. Many, perhaps most, had never before savoured the magic of this moment when the busy life of a warship is hushed and the evening comes. Others of us, standing at the salute, were in tears as we remembered those who would never again see 'Colours' in the morning or hear the bugles sound 'Sunset' at dusk. I thought of all those friends in *Hood* who had come to see me off and the many many others … As the White Ensign came into the hands of our Chief Yeoman and the 'Carry on' sounded, we realised that on board all the great US ships around us every activity had stopped, their sailors facing towards the British flagship and saluting us.

In the years that followed Band Corporal Wally Rees RM, he of the effervescent trumpet, could never speak of his companions in the transmitting station without tears welling in his eyes. For Rear Admiral Joseph H Wellings, who learnt the news in the *Rodney*, shock and sadness were accompanied by a sense that things had changed for ever: 'I was shocked because the *Hood* had been the symbol of British naval supremacy for over 20 years, and saddened because of the loss of so many friends.'

And so the *Hood* passed into history. Her epitaph? Leonard Williams:

It was a very long time before I got over the shock of *Hood*'s loss. As a ship's company we had been together a very long time. We had shared the joys and excitement of peace. In war we had welded ourselves into true comradeship that had weathered the Arctic gales and outshone the Mediterranean sun. As long as sea history is written, *Hood* and her gallant band of men will be remembered, and theirs will be a golden page in the book of time.

*

There is a special quality about the battlecruiser *Hood* which resists any single definition. It has to do with her beauty and her destructive power, with her gilded years of peace and then her annihilation in war, of sinuous strength and desperate fragility. Most of all, perhaps, it has to do with the association between these elements and what she represented. The *Hood* came to symbolise two things above all: the perpetuation of the British Empire and all that the Royal Navy wished for itself. Once she had gone, nothing would or could ever be quite the same again and the passage of time has only sharpened that impression. In the fifteen months that separate the destruction of the *Hood* in May 1941 and Operation PEDESTAL in August 1942, the Royal Navy lost many of her most famous ships: the *Barham* off North Africa and *Ark Royal* off Gibraltar; *Repulse* and *Prince of Wales* off Malaya; *Hermes* in the Indian Ocean and *Eagle* in the western Mediterranean; and of course *Hood* herself at the beginning of this period together with dozens of cruisers, destroyers, submarines and escorts. Though these disasters did not alter the outcome of the war they encapsulate a loss of power and prestige from which there would be no recovery. And of these blows none fell heavier than that of *Hood*, destroyed with virtually her entire company in a tragedy which has come to stand for the Calvary of the Royal Navy as a whole during the Second World War.

Nor is this all. For many, the passing of the *Hood* represents not only the closing phase in the Royal Navy's age of greatness but also a vanished era in

British industrial power. One needs to look back beyond the forcing of the railways across England to the age of the great cathedrals and monasteries to find a parallel for the immense endeavour represented by the 'Great Naval Race' of the early twentieth century. As in the High Middle Ages, the construction of the *Hood* united the zeal, treasure, skills and energy of entire communities and, as then, the scale of the enterprise reflects the confidence and vaulting ambition of her creators, to build bigger and better to an end and for a purpose greater than themselves. Despite her flaws, this circumstance makes the *Hood* as much a triumph of the shipbuilder's art and organisation as she was of naval power and administration, and it must be a source of profound sadness that not one of the great British warships of the first half of the twentieth century has survived to mark this achievement for posterity.

There is another tragedy, too, and this is that *Hood* went ill-prepared to her moment of reckoning in the Denmark Strait. This circumstance had not only to do with unsatisfactory protection, a motley assemblage of secondary armament and the inscrutable turns of Fortuna's wheel. It was also the product of economic decline and financial parsimony, diplomatic incompetence and political upheaval; a result of the strategic and military failure that placed her under *Bismarck*'s guns when she might otherwise have been quietly scrapped or in the throes of reconstruction. Then there is the Battle of the Denmark Strait itself, a particularly stark example of the dichotomy between strength and power in capital-ship design. Here, after a brief engagement between two ships of comparable armament, the *Hood* blew up with the loss of virtually her entire crew before she could land a single hit on the enemy. Over the next three days the *Bismarck* was hunted down and finally battered to destruction without inflicting any significant damage on her tormentors. There are lessons to be drawn from the experience of both vessels: that what makes a ship in peace is assuredly not what makes her in war; that the power of a capital ship equates to the strength which permits her to suffer a measure of the punishment she would mete out to others; and that a clear distinction must be drawn between what keeps a ship fighting and what keeps her from sinking. For *Bismarck* that distinction was very great though ultimately not great enough; for *Hood* it was barely perceptible. Two great ships, each vulnerable in her own way.

To have witnessed the collapse of the World Trade Center on 11 September 2001 is to appreciate how a great entity many years in the making can be destroyed in the passage of a few seconds. But the tragedy is not one of structure so much as of humanity. With *Hood* as with *Bismarck*, *Arizona* and *Yamato*, it was less a ship than a community that was destroyed, the community evoked here by LS Leonard Williams (1936–41):

Here we lived together as a giant family. We knew each other's failings and weaknesses, and liked each other in spite of them. We slept in close proximity, in swaying hammocks. We even bathed together in the communal bathrooms.

In fact we lived candidly with one another, accepting the rough with the smooth. This sharing and living together forged a comradeship which one can never find in civilian life. Nor was the ship herself left out of our lives, for everything we did was for her. On our smartness, the way we dressed, in fact everything we did depended our ship's efficiency rating in the fleet. She was our constant task mistress. While we could, and often did, call her all the rough names under the sun when things went wrong, heaven help those, not of our company, who tried to do the same. This is the team spirit we miss when we leave the service, for it is something very fine. Something which, through countless ages, has scaled the highest mountains, fought and won hopeless battles ...

It was her men who breathed life into her, made her rich in history, character and memory from the splendours of Rio de Janeiro to the Stygian waters of the North Atlantic. In *Hood*, the notion of the warship as a tool of peaceful diplomacy reached its maximum expression, not only in her graceful form, speed and armament but also in the qualities of her people. The *Hood* was undeniably an engine of war, but as with the greatest weapons her career was as much about preserving life as about taking it. Of her many legacies this shall perhaps prove the most enduring.

Roll of Honour

HMS *Hood*, 24 May 1941

Holland, Lancelot E, CB – Vice Admiral, Battle Cruiser Squadron
Kerr, Ralph, CBE – Captain

Abbott, Frederick – Marine
Abbott, Kenneth – Ordinary Coder
Ablett, Wallace A – Marine
Abrams, Robert G – Marine
Acton, Percival C H – Able Seaman
Adams, Frank P – Musician
Adams, Keith H – Corporal, RM
Adams, Nigel N – Midshipman, RNR
Adams, Victor E – Ordinary Seaman
Adams, Victor H – Leading Stoker
Ainsworth, Frederick J – Able Seaman
Akehurst, Rodney G – Stoker 1st Class
Aldred, Gerald A – Ordinary Telegraphist
Algate, Alfred K – Canteen Assistant, NAAFI
Alger, Eric – Ordinary Seaman
Alland, Henry C – Petty Officer
Allcock, William S – Boy 1st Class
Allen, Arthur F J – Leading Stoker
Allen, Charles W – Leading Seaman
Allen, Edward B – Ordinary Seaman
Allen, James E – Stoker 1st Class
Allen, John G – Marine
Allen, William E S – Able Seaman
Allott, George – Marine

Almond, Frederick – Able Seaman
Altham, Arthur – Stoker 2nd Class
Ambridge, Walter C – Sergeant, RM
Ambrose, John – Able Seaman
Amery, Thomas C F – Able Seaman
Anderson, Arthur D – Able Seaman
Anderson, John – Chief Engine Room Artificer
Anderson, Joseph M – Ordinary Seaman
Andrews, Cecil V – Ordinary Seaman
Annis, James E – Stoker 1st Class
Applegarth, Richard – Leading Signalman
Appleyard, John A F – Ordinary Seaman
Ardley, Jack C – Boy 1st Class
Arkinstall, John – Leading Seaman
Armstrong, John C – Leading Stoker
Armstrong, Norman – Able Seaman
Arnold, William A – Petty Officer Stoker
Ashley, Robert G – Able Seaman
Assirati, Albert F G – Petty Officer Stoker
Aston, John – alias of André Blondel
Atkins, William E – Chief Petty Officer Steward
Atkinson, John H – Able Seaman
Atkinson, Robert – Petty Officer Stoker

Austin, Albert G L – Able Seaman

Avery, Albert G – Able Seaman

Awdry, Charles D – Lieutenant Commander

Ayling, Frank R – Canteen Assistant

Ayling, Ronald – Able Seaman

Ayres, Henry D – Ordinary Signalman

Badcock, John H – Stoker 2nd Class

Baildon, Frank – Able Seaman

Bailey, Frederick W – Marine

Bailey, Leonard W J – Ordinary Signalman

Baines, Godfrey J – Leading Seaman

Baker, Andrew L – Ordinary Seaman

Baker, George E – Leading Stoker

Baker, Kenneth A – Petty Officer Telegraphist

Balch, Percy H – Able Seaman

Baldwin, Kenneth E G – Stoker 1st Class

Baldwin, Phillip R – Ordinary Seaman

Ball, Charles F D – Able Seaman

Ball, Phillip A – Stoker 1st Class

Ball, William – Leading Stoker

Ballard, Arthur – Boy 1st Class

Balsdon, Ernest F – Stoker 1st Class

Bamford, Anthony B J – Able Seaman

Banfield, Kenneth J – Boy 1st Class

Banks, George H – Stoker 1st Class

Banks, Sidney T – Leading Cook (S)

Barclay, Alex C – Leading Cook (S)

Barker, Thomas – Ordinary Seaman

Barnes, Thomas G – Petty Officer Stoker

Barnes, Walter J – Able Seaman

Barnet, William L – Cook (O)

Barnett, Ivor G – Stoker 2nd Class

Barrie, Walter R – Able Seaman

Barringer, William H – Marine

Bartley, Archibald E T – Signal Boatswain

Barton, Kenneth C F – Petty Officer

Basham, Howard – Ordinary Seaman

Bassett, Charles G – Petty Officer

Basstone, Jack – Marine

Batchelor, Arthur R – Yeoman of Signals

Bates, Frederick G – Leading Seaman

Bates, Leonard A – Marine

Bates, Reginald S – Wireman

Batley, A Roger T – Lieutenant Commander, RNVR

Batten, Herbert W L – Ordinary Seaman

Battersby, Clifford – Able Seaman

Baxter, John K – Petty Officer

Baylis, Herbert J – Ordinary Signalman

Beard, R Alan – Marine

Beard, Thomas N K – Midshipman, RCN

Beardsley, Geoffrey V – Joiner 4th Class

Belcher, Cyril S V – Electrical Artificer 3rd Class

Bell, Cyril K – Ordinary Signalman

Bell, Ronald T L – Ordinary Signalman

Bell, William – Able Seaman, RNVR

Belsham, James R – Able Seaman

Bembridge, Percy A – Ordinary Seaman

Bennett, Ernest – Marine

Bennett, Percival – Boy 1st Class

Benoist, Donald G – Able Seaman

Benton, Leonard – alias of Leonard Goulstine

Benwell, Ernest F T – Sick Berth Chief Petty Officer

Beresford, Kenneth – alias of Kenneth Radley

Berner, Robert V – Leading Writer

Betts, Robert – Stoker 1st Class

Beveridge, Roy – Ordnance Artificer 4th Class

Biggenden, Walden J – Chief Stoker

Binnie, John E – Petty Officer Stoker

Bird, Herbert G A – Ordnance Artificer 3rd Class

Bishop, Charles J – Chief Stoker

Bishop, Edward J P – Petty Officer (Pensioner)

Bispham, Leslie W – Ordinary Seaman

Biss, John – Able Seaman

Blake, Harold G – Leading Stoker

Blann, Kenneth A F – Able Seaman

Bleach, Arthur B – Able Seaman

Blondel, André – Electrical Artificer 4th Class

Bloodworth, Herbert W – Able Seaman

Blow, Leonard – Ordinary Seaman

Blunt, William H T – Leading Cook (S)

Boardman, Stanley – Petty Officer

Bocutt, Alfred A – Marine

Boncey, William L – Petty Officer

Bond, Sidney W – Able Seaman

Boneham, Norman – Marine

Boniface, Jack – Able Seaman

Bonner, Colin A – Able Seaman

Boone, Bernard J – Engine Room Artificer 4th Class

Booth, George H – Stoker 2nd Class

Borrer, Harold T – Able Seaman

Borsberry, George – Petty Officer Cook (S)

Bosley, Frank W – Leading Sick Berth Attendant

Bostock, Charles W – Chief Mechanician

Bower, Reginald P – Able Seaman

Bower, Ronald – Stoker 1st Class

Bowers, Leo S – Ordinary Seaman

Bowie, Duncan – Able Seaman, RNVR

Bowyer, Thomas R – Ordinary Telegraphist

Bowyer, Walter F – Stoker 1st Class

Bradley, Harold – Ordinary Seaman

Bradley, Kenneth J – Able Seaman

Bradshaw, Thomas F – Stoker 2nd Class

Bramhall, Harold – Joiner 4th Class

Brand, William H – Corporal, RM

Brandon, Albert A – Ordinary Telegraphist

Bransden, Paul D – Able Seaman

Brett, Benjamin A – Ordinary Seaman

Brewer, Arthur W – Ordinary Seaman

Brewer, George – Ordinary Seaman

Bridge, Arthur T – Telegraphist

Bridges, Kenneth C – Ordinary Telegraphist, RNVR

Bridges, Ronald W – Wireman

Brierley, William L – Leading Steward

Bristow, Harry – Wireman

Britton, Clarence V – Marine

Broadhurst, Dennis C – Wireman

Broadley, William N – Leading Seaman

Brookes, Donald A – Telegraphist

Brooks, Gordon B – Stoker 1st Class

Brooks, Jack – Stoker 1st Class

Brooks, Terrence L – Marine

Broom, George W – Shipwright 3rd Class

Brown, Arthur – Marine

Brown, Eric F – Boy 1st Class

Brown, Ernest – Stoker 2nd Class

Brown, George W – Steward

Brown, Henry J – Able Seaman

Brown, John L – Leading Seaman

Brown, Robert K – Petty Officer Stoker

Browne, Robert H P – Paymaster Lieutenant

Brownrigg, John G P – Lieutenant Commander

Bryant, Denis M – Midshipman

Buck, Arthur E J – Mechanician 2nd Class

Buck, Herbert T J – Petty Officer Stoker

Buckett, Philip J – Midshipman, RNVR

Bull, Percival H – Leading Seaman

Bull, Robert J – Able Seaman

Bullock, Edward H – Able Seaman

Bullock, Henry W – Marine

Bullock, William F – Able Seaman

Bulman, Kenneth F – Petty Officer

Burckitt, John B E – Petty Officer Cook

Burgess, Henry – Warrant Ordnance Officer

Burkin, Robert H – Marine

Burnell, Gordon R – Ordinary Seaman

Burningham, William F R – Chief Petty Officer

Burns, Albert S – Able Seaman

Bussey, Harry F – Able Seaman

Butler, Horace A – Able Seaman

Butterworth, Alfred N – Able Seaman

Byrne, Francis – Boy 1st Class

Byrne, Thomas G – Stoker 1st Class

Cabell, Percy A – Chief Petty Officer Cook

Cabrin, Roy V – Stoker 2nd Class

Callon, William J – Boy 1st Class

Cambridge, John H – Sub Lieutenant (E), RNVR

Campbell, Albert G – Leading Seaman

Cann, Herbert R – Marine

Cantrill, Joshua – Petty Officer Stoker

Canty, William D – Yeoman of Signals

Capon, Leslie A – Ordinary Seaman

Capstick, Arthur J – Marine

Carey, Arthur T – Ordinary Seaman

Carey, Daniel A B – Supply Assistant

Carlin, George V – Paymaster Lieutenant Commander, RNVR

Carn, George H K – Chief Yeoman of Signals

Carpenter, Robert S – Marine

Carr, John – Stoker 2nd Class

Carter, Robert J W – Marine

Cartwright, Thomas D – Captain, RM

Cavell, Percy H – Stoker 1st Class

Chamberlain, Henry S – Corporal, RM

Chandler, Alfred J – Master-at-Arms

Chaplin, Albert E – Boy 1st Class

Chapman, James A – Commissioned Gunner

Chappell, Robert E – Able Seaman

Charker, Albert W – Able Seaman

Charlton, Robert A – Able Seaman

Chatfield, Edwin H – Able Seaman

Cheadle, Henry J – Petty Officer

Chivers, William A – Engine Room Artificer 3rd Class

Choules, Sydney J – Chief Petty Officer

Chowney, William H – Chief Petty Officer

Churchill, Ronald J – Ordinary Seaman

Claringbold, Leon J – Able Seaman

Clark, Jack C P – Ordinary Seaman

Clark, John F – Leading Seaman

Clark, Leonard A – Marine

Clark, Robert G – Marine

Clarke, David W – Ordinary Seaman

Clarke, Leslie H – Electrical Artificer

4th Class

Clarke, Stanley W – Wireman

Clayton, Stanley – Wireman

Clayton, William A – Ordinary Seaman

Cleeter, William G – Able Seaman

Clements, Thomas W – Able Seaman

Cleton, Peter V – Engine Room Artificer 4th Class

Clitherow, Charles F – Stoker 2nd Class

Clothier, Kenneth R J – Ordinary Coder

Clout, Cecil G – Able Seaman

Cobb, William H – Ordinary Seaman

Cockhead, Alfred J – Leading Stoker

Cogger, Thomas E – Marine

Cole, Albert E – Ordinary Seaman

Cole, George D – Marine

Cole, John J – Able Seaman

Cole, William G – Marine

Coleman, Dennis J – Marine

Collett, Stanley J – Able Seaman

Collings, John P – Paymaster Midshipman

Collins, Arthur R – Petty Officer

Collins, Reginald J – Able Seaman

Collinson, Robert E – Boy 1st Class

Collis, Gordon V – Boy 1st Class

Collyer, Percy W L – Boy 1st Class

Comber, James D – Leading Seaman

Combes, Richard A L – Ordinary Seaman

Compton, William A – Leading Stoker

Conchie, William M – Boy 1st Class

Conroy, Cornelius – Stoker 2nd Class

Constable, Alan R – Boy 1st Class

Cook, James E – Chief Stoker

Cook, Joseph R – Able Seaman

Cook, Vernon – Blacksmith 4th Class

Coombes, Gerald E – Sergeant, RM

Cooper, Alan C – Able Seaman

Cooper, Frederick G D – Mechanician 2nd Class

Cooper, Geoffrey G – Able Seaman

Cooper, George W – Ordinary Coder

Cooper, John – Marine

Cope, George R – Boy 1st Class

Cope, Sidney J – Commissioned Gunner (T)

Corddell, Harold L – Chief Petty Officer

Corlett, John – Engine Room Artificer 4th Class

Cornock, James – Able Seaman

Cotton, Lewis A – Stoker 2nd Class

Cottrell, Albert E – Ordinary Seaman

Coulson, John – Musician

Coulthurst, Francis B – Stoker 2nd Class

Court, William R – Able Seaman

Cowie, John E L – Shipwright 4th Class

Cox, Arthur J – Ordinary Seaman

Cox, Cyril A – Stoker 1st Class

Cox, John F – Wireman

Cox, Leslie L – Ordinary Coder

Cox, Stanley K – Leading Seaman

Craft, Thomas E – Able Seaman

Cranston, Aylmer N J – Stoker 1st Class

Crawford, William M – Boy 1st Class

Crawley, Lawrence – Stoker 1st Class

Crawte, Alfred E J – Musician

Crellin, William – Stoker 1st Class

Cresswell, Henry R – Marine

Cross, Joseph B – Petty Officer

Cross, Robert C – Cook (O)

Cross, William K R – Commander

Crouch, Cecil H – Regulating Petty Officer

Croucher, Lambert E – Able Seaman
Crow, George L – Leading Stoker
Crumpton, Laurence – Leading Stoker
Cruttenden, John E – Able Seaman
Cunningham, John – Able Seaman
Cunningham, Richard F – Ordinary Seaman
Currie, George – Stoker 1st Class
Currie, Robert – Stoker 1st Class
Cuthbert, Albert T – Corporal, RM
Czerny, Stanisław – Marynarz Podchorąży (Midshipman), Polish Navy
d'Abry de l'Arves, Robert C – Able Seaman
Dade, William F L – Petty Officer Steward
Dakers, William B – Sick Berth Attendant
Dale, Richard H – Lieutenant (E)
Dall, Francis O'N – Able Seaman
Dalziel, Thomas – Ordinary Signalman
Daniels, Charles G – Stoker 1st Class
Darby, Leonard – Ordinary Signalman
Davey, Frederick G – Leading Telegraphist
Davey, Reginald J – Able Seaman
Davies, Douglas A – Able Seaman
Davies, Frederick M – Able Seaman
Davies, Hamilton K – Midshipman, RNVR
Davies, Horace D – Lieutenant, RM
Davies, Kenneth J – Boy Bugler
Davies, Ronald T – Senior Master Commissioned Warrant Officer
Davis, Gordon E – Able Seaman
Davis, Herbert A – Marine
Davis, Percy J – Stoker 1st Class
Dawson, Philip J – Signal Boy
Day, Frederick J – Marine
Day, William S W – Chief Electrical Artificer
De Gernier, James B – Able Seaman, RNVR
De St George, Edward O – Able Seaman
De Ste Croix, Cyril R – Leading Stoker
Dean, Cyril A J – Stoker 1st Class
Dean, George A – Signalman
Dear, Nelson L – Musician
Dempsey, Martin – Able Seaman
Denault, Benjamin – Stoker 2nd Class
Dennis, Ronald – Able Seaman
Dent, Christopher H C – Surgeon Lieutenant, RNVR
Derrick, Charles T – Leading Supply Assistant
Devereaux, Albert – Ordinary Seaman
Dewey, Edward D G – Boy 1st Class
Diggens, James B – Able Seaman
Dilly, John H C – Stoker 1st Class
Dinsdale, Stanley – Stoker 1st Class
Discombe, Archie A J – Musician
Dixon, Albert – Leading Stoker
Dixon, William – Able Seaman
Doak, Walter W – Petty Officer
Dobeson, Nicholas – Chief Petty Officer (Pensioner)
Dobson, Charles W – Able Seaman
Dodd, Henry – Stoker 1st Class
Donaghy, Walter – Able Seaman
Donald, James H – Boy 1st Class
Donaldson, Walter M H – Ordinary Seaman
Doolan, Francis – Stoker 2nd Class
Douglas, Neil H – Able Seaman
Douglass, Mark R – Boy 1st Class
Dowdell, William F S – Leading Seaman
Dowdles, Malcolm M – Able

Seaman, RNVR

Down, John R – Sub Lieutenant, RNVR

Druken, Valentine – Ordinary Seaman

Drury, Ernest – Ordinary Signalman

Duckworth, Kenneth R R – Able Seaman

Dudman, Caleb A W – Mechanician 1st Class

Duffield, John – Stoker 2nd Class

Dunn, Stephen E – Able Seaman

Dunne, Patrick L – Petty Officer

Dunnell, Graham G – Marine

Dunwell, William S – Able Seaman

Dyas, Richard J – Stoker 2nd Class

Dyment, Herbert R – Ordinary Seaman

Eagles, George R – Midshipman

Earl, Joseph W – Stoker 2nd Class

Earwaker, Ronald C – Able Seaman

Eastwood, Walter C – Marine

Eaton, Raymond K J – Leading Stoker

Eaves, Leonard – Wireman

Edes, Henry M – Able Seaman

Edmiston, Reginald F – Chief Engine Room Artificer

Edmonds, Alfred G – Able Seaman

Edmonds, Anthony R – Writer

Edwards, Melville – Marine

Edwards, Robert – Stoker 2nd Class

Edwards, Thomas W G – Able Seaman

Eldred, Eric C – Stoker 1st Class

Eldridge, Bertie D M – Stoker 2nd Class

Elliott, John G – Petty Officer Stoker

Eltis, Donald O – Ordinary Seaman

Emery, Lawrence A – Musician

Emery, Richard C – Petty Officer Stoker

Erridge, Frank A – Telegraphist

Erskine, John G M – Lieutenant Commander (E)

Erskine, Roy D – Signalman

Escott, Robert W – Stoker 2nd Class

Evans, David M – Stoker 2nd Class

Ewart-James, David E – Ordinary Seaman

Eyres, Thomas W W – Able Seaman

Fair, George W – Shipwright 4th Class

Fairlie, Percy W – Stoker 1st Class

Farmer, Albert V – Leading Seaman

Farnish, Frederick N – Petty Officer Telegraphist

Farrar, Clifford – Marine

Faulkner, Ronald E – Stoker 1st Class

Fenner, Henry J – Marine

Field, Edgar C – Ordinary Signalman

Fielder, Jack H – Able Seaman

Fielding, James O – Surgeon Lieutenant

Finch, John L – Boy 1st Class

Finlayson, David A – Able Seaman, RNVR

Fisher, Leslie – Blacksmith 3rd Class

Fitch, Edward G – Able Seaman

Fitchew, Cecil A – Ordinary Seaman

Fitzgerald, Joseph V – Ordinary Seaman

Fletcher, Peter – Petty Officer Stoker

Fletcher, Victor W J – Able Seaman

Flint, Sydney G – Able Seaman

Floyd, Charles – Wireman

Flynn, John T – Stoker 2nd Class

Foden, Leslie J – Leading Seaman

Foley, Rodney A – Chief Stoker

Foot, Charles – Leading Stoker

Ford, Douglas C – Midshipman, RNR

Ford, Harold E – Ordinary Seaman

Ford, Jack – Able Seaman

Forrest, Ernest W – Writer
Forrest, George M D – Wireman
Forrest, Victor – Petty Officer
Steward
Forrester, John J – Chief Petty
Officer Writer
Forster, Frederick G – Engine Room
Artificer 3rd Class
Foster, Algernon T – Able Seaman
Foster, Colin E – Ordinary Seaman
Foster, Kenneth J – Able Seaman
Foster, Ralph – Ordinary Seaman
Foster, Reginald – Able Seaman
Fotheringham, George – Marine
Fowle, Henry J – Able Seaman
Fowler, Frank S – Ordinary
Signalman
Fowler, Robert H – Musician
Francis, Charles A – Boy 1st Class
Francis, Victor R – Leading Stoker
Freeborn, Frederick C – Warrant
Supply Officer
Freeman, Douglas E – Ordinary
Seaman
Freeman, Mark H P – Midshipman,
RNR
French, Leslie V – Ordinary Seaman
French, Ronald M – Ordnance
Artificer 4th Class
Friend, Leslie E – Lieutenant, RNVR
Frodsham, Neville H – Sub
Lieutenant
Fry, John C – Ordinary Coder
Fullick, Frederick R – Able Seaman
Funnell, Kenneth G – Ordinary
Seaman
Gabbett, Cecil P – Ordinary Seaman
Gale, Ronald M – Stoker 1st Class
Gallacher, Cornwall – Ordinary
Signalman
Gallant, Joseph – Ordinary Seaman
Gallant, William – Ordinary Seaman
Galliott, Howard W – Ordinary

Seaman
Galloway, Arthur – Engine Room
Artificer 4th Class
Gardner, James D – Petty Officer
Telegraphist
Garman, Victor G – Leading Stoker
Garroway, Robert L – Steward
Garry, Neville W H – Ordinary
Telegraphist
Gascoine, Thomas R – Able Seaman
Gaudet, Samuel – Ordinary Seaman
Genaway, Victor W – Ordinary
Seaman
Gibb, Stanley D – Wireman
Gibbon, Isaac G – Chief Ordnance
Artificer
Gibbs, Charles W E – Leading
Signalman
Gibson, James – Stoker 2nd Class
Gibson, John H – Signalman
Gibson, Thomas – Marine
Giffen, John A – Stoker 2nd Class
Gilbert, Charles E G – Stoker 1st
Class
Gilbert, Harold – Able Seaman
Gillan, Joseph – Marine
Gillett, George P – Ordinary
Seaman
Gillis, John R – Ordinary Seaman
Glass, Leslie G V – Able Seaman
Gledhill, James E – Corporal, RM
Glenn, Robert – Petty Officer Stoker
Goddard, Sidney – Able Seaman
Goff, Jack – Boy 1st Class
Goldsmith, Horace W – Petty
Officer
Gomer, Harry – Marine
Gomershall, Royston – Ordinary
Seaman
Good, Bernard E C – Marine
Good, Frederick A – Petty Officer
Goodbody, John W – Stoker 1st
Class

Goodenough, Herbert H – Cook (S)

Gordon, Leslie S – Able Seaman

Gough, John M – Colour Sergeant, RM

Goulstine, Leonard – Able Seaman

Graham, Donald – Supply Assistant

Graves, John R – Paymaster Lieutenant, RNVR

Gray, Alfred E E – Able Seaman

Gray, John C – Ordinary Seaman

Green, Benjamin L – Marine

Green, Harry – Able Seaman

Green, Herbert – Signal Boy

Green, John H – Ordinary Signalman

Green, William James – Ordinary Signalman

Green, William John – Leading Stoker

Greene, Derek A – Ordinary Signalman

Gregory, Arthur H – Leading Seaman

Gregory, John – Marine

Gregson, Edward H G – Commander (G)

Griffin, Charles A – Marine

Griffiths, Leonard F – Ordinary Seaman

Grogan, Robert T – Commander (E)

Groucott, Roland D – Able Seaman

Groves, Stedman B – Musician

Groves, Thomas – Able Seaman

Grundy, Frederick E – Wireman

Guest, Alan – Bandboy

Gulliver, Edward G V – Leading Seaman

Haden-Morris, Alec B-H – Supply Assistant

Hadley, Alan E – Ordinary Seaman

Hadow, Norman W A – Ordinary Seaman

Haeger, Edward G – Sergeant, RM

Hales, Edward – Able Seaman

Hall, David G – Ordinary Seaman, RANVR

Hall, George W – Ordinary Seaman, RANVR

Hall, Henry G – Able Seaman

Hall, John W – Lieutenant Commander (Ret)

Hall, Neville T – Signalman

Hall, Norman V – Stoker 1st Class

Hall, Thomas – Marine

Halls, Wilfred C – Ordinary Signalman

Hambley, Thomas H – Able Seaman

Hanna, Robert – Plumber 3rd Class

Hannaway, Edward J – Ordinary Telegraphist

Hannay, James D – Stoker 2nd Class

Hanwell, Tom – Chief Stoker

Harding, John S – Able Seaman

Harding, William – Stoker 1st Class

Hardy, Henry F M – Cook (S)

Harkess, Robert W – Stoker 1st Class

Harkison, Thomas – Able Seaman

Harler, Douglas B – Able Seaman

Harmer, George – Engine Room Artificer 4th Class

Harris, Charles A – Chief Mechanician

Harris, Desmond S R – Lieutenant, RM

Harris, Frank R – Ordnance Artificer 4th Class

Harris, James H – Marine

Harrison, Robert C – alias of Robert C d'Abry de l'Arves

Hartley, Arthur – Boy 1st Class

Hartley, Norman – Stoker 2nd Class

Hartmann, Geoffrey H – Ordinary Coder

Harty, Jack – Leading Seaman

Harvey, Edward R – Leading Cook (O)

Harvey, Eric O – Stoker 2nd Class

Hastings, Joseph – alias of Joseph Rannou

Hatherill, William H – Marine

Haughton, Cyril – Warrant Engineer

Hawkey, Derrick B, DSM – Signalman

Hawkins, Ernest H – Shipwright 1st Class

Hawthorne, Arthur W – Wireman

Hawthorne, John W – Chief Petty Officer Cook (O)

Hayde, Joseph A – Leading Seaman

Haynes, Albert E – Leading Stoker

Hayton, John W – Able Seaman

Heath, David J – Ordinary Seaman

Heaton, Albert – Able Seaman

Hellens, Joseph S – Engine Room Artificer 4th Class

Hemmings, Bertie – Engine Room Artificer 1st Class

Henderson, John – Signalman

Hendry, William – Marine

Hennessy, David T – Boy 1st Class

Henshaw, Owen W – Stoker 1st Class

Henshaw, Ronald – Boy 1st Class

Heptonstall, George A – Able Seaman

Herbert, Sidney J – Captain (E)

Hermon, Eric D – Marine

Herod, Maurice H E – Bandmaster 1st Class

Heys, William W – P/Sick Berth Attendant

Hibbs, Francis H F – Corporal, RM

Hibbs, Richard A – Midshipman, RNVR

Hickman, Leonard A – Stoker 2nd Class

Hickmott, William J – Boy 1st Class

Higginson, William – Stoker 1st Class

Higgott, John N – Engine Room Artificer 3rd Class

Hill, Eric J R – Marine

Hilton, Albert F – Stoker 1st Class

Hiscock, Frederick J – Marine

Hiscock, William A – Petty Officer

Hives, Ronald – Stoker 1st Class

Hoare, Cyril A – Stoker 2nd Class

Hoare, Norris H – Paymaster Lieutenant, RNVR

Hobbs, Frederick J – Chief Stoker

Hobbs, Robert – Engine Room Artificer 4th Class

Hogan, John M – Paymaster Commander

Holdaway, Frank – Joiner 1st Class

Holland, Charles – Marine

Holland, Francis H – Stoker 2nd Class

Hollis, Bramwell G – Ordinary Signalman

Holmes, Edward J – Boy 1st Class

Holmes, George – Leading Stoker

Holmes, Harold – Able Seaman

Holroyd, Arthur – Sailmaker's Mate

Homer, Harold – Chief Mechanician

Honeybun, Richard J – Chief Stoker

Hoole, Horace – Leading Stoker

Hope, Ernest J – Leading Stoker

Horner, Leslie – Able Seaman

Horsman, Lawrence – Leading Cook (S)

Horton, George W – Petty Officer Steward

Howard, Eric S – Ordinary Seaman

Howe, Reginald E – Stoker 2nd Class

Howie, Robert G W – Marine

Howlett, Patrick – Ordinary Seaman

Hows, Gordon – Marine

Howse, Thomas – Leading Seaman

Hoyle, Sidney – Ordinary Seaman

Hughes, Hugh – Leading Stoker

Hughes, William F – Marine

Hull, Arthur W – Able Seaman

Hulme, Arthur – Wireman

Hulme, Owen E – Able Seaman

Humphrey, Michael S T – Lieutenant (E)

Humphreys, William – Marine

Hunns, John A C – Marine

Hunt, George – Stoker 2nd Class

Hunt, William N – Ordnance Artificer 1st Class

Hunter, John M J – Ordinary Seaman

Huntington, Ernest S – Sergeant, RM

Huntley, Henry F – Plumber 1st Class

Hurle, Ronald C – Supply Assistant

Hurst, Christopher W – Coder

Hurst, Henry – Surgeon Commander

Huskinson, Sydney – Able Seaman

Hutchings, Leslie W R – Painter 3rd Class

Hutchins, Albert J – Petty Officer

Iago, John M – Electrical Lieutenant, RNVR

Ierston, Kenneth W – Ordinary Seaman

Ingram, John W – Able Seaman

Ingram, Leslie R – Able Seaman

Inkpen, Reginald S – Stoker 1st Class

Innes, Alexander – Able Seaman

Jack, George – Ordinary Seaman

Jackson, George S – Marine

Jaggers, Eric – Stoker 2nd Class

James, Leonard A – Leading Stoker

James, Phillip A – Ordinary Seaman

Jarvis, Arthur C – Able Seaman

Jarvis, Leonard R – Able Seaman

Javan, Kenneth W – Ordinary Seaman

Jeffs, Norman – Stoker 1st Class

Jelley, Stanley A – Boy 1st Class

Jennings, Walter H W – Chief Petty Officer

Jesse, Harold – Chief Electrical Artificer

John, Thomas – Marine

Johnson, Frederick – Leading Cook

Johnson, Ralph – Stoker 1st Class

Johnson, Stanley F – Leading Writer

Johnson, William F – Petty Officer

Johnson, William St C – Petty Officer Stoker

Johnston, James – Able Seaman

Johnston, William – Assistant Steward

Jones, Albert J – Able Seaman

Jones, David J – Leading Stoker

Jones, Francis L L – Midshipman, RCN

Jones, Frederick R – Able Seaman

Jones, Gordon H – Stoker 1st Class

Jones, Gwilym – Able Seaman

Jones, Harold H – Able Seaman

Jones, Hayden J – Stoker 1st Class

Jones, James W – Petty Officer Stoker

Jones, John W – Petty Officer

Jones, Kenneth – Ordinary Seaman

Jones, Richard – Seaman, RNR

Jones, Robert W – Boy 1st Class

Jones, Ronald G S – Ordinary Seaman

Jones, Roy T R – Boy 1st Class

Jordan, Geoffrey W – Canteen Assistant, NAAFI

Jordan, Kenneth F A – Leading Cook (S)

Joyce, Leslie R – Boy 1st Class

Julier, Alfred E – Marine

Kay, Norman – Engine Room Artificer 3rd Class

Kay, Samuel – Ordinary Seaman

Keal, George F – Leading Stoker

Kean, Albert A – Petty Officer

Telegraphist

Kearney, Thomas P – Seaman, RNR

Keating, Kenneth H W – Able Seaman

Keenan, Robert J – Stoker 2nd Class

Keens, Eric G – Boy Telegraphist

Keers, Robert – Boy 1st Class

Keith, Arthur W – Marine

Kelly, Cornelius – Ordinary Signalman

Kelly, Jack V K – Able Seaman

Kelly, John – Ordnance Artificer 4th Class

Kelly, Robert – Petty Officer Stoker

Kemish, Colin H T – Boy 1st Class

Kempton, Sylvius L – Ordinary Signalman

Kendall, Albert J – Able Seaman

Kerr, Alexander – Engine Room Artificer 5th Class

Kerr, Raymond W – Boy 1st Class

Kerridge, Herbert – Stoker 1st Class

Kersley, Albert S – Marine

King, Ernest H – Able Seaman

King, Howard L C – Signalman, RNVR

King, William A – Able Seaman

Kingston, Jack – Able Seaman

Kinmond, Charles H – Able Seaman

Kirk, Alfred – Ordinary Telegraphist

Kirk, Russell G – Marine

Kirkland, John D – Able Seaman

Kitchener, Reginald J – Able Seaman

Knapper, Joseph W – Able Seaman

Knight, James A P – Stoker 1st Class

Knight, John – Engine Room Artificer 4th Class

Knight, Roy F – Midshipman, RNR

Knight, Stanley R – Joiner 4th Class

Knox, John A – Ordinary Seaman

Knox, John D – Stoker 2nd Class

Ladd, Charles J – Stoker 2nd Class

Laidman, Reginald A – Able Seaman

Laing, John – Ordinary Seaman

Laking, Andrew – Stoker 2nd Class

Lambert, Thomas W – Ordinary Seaman

Lancaster, Howard – Able Seaman

Lane, Cyril F – Shipwright 2nd Class

Lane, Herbert F W – Able Seaman

Langley, James – Ordinary Coder

Lansdowne, Cecil R E – Canteen Assistant, NAAFI

Lapthorn, Peter R – Midshipman, RNVR

Latimer, Walter S – Ordinary Seaman

Laughlin, John C A – Boy 1st Class

Laws, Albert E – Chief Stoker

Lawson, Jack – Cook (S)

Laycock, Henry – Marine

Layton, Sidney G – Marine

Le Bosquet, Cecil E – Able Seaman

Le Noury, Alfred N – Able Seaman

Le Page, Edwin H G – Able Seaman

Leach, Harold G – Mechanician 1st Class

Leaney, Robert T – Boy 1st Class

Leason, Harry V – Engine Room Artificer 3rd Class

Lee, Wilfred – Assistant Steward

Leggatt, George F S – Stoker 1st Class

Leggett, Cyril A – Ordinary Seaman

Leishman, William – Chief Stoker

L'Enfant, Bertram H – Leading Stoker

Levack, John S L – Marine

Lever, Stanley R – Stoker 1st Class

Levy, Albert P – Ordinary Seaman

Lewington, George C – Yeoman of Signals

Lewis, Alfred G – Stoker 1st Class

Lewis, Edward P S – Lieutenant

Lewis, Michael E – Petty Officer Stoker

Lewis, Thomas – Able Seaman

Liddell, Archibald T – Stoker 1st Class

Liddle, Harold – Leading Seaman

Lifford, Henry G – Supply Assistant

Lightbody, Robert – Boy 1st Class

Lihou, Owen F C – Able Seaman

Livingstone, Robert J – Stoker 2nd Class

Lloyd, Philip – Stoker 1st Class

Lock, Herbert H – Petty Officer Stoker

Lock, Robert H – Marine

Lockhart, Archibald W – Boy 1st Class

Locklin, James – Able Seaman

London, Reginald J C – Sergeant, RM

Long, George H – Musician

Long, Percy C B – Boy 1st Class

Lott, Frederick C – Able Seaman

Love, Herbert W – Leading Stoker

Lovegrove, Herbert E – Leading Seaman

Lovelock, Charles W – Stoker 1st Class

Lownds, John – Able Seaman

Luckhurst, John H J – Able Seaman

Lumley, Heaton – Major, RM

Luxmoore, Thomas G P – Paymaster Lieutenant

Luxton, Denis W A – Engine Room Artificer 4th Class

Lyle, James P – Able Seaman

Lynch, Augustine P – Able Seaman

Lynch, James F – Supply Petty Officer

Macdonald, Alastair D – Boy 1st Class

Machin, John L – Lieutenant Commander

Mackay, John – Seaman, RNR

Mackin, Ronald W – Able Seaman

Maclean, Hugh W P – Ordinary Coder

Macnamara, Robert T – Able Seaman

Madden, John F – Ordinary Seaman

Maidment, Harold L – Ordinary Seaman

Maitland, John W – Chief Shipwright

Malcolmson, Alexander – Ordinary Seaman

Malin, Walter G – Telegraphist

Mann, Arthur J – Ordinary Seaman

Manser, Richard A – Marine

Manton, Ernest P – Cook (S)

Markey, Harold E – Joiner 2nd Class

Marr, Ian C C – Able Seaman

Marsh, Eric – Leading Seaman

Marsh, Eric – Supply Assistant

Marsh, Joseph S – Able Seaman

Marsh, Percy G – Marine

Marsh, Robert J A – Leading Stoker

Martin, John W – Boy 1st Class

Martin, Thomas G – Stoker 1st Class

Martin, William R – Sergeant, RM

Martindale, Norman – Boy 1st Class

Maskell, John N – Able Seaman

Mason, Vernon R K – Boy 1st Class

Masters, Gordon H T – Boy 1st Class

Matthews, Albert G – Stoker 2nd Class

Matthews, Stanley G – Ordinary Telegraphist

Matthews, William D – Able Seaman

Maycock, Ernest V – Able Seaman

McAllen, John W F – Stoker 2nd Class

McAteer, William – Stoker 1st Class

McCart, George – Telegraphist

McCaughey, Daniel – Stoker 1st Class

McCaw, Robert W – Ordinary

Seaman

McCleary, William – Able Seaman

McCormac, John – Signal Boy

McCullagh, John – Engine Room Artificer 4th Class

McDonald, Ewen – Able Seaman

McDonald, Harold – Able Seaman

McDonald, Wallace – Able Seaman

McDowell, Albert – Ordinary Seaman

McDuell, Alfred – Able Seaman

McEvoy, Patrick J – Able Seaman

McEwan, Mark – Assistant Steward

McFadyen, Walter E – Sergeant, RM

McGhee, John – Ordinary Seaman

McGregor, Alfred – Stoker 1st Class

McGuire, Arthur T – Chief Engine Room Artificer

McIlwraith, Geoffry J – Stoker 1st Class

McKim, William – Boy 1st Class

McLaren, John B – Midshipman, RNR

McLatchie, William – Ordinary Seaman

McLean, Alexander – Leading Stoker

McLeod, Ian M – Able Seaman

McNulty, John G – Chief Petty Officer Telegraphist

McQuaid, Ernest G – Marine

McRae, William R – Boy Telegraphist

Meakin, Harry – Ordinary Seaman

Mellalieu, Frank – Stoker 2nd Class

Melville, John – Stoker 2nd Class

Mendham, Frederick G – Boy 1st Class

Mepham, Henry J – Engine Room Artificer 3rd Class

Metcalfe, Matthew – Leading Seaman

Middleton, Frank R – Petty Officer

Milburn, Samuel C – Able Seaman

Miles, Francis B – Able Seaman

Miles, Ronald S – Marine

Miles, Vernon G – Chief Petty Officer

Millard, David T H – Able Seaman

Millard, George K – Able Seaman, RNVR

Miller, James A K – Stoker 1st Class

Miller, Thomas – Able Seaman, RNVR

Mills, Campbell R F – Ordinary Seaman

Mills, Harry J – Ordinary Seaman

Mills, Montague D – Marine

Mills, Raymond E – Stoker 2nd Class

Mills, Ronald W – Stoker 1st Class

Minard, André – Leading Signalman

Mitchell, Frank – Electrical Artificer 4th Class

Mitchell, Frederick R – Able Seaman

Mitchell, John – Able Seaman

Mitchell, Leonard F W – Able Seaman

Moat, Norman – Ordinary Seaman

Mochan, John C – Ordinary Seaman

Monument, Harry – Joiner 4th Class

Moody, Walter – Ordinary Signalman

Moon, Jack E – Petty Officer

Moon, Walter – Able Seaman

Moore, Brian R – Ordinary Seaman

Moore, Edward A P – Stoker 2nd Class

Moore, Hugh T H – Petty Officer

Moore, James K – Boy 1st Class

Morgan, Albert H – Marine

Morgan, Ronald – Marine

Morley, Sidney V – Chief Petty Officer

Morrell, Ronald F – Stoker 2nd Class

Morten, Thomas A – Engine Room Artificer 4th Class

Mortimer, Robert E G – Able Seaman

Mortimer, Stanley E – Stoker 2nd Class

Mould, Geoffrey J W – Able Seaman

Moultrie, Edward H F – Lieutenant Commander

Mullen, John – Telegraphist

Mulligan, James – Stoker 1st Class

Mullins, Edgar W F – Ordinary Seaman

Munday, Harold J – Wireman

Murphy, Frank E – Stoker 1st Class

Murray, Frederick C – Marine

Murray, Hugh – Able Seaman

Murray, Sidney – Electrical Artificer 5th Class

Murrell, George P – Shipwright 4th Class

Myers, Gordon W – Ordinary Seaman

Myers, Sidney C S – Ordinary Seaman

Myram, Maurice A – Shipwright 4th Class

Nally, Joseph – Leading Stoker

Nash, Kenneth R – Stoker 1st Class

Naylor, Rodney J – Chief Petty Officer Cook (O)

Naylor, Ronald – Able Seaman

Neal, Edward R – Supply Assistant

Neal, Ronald W – Able Seaman

Neale, Robert S – Marine

Neave, Peter F A – Able Seaman

Nelson, William – Stoker 2nd Class

Nevett, Arthur L – Yeoman of Signals

Neville, William A – Petty Officer

Newell, Charles J – Able Seaman

Newey, Cedric B N – Lieutenant, RNVR

Newnham, Robert – Able Seaman

Nicholl, Donald W – Able Seaman

Nicholls, Douglas H – Stoker 2nd Class

Nichols, Thomas F – Ordinary Seaman

Nicholson, Alfred F – Petty Officer

Nicholson, Andrew – alias of André Minard

Nicholson, Thomas W – Cook

Noble, Alexander – Marine

Norman, Christopher J B – Midshipman, RCN

Norris, Thomas F – Stoker 2nd Class

Northam, William A – Able Seaman

Nuding, Albert V – Supply Assistant

Nugent, William J – Stoker 1st Class

Oborne, Reginald G H – Petty Officer Steward

O'Connell, John F – Petty Officer

Ogden, Robert – Able Seaman

Oldershaw, Arthur – Leading Stoker

O'Leary, Leslie S D – Stoker 1st Class

Olive, Ronald McC – Cook (O)

O'Neil, Owen – Ordinary Seaman

O'Reilly, Dennis P – Stoker 2nd Class

O'Rourke, Patrick C – Leading Seaman

Orrell, Walter J – Marine

Ovenden, Jack – Canteen Assistant, NAAFI

Owen, Harold – Petty Officer

Owens, George E M – Lieutenant Commander

Pacy, Ronald – Engine Room Artificer 4th Class

Paddock, Stanley A – Stoker 1st Class

Pae, James – Able Seaman

Page, Victor E F – Stoker 2nd Class

Palmer, Frank – Stoker 1st Class

Palmer, Frederick W J – Regulating Petty Officer

Palmer, James A – Marine

Palmer, Reginald W – Sergeant, RM

Palmer, Stephen – Able Seaman, RNVR

Papworth, Robert G – Yeoman of Signals

Pares, Anthony – Lieutenant Commander (T)

Park, Raymond – Able Seaman

Parker, Gordon – Steward

Parratt, Albert H – Stoker 1st Class

Parton, Stanley G – Stoker 1st Class

Passells, Keith C – Chief Petty Officer Supply

Passey, Aubrey R – Sick Berth Attendant

Patton, Owen – Able Seaman

Pay, James L – Able Seaman

Payne, Harry T – Able Seaman

Payne, John W – Leading Stoker

Peace, Denzil S – Marine

Peacock, John E C – Surgeon Lieutenant (D)

Peacock, William – Stoker 2nd Class

Pearce, Arthur S – Stoker 1st Class

Pearce, Harry R – Engine Room Artificer 3rd Class

Pearce, Ronald J – Leading Supply Assistant

Pearce, William F – Petty Officer

Pearse, John F F, BEM – Electrical Artificer 1st Class

Pearse, Sidney C – Able Seaman

Pearson, George – Cook (O)

Peck, Owen O'R – Able Seaman

Peckham, Leonard M – Ordinary Seaman

Pedder, Ernest A J – Able Seaman

Peden, David G – Ordinary Seaman

Peel, Reginald K – Assistant Steward

Peirce, James P – Chief Petty Officer Steward

Pemberton, Frederick S – Engine Room Artificer 4th Class

Pennycook, William R – Stoker 2nd Class

Percival, Stanley E P – Stoker 2nd Class

Perkins, William G – Marine

Perman, Roland G C – Midshipman, RIN

Perrin, Alfred J – Cook (S)

Perry, Aubrey J W – Steward

Perry, Leonard – Marine

Perry, William H – Petty Officer Cook (O)

Pescod, Thomas C – Boy 1st Class

Petch, Roy V – Able Seaman

Petty, Edmund J – Able Seaman

Phelps, Henry F – Blacksmith 1st Class

Phillips, George T E – Ordinary Seaman

Phillips, Horace E – Leading Seaman

Phillips, Lancelot J – Ordinary Seaman

Phillips, Norman – Stoker 2nd Class

Phillips, Raymond T – Ordinary Seaman

Phillips, Ronald G – Paymaster Lieutenant

Pickering, Harry – Petty Officer Stoker

Pierce, Robert D – Marine

Pike, William A – Musician

Pink, Harold J – Able Seaman

Pinkerton, Robert R – Wireman

Piper, Fred H – Ordinary Signalman, RNVR

Pitts, Henry G – Ordinary Seaman

Plant, Edwin – Marine

Plimbley, Edward C – Leading Steward

Plumley, Reginald A H – Warrant Engineer

Poar, Reginald J – Marine

Pope, Geoffrey C – Chief Petty Officer Supply

Porter, Cyril L D – Ordinary Signalman

Porter, Frederick A – Marine

Porter, Reginald J – Musician

Porter-Fausset, Frederick A P – Paymaster Lieutenant

Potts, Frank S – Writer

Power, Alfred – Able Seaman

Powley, Herbert W – Chief Engine Room Artificer

Prangnell, Maurice R – Able Seaman

Pratt, Albert W C – Marine

Prescott, Marcus R – Petty Officer Stoker

Price, Alfred C J – Shipwright 4th Class

Price, William A – Warrant Shipwright

Pringle, Robert H W – Stoker 1st Class

Print, Dennis C B – Engine Room Artificer 4th Class

Proudlock, Eric – Able Seaman

Pulling, Edward – Petty Officer Stoker

Punter, Jack A – Able Seaman

Puttick, William F – Stoker 1st Class

Puttock, Maurice J E – Signalman, RNVR

Quigley, John J – Ordinary Seaman

Radley, Kenneth – Stoker 1st Class

Rae, Hector R – Plumber 3rd Class

Ramsbotham, William L, MM – Shipwright 4th Class

Rance, John – Leading Stoker

Randall, Cyril W – Able Seaman

Randall, Maurice P – Boy 1st Class

Randall, Stanley R – Marine

Randall, Victor J – Stoker 1st Class

Rannou, Joseph – Able Seaman

Rant, Leonard V – Stoker 2nd Class

Raw, Dennis A – Engine Room Artificer 4th Class

Raw, Irving T – Able Seaman

Raw, Roderick M – Stoker 1st Class

Rawlinson, Albert G E – Stoker 1st Class

Rawlinson, Leonard – Able Seaman

Raynor, Francis – Signalman

Read, Anthony V – Ordinary Seaman

Read, Douglas – Boy 1st Class

Reay, William E, DSM – Petty Officer

Reddall, Peter E A – Signal Boy

Reed, Hector L – Corporal, RM

Rees, Vernon J – Stoker 1st Class

Reeve, Robert E – Leading Steward

Reeves, Cyril A – Able Seaman

Reeves, Stanley E – Ordinary Seaman

Rendell, Stewart R J – Able Seaman

Reveler, Thomas S – Engine Room Artificer 4th Class

Reynolds, John A – Stoker 2nd Class

Rhodes, John – Steward

Rice, Herbert F – Stoker 2nd Class

Richards, Alfred W – Stoker 1st Class

Richardson, Henry F D – Ordinary Signalman

Richardson, Snowden F O – Stoker 1st Class

Richer, Harold E – Petty Officer

Ridge, Merlin F – Writer

Riding, Walter K – Ordinary Seaman

Rigby, Benjamin G – Boy 1st Class

Rigglesford, Arthur P – Stoker 1st Class

Riley, George P – Stoker 1st Class

Ritchie, James S – Petty Officer Telegraphist

Ritchie, Thomas B – Electrical Artificer 4th Class

Roach, Bryan C J – Lieutenant (E)

Robarts, Frederick J – Ordinary Telegraphist

Robb, James G – Able Seaman

Robbins, Robert S – Ordinary Seaman

Roberts, Ernest G – Mechanician 2nd Class

Roberts, Frederick C – Leading Seaman

Roberts, Gordon R – Able Seaman

Roberts, Lewis G – Able Seaman

Roberts, Reginald C – Ordinary Seaman

Robins, Anthony C R – Sub Lieutenant, RNR

Robins, Charles V – Yeoman of Signals

Robinson, Arthur E – Able Seaman

Robinson, Percival T – Petty Officer Cook

Robinson, Peter J – Boy 1st Class

Robotham, Charles – Able Seaman

Rodgman, Claude B – Able Seaman

Rodley, Samuel J – Marine

Roe, Donovan C – Paymaster Commander

Rootham, Peter – Ordinary Seaman

Rorrison, Hugh F – Boy 1st Class

Rose, Reginald T – Stoker 1st Class

Rose, William J – Stoker 2nd Class

Rose, William R – Leading Seaman

Rosenthal, Henry C – Marine

Routledge, Walter – Boy 1st Class

Rowe, Stanley G S – Marine

Rowlands, Daniel J – Marine

Rowntree, George W – Stoker 1st Class

Rowsell, Graham H – Able Seaman

Rowsell, Leslie D – Boy 1st Class

Roy, Ian A – Boy 1st Class

Rudd, Edwin A – Ordnance Artificer 4th Class

Rundle, Arthur F – Marine

Runnacles, Frederick E – Marine

Russell, Charles A – Able Seaman

Russell, David L – Musician

Russell, John A G – Petty Officer

Russell, Leonard W – Able Seaman

Russell, Walter F – Petty Officer

Ryder, Leonard – Petty Officer Telegraphist

Sadler, Edward R – Marine

Saiger, John G – Stoker 1st Class

Sammars, Thomas J B – Boy 1st Class

Sanderson, Peter – Able Seaman

Sargeaunt, Henry E J – Stoker 2nd Class

Saul, Charles – Leading Stoker

Saunders, Albert – Corporal, RM

Saunders, Arthur W – Engine Room Artificer 4th Class

Saunders, James G – Stoker 2nd Class

Savage, Edwin J – Chief Engine Room Artificer

Sayers, Robert M – Ordinary Seaman

Scammell, Walter G – Leading Stoker

Scattergood, Frederick J – Stoker 1st Class

Scott, Andrew B – Seaman, RNR

Scott, Jack – Ordinary Seaman

Scott, James – Leading Stoker

Scott, Robert C – Marine

Scott, William P – Stoker 2nd Class

Scott-Kerr, John H A – Sub Lieutenant

Senior, Reuben – Stoker 2nd Class

Sewell, Gilbert W – Marine

Shadbolt, Maurice H – Marine

Shand, Robert – Able Seaman

Shannon, John D – Ordinary Seaman, RANVR

Sharp, John S – Steward

Sharpe, Albert J – Stoker 2nd Class

Shawe, Robert B – Able Seaman

Shearer, George B B – Leading Cook (S)

Shepherd, Cyril H – Ordinary Seaman

Shepherd, George V – Chief Engine Room Artificer

Shepherd, Lambert C – Ordinary Seaman

Shepherd, Percy R – Able Seaman

Sheppard, Leonard F G – Petty Officer

Sherval, William R – Chief Stoker

Shiers, William H – Petty Officer Supply

Shipp, Leslie F – Stoker 1st Class

Shorrock, Stanley H A – Able Seaman

Short, Arthur E – Engine Room Artificer 4th Class

Shuck, William B – Ordnance Artificer 5th Class

Shuker, Archibald – Leading Seaman

Shute, Harry L – Leading Cook (O)

Siddall, John – Able Seaman

Sidley, Robert B P – Petty Officer Stoker

Silk, Jack C R – Stoker 2nd Class

Sim, Alexander E – Sick Berth Attendant

Simmons, Ernest A – Stoker 1st Class

Simpson, Peter – Ordinary Seaman

Sims, William – Engine Room Artificer 4th Class

Sinnott, Frederick W – Able Seaman

Skett, Raymond L – Ordnance Artificer 4th Class

Skipper, John FW – Able Seaman

Slade, Ronald A – Able Seaman

Slowther, George – Petty Officer Stoker

Smart, Leslie E V – Able Seaman

Smith, Alexander G – Steward

Smith, Andrew K – Able Seaman

Smith, Benjamin T – Marine

Smith, Charles L S – Able Seaman

Smith, Dick – Able Seaman

Smith, Eric T – Ordinary Seaman

Smith, Frederick A – Able Seaman

Smith, Frederick H S – Petty Officer Stoker

Smith, George F – Stoker 1st Class

Smith, Harold G E – Lieutenant (E)

Smith, James – Able Seaman

Smith, James McL – Able Seaman

Smith, John C – Ordinary Seaman

Smith, John H – Chief Petty Officer

Smith, John H – Supply Assistant

Smith, John H – Regulating Petty Officer

Smith, Peter W C – Supply Assistant

Smith, Stanley C – Leading Cook

Smith, Stephen R – Able Seaman

Smith, Thomas – Ordinary Seaman

Smith, Thomas N – Stoker 1st Class

Smith, Walter H – Leading Seaman

Smith, William G – Able Seaman

Smith-Withers, Stephen J – Wireman

Snelgrove, Colin – Leading Seaman

Snell, John – Chief Engine Room Artificer

Snook, George A – Marine

Snooks, William H – Ordinary Seaman

Snow, David J – Boy 1st Class

Solman, Murdoch McL – Able Seaman

Southgate, Thomas E – Marine

Sowerby, Curzon – Writer

Sparkes, Ernest – Marine

Spence, Tristram F – Lieutenant (E)

Spencer, Arthur – Mechanician 2nd Class

Spinner, George D – Stoker 1st Class
Sprakes, John – Chief Stoker
Spreadbury, Jack F W – Ordinary Seaman
St Clair-Tracy, Albert E – Electrical Artificer 2nd Class
Stanley, Leonard – Able Seaman
Stannard, George W – Sick Berth Petty Officer
Startup, Ian G E – Ordinary Seaman, RANVR
Steel, Douglas M – Instructor Commander
Steele, Alexander – Able Seaman
Steele, Joseph W – Ordinary Seaman
Steptoe, John H – Marine
Sterne, Benjamin S – Able Seaman
Steven, Arthur – Stoker Petty Officer
Stevenson, Basil P – Midshipman, RNR
Stevenson, Noel – Ordnance Artificer 5th Class
Stewart, Albert M – Able Seaman
Stewart, R J Patrick – Chaplain
Stewart, Thomas – Able Seaman
Stibbs, Charles T – Ordinary Seaman
Stocker, Norman G L – Boy 1st Class
Stoddard, George H P – Marine
Stokes, John E – Able Seaman
Stone, Arthur W – Petty Officer
Stothers, Hugh – Able Seaman
Stoyles, Sydney S – Chief Stoker
Strange, Edward J – Stoker 1st Class
Stringer, Cecil A B – Able Seaman
Strong, Arthur J – Leading Writer
Stubbings, Douglas H – Marine
Stubbs, Charles F B – Lieutenant, RNVR
Sturgess, Cyril L – Able Seaman
Sturgess, John P – Boy 1st Class
Sulley, John C – Commissioned Ordnance Artificer

Sullivan, Albert – Petty Officer Stoker
Sullivan, Frank D – Stoker 2nd Class
Surrey, Archibald H – Chief Petty Officer Writer
Swain, James F – Leading Writer
Swain, Ronald W – Ordinary Telegraphist
Swanborough, Rupert T – Cook (O)
Swatton, Bertram C – Petty Officer
Swinson, Ernest J – Ordnance Artificer 3rd Class
Switzer, Albert – Ordinary Seaman
Sylvester, James – Ordinary Telegraphist
Symes, Reginald C – Wireman (L)
Szymalski, Kazimierz – Marynarz Podchorąży (Midshipman), Polish Navy
Taggart, Robert – Assistant Cook (O)
Tallett, Ronald L W – Leading Seaman
Tamarelle, Marius – Electrical Artificer 4th Class
Tapsell, Albert E – Marine
Tawney, David R – Musician
Taylor, Arnold E – Ordinary Seaman
Taylor, Charles – Leading Seaman
Taylor, Charles A – Telegraphist
Taylor, Clifford – Leading Stoker
Taylor, David – Wireman
Taylor, Frederick – Able Seaman
Taylor, Henry C – Stoker 1st Class
Taylor, James – Stoker 2nd Class
Taylor, Lewis J – Marine
Taylor, Michael – alias of Marius Tamarelle
Taylor, Reginald L – Musician
Taylor, William C – Ordinary Telegraphist
Taylor, William O – Commissioned Telegraphist

Telford, Charles – Marine

Terry, Gordon V – Telegraphist

Thomas, Francis J – Able Seaman

Thomas, Harold J – Able Seaman

Thompson, Harold – Able Seaman

Thompson, Robert – Boy 1st Class

Thomson, Hugh – Able Seaman

Thorpe, George E – Leading Stoker

Thorpe, Joseph – Marine

Thorpe, Richard – Ordinary Seaman

Thurogood, John F – Cook (S)

Till, Jack C – Telegraphist

Till, William E C – Shipwright 3rd Class

Tipping, Alfred J E – Able Seaman

Titheridge, Jack R – Canteen Assistant, NAAFI

Tocher, Edwin – Ordinary Seaman

Todd, William C – Stoker 1st Class

Tomlins, George – Leading Seaman

Tomlinson, William T – Boy 1st Class

Toogood, Leslie B – Marine

Topham, Thomas – Able Seaman

Townley, William J – Stoker 2nd Class

Tozer, Harry G H – Commissioned Gunner

Treloar, Walter J B – Leading Seaman

Trevarthen, William – Canteen Manager, NAAFI

Trollope, Clifton W – Stoker 2nd Class

Trotter, Ralph W – Petty Officer Telegraphist

Trowbridge, William C – Petty Officer

Trzebiatowski-Zmuda, Leon – Marynarz Podchorąży (Midshipman), Polish Navy

Tucker, Leslie – Ordinary Seaman

Turnbull, William S – Able Seaman

Turner, George F – Stoker 1st Class

Turner, George H F – Stoker 1st Class

Turner, John – Stoker 1st Class

Tuxworth, Frank A – Ordinary Signalman

Twigg, Charles J – Stoker 1st Class

Underwood, John – Stoker 2nd Class

Upton, Roy R – Ordinary Telegraphist

Utteridge, Raymond H – Petty Officer Telegraphist

Vacher, Geoffrey D B – Paymaster Midshipman

Varlow, Albert C – Commissioned Gunner

Varndell, Arthur G – Petty Officer Stoker

Veal, Richard E – Stoker 1st Class

Vickers, Herbert G – Chief Petty Officer Cook

Viney, Albert E – Marine

Wagstaff, William – Able Seaman

Walker, Albert C – Petty Officer

Walker, George T – Ordinary Signalman

Walker, Thomas – Stoker 1st Class

Wallace, James W – Leading Stoker

Waller, William J – Stoker 2nd Class

Wallis, Michael H St J – Marine

Walsh, John F – Assistant Cook (S)

Walter, William F P – Warrant Engineer

Walters, Douglas T – Assistant Cook (S)

Walton, Clifford – Marine

Walton, John – Leading Seaman

Walton, Josiah T – Chief Stoker

Wannerton, Henry J – Leading Stoker

Ward, Frederick W – Painter 3rd Class

Ward, George – Signalman

Ward, Joseph – Ordinary Telegraphist

Warden, Kenneth G – Midshipman, RNR

Warrand, S John P – Commander (N)

Warren, Donald – Marine

Warwick, Benjamin – Boy 1st Class

Waterhouse, Reginald G – Able Seaman

Waterlow, Antony A – Ordinary Signalman

Waterman, Albert D – Able Seaman

Waters, William F – Stoker 1st Class

Waterson, Thomas J B – Leading Stoker

Watkins, John – Petty Officer Stoker

Watkinson, Stanley – Paymaster Sub Lieutenant, RNZN

Watson, Alexander – Seaman, RNR

Watson, Harry, BEM – Chief Stoker

Watson, John C – Able Seaman

Watson, Robert – Able Seaman, RNVR

Watson, Robert G – alias of Robert G W Howie

Watt, Charles J J – Stoker 1st Class

Watt, Robert A E – Steward

Watts, Edward A H – Chief Petty Officer

Wearn, Arthur – Marine

Wearne, Harry E – Able Seaman

Weaver, Henry E – Marine

Webb, Albert – Able Seaman

Weddle, William – Able Seaman

Welch, Albert C W – Stoker 1st Class

Welch, Reginald A – Petty Officer

Welch, Sidney C T – Marine

Weldon, Eric – Able Seaman

Wellman, Arthur C – Petty Officer Stoker

Wells, Henry – Stoker 2nd Class

Wells, Herbert W – Ordinary Seaman

Wells, Horace W – Stoker 1st Class

Wells, Philip J – Corporal, RM

Wells, Ronald D G – Able Seaman

Wells, Stanley A – Boy 1st Class

West, Alfred P – Petty Officer Cook (S)

West, Robert W – Chief Engine Room Artificer

Wharfe, Cyril P – Petty Officer

Wheeler, Ernest F – Gunner (T)

Wheeler, Francis W – Able Seaman

White, Arthur – Wireman

White, Edward H – Petty Officer Telegraphist

White, Harry – Marine

Whitehead, Reginald C – Sergeant, RM

Whiteman, John W – Petty Officer Stoker

Whitewood, Cyril J – Able Seaman

Whitfield, Victor V – Petty Officer

Wicks, Hubert G – Able Seaman

Wigfall, Leslie A – Engine Room Artificer 3rd Class

Wiggett, James K – Stoker 2nd Class

Wigzell, Norman F H – Ordinary Coder

Wilcocks, Eric C – Able Seaman

Wilcockson, Harry R – Stoker 1st Class

Wilkins, George H – Able Seaman

Wilkinson, Frederick J R – Boy 1st Class

Wilkinson, James W – Stoker 1st Class

Wilkinson, Stanley – Leading Seaman

Willetts, Tom – Sub Lieutenant, RNVR

Williams, Frederick P – Ordinary Seaman

Williams, Horace A – Painter 3rd Class

Williams, Leonard J – Able Seaman

Williams, Lloyd – Electrical Artificer 4th Class

Williams, Roderick G – Midshipman, RNVR

Williams, Roland M – Writer

Williams, Tom G J – Able Seaman

Williamson, Harry – Leading Stoker

Willis, Albert T – Stoker 1st Class

Willis, Herbert – Marine

Wilmshurst, George H – Leading Seaman

Wilson, George – Able Seaman

Wilson, Gordon A C – Able Seaman

Wilson, Herbert G – Leading Seaman

Wilson, John V – Ordinary Seaman

Wilson, Walter – Signalman

Windeatt, Ralph F – Boy Telegraphist

Wingfield, Charles H – Petty Officer Cook (S)

Winkfield, Victor M – Leading Stoker

Wishart, Jack E – Marine

Woelfell, Edward J E – Writer

Wood, William E – Able Seaman

Woodward, Frederick J – Warrant Electrician

Wootton, Desmond T – Boy 1st Class

Worboys, Robert M – Stoker 1st Class

Worrall, Arthur – Stoker 2nd Class

Worsfold, Sydney G – Band Corporal, RM

Worwood, Raymond F – Able Seaman

Wright, Alfred W – Ordinary Seaman

Wright, Charles E – Petty Officer Telegraphist

Wright, George – Yeoman of Signals

Wright, Stanley W F – Supply Assistant

Wright, Thomas C – Leading Seaman

Wrighting, Douglas H W – Stoker 2nd Class

Wyatt, Jeffrey A F – Marine

Wyldbore-Smith, Hugh D – Lieutenant Commander

Yarrow, Peter M – Ordinary Seaman

Yates, Robert G – Boatswain

Young, John O – Signalman

Young, Percy A – Boy Bugler

Younger, Albert – Marine

Żurek, Kazimierz – Marynarz Podchorąży (Midshipman), Polish Navy

Quis separabit?

233

Further Reading

A FULL LISTING of sources (published and unpublished) consulted in the preparation of this work can be found in *The Battlecruiser* HMS Hood: *An Illustrated Biography, 1916–1941* (London: Chatham Publishing, 2005; revised edn Barnsley, S Yorks: Seaforth Publishing, 2008).

The first port of call for enthusiasts and researchers is the website of the HMS *Hood* Association: http://www.hmshood.com/

Histories of the Ship

Bradford, Ernle, *The Mighty* Hood (London: Hodder and Stoughton, 1959)

Coles, Alan, & Ted Briggs, *Flagship* Hood: *The Fate of Britain's Mightiest Warship* (London: Robert Hale, 1985)

Robertson, Lt R G, 'HMS *Hood*: Battle-Cruiser 1916–1941' in John Wingate, ed, *Warships in Profile*, vol II (Windsor: Profile Publications, 1973), pp 145–72; also published separately as HMS Hood [Warships in Profile, no 19]

Origins, Design, Fabric and Construction

Burt, R A, *British Battleships, 1919–1939* (London: Arms and Armour Press, 1993)

Campbell, N J M, *Naval Weapons of World War Two* (London: Conway Maritime Press, 1985)

Friedman, Norman, *Naval Firepower: Battleship Guns and Gunnery in the Dreadnought Era* (Barnsley, S Yorks: Seaforth Publishing, 2008)

Hodges, Peter, *The Big Gun: Battleship Main Armament, 1860–1945* (London: Conway, 1981)

Johnston, Ian, *Ships for a Nation: John Brown & Company Clydebank, 1847–1971* (Glasgow: West Dunbartonshire Libraries & Museums, 2000)

_____, *Clydebank Battlecruisers: Forgotten Photographs from John Brown's Shipyard* (Barnsley, S Yorks: Seaforth Publishing, 2011)

Lambert, Nicholas A, *Sir John Fisher's Naval Revolution* (Columbia, SC: University of South Carolina Press, 1999)

Northcott, Maurice, HMS Hood [Man O'War, vol 6] (London: Bivouac Books, 1975)

Raven, Alan, & John Roberts, *British Battleships of World War Two: The Development and Technical History of the Royal Navy's Battleships and Battlecruisers from 1911 to 1946* (London: Arms and Armour Press, 1976)

Roberts, John, *The Battlecruiser* Hood [Anatomy of the Ship] (London: Conway, 1982)

_____, *Battlecruisers* (London: Chatham Publishing, 1997)

Sumida, Jon Tetsuro, *In Defence of Naval Supremacy: Finance, Technology and British Naval Policy, 1889–1914* (Boston: Unwin Hyman, 1989)

Weldon, D G, 'HMS *Hood*' in *Warship International*, 9 (1972), no 2, pp 114–58

Life Aboard and at Sea

Arnold-Forster, Rear Admiral D, *The Ways of the Navy* (London: Ward, Lock, c1932)

Bacon, Admiral Sir Reginald H S, ed, *Britain's Glorious Navy* (London: Odham's, c1943)

Campbell, Cdr A B, *Customs and Traditions of the Royal Navy* (Aldershot: Gale & Polden, 1956)

McKee, Christopher, *Sober Men and True: Sailor Lives in the Royal Navy, 1900–1945* (Cambridge, Mass: Harvard University Press, 2002)

O'Conor, Capt Rory, *Running a Big Ship on 'Ten Commandments' (With Modern Executive Ideas and a Complete Organisation)* (Portsmouth: Gieves, 1937)

Owen, Cdr Charles, *Plain Yarns from the Fleet: The Spirit of the Royal Navy during its Twentieth-Century Heyday* (Stroud, Glos: Alan Sutton, 1997)

Twiss, Admiral Sir Frank, *Social Change in the Royal Navy, 1924–1970: The Life and Times of Admiral Sir Frank Twiss, KCB, KCVO, DSC* (Stroud, Glos: Alan Sutton/Royal Naval Museum, 1996)

Wells, Capt John, *The Royal Navy: An Illustrated Social History, 1870–1982* (Stroud, Glos: Alan Sutton/Royal Naval Museum, 1994)

The Royal Navy between the Wars

Bell, Christopher M, *The Royal Navy, Seapower and Strategy between the Wars* (London: Macmillan, 2000)

Chatfield, Ernle, Admiral of the Fleet Lord, *The Navy and Defence* (London: Heinemann, 1942)

_____, *It Might Happen Again* (London: Heinemann, 1947)

Moretz, Joseph, *The Royal Navy and the Capital Ship in the Interwar Period* (London: Frank Cass, 2002)

Roskill, Capt Stephen W, *Naval Policy between the Wars* (2 vols, London: Collins, 1968–76)

The Invergordon Mutiny

Carew, Anthony, *The Lower Deck of the Royal Navy, 1900–39: The Invergordon Mutiny in Perspective* (Manchester: Manchester University Press, 1981)
Coles, Alan, *Invergordon Scapegoat: The Betrayal of Admiral Tomkinson* (Stroud, Glos: Alan Sutton, 1993)
Divine, David, *Mutiny at Invergordon* (London: MacDonald, 1970)
Edwards, Lt Cdr Kenneth, *The Mutiny at Invergordon* (London: Putnam, 1937)
Ereira, Alan, *The Invergordon Mutiny* (London: Routledge & Kegan Paul, 1981)
Wincott, Len, *Invergordon Mutineer* (London: Weidenfeld & Nicolson, 1974)

The War at Sea

Connell, G G, *Jack's War: Lower-Deck Recollections from World War II* (London: William Kimber, 1985)
Coward, Cdr B R, *Battleship at War* (London: Ian Allan, 1987)
Lavery, Brian, *Hostilities Only: Training the Wartime Royal Navy* (Greenwich: National Maritime Museum, 2004)
_____, *Churchill's Navy: The Ships, Men and Organisation, 1939–1945* (London: Conway, 2006)
Poolman, Kenneth, *The British Sailor* (London: Arms and Armour Press, 1989)
Prysor, Glyn, *Citizen Sailors: The Royal Navy in the Second World War* (London: Penguin, 2011)
Roskill, Capt Stephen W, *The War at Sea, 1939–1945* (3 vols in 4 tomes, London: HMSO, 1954–61)
_____, *Churchill and the Admirals* (London: Collins, 1977)

Hood *at War*

Geary, Lt Stanley, HMS Hood (London: Robert Ross & Co, c1942)
Hore, Capt Peter, *Sea Power Ashore* (London: Chatham Publishing, 2001)
Tute, Warren, *The Deadly Stroke* (London: Collins, 1973)

The Sinking

Allen, Frank, & Paul Bevand, 'The Pursuit of *Bismarck* and the Sinking of HMS *Hood*' on http://www.hmshood.com/history/denmarkstrait/bismarck1.htm
Grenfell, Capt Russell, *The* Bismarck *Episode* (London: Faber and Faber, 1949)

Jurens, W J, 'The Loss of HMS *Hood* – A Re-examination' in *Warship International*, 24 (1987), no 2, pp 122–61

Kennedy, Ludovic, *Pursuit: The Chase and Sinking of the* Bismarck (London: Collins, 1974)

Mearns, David, & Rob White, Hood *and* Bismarck: *The Deep-Sea Discovery of an Epic Battle* (London: Pan Macmillan/Channel 4 Books, 2001)

von Müllenheim-Rechberg, Baron Burkard, *Battleship* Bismarck: *A Survivor's Story* (2nd edn, Annapolis: Naval Institute Press, 1990)

Rhys-Jones, Graham, *The Loss of the* Bismarck: *An Avoidable Disaster* (London: Cassell, 1999)

Stephen, Martin, *The Fighting Admirals: British Admirals of the Second World War* (London: Leo Cooper, 1991)

Thompson, Major General Julian, *The Imperial War Museum Book of the War at Sea* (London: Sidgwick & Jackson, 1996)

Memoirs

1920s

Benstead, Instructor Lt C R, *Round the World with the Battle Cruisers* (London: Hurst & Blackett, c1925)

Connor, W, *To Rio and Back with HMS* Hood (London: The Westminster Press, 1922)

Dreyer, Admiral Sir Frederic C, *The Sea Heritage: A Study of Maritime Warfare* (London: Museum Press, 1955)

Fairbairn, Lt Cdr Douglas, *The Narrative of a Naval Nobody* (London: John Murray, 1929)

O'Connor, V C Scott, *The Empire Cruise* (1st edn, London: Riddle, Smith & Duffus [for the author], 1925; there is a second printing with a foreword by Leo Amery MP)

Wells, Lt (E) Geoffrey, Unpublished diary (private collection)

1930s

Coombes, Boy Fred, Unpublished memoirs (Imperial War Museum, London, 91/7/1)

Cunningham of Hyndhope, Admiral of the Fleet Viscount, *A Sailor's Odyssey* (London: Hutchinson, 1951)

James, Admiral Sir William, *The Sky Was Always Blue* (London: Methuen, 1951)

Le Bailly, Vice Admiral Sir Louis, *The Man Around the Engine: Life Below the Waterline* (Emsworth, Hants: Kenneth Mason, 1990)

Pridham, Admiral Sir Francis, Unpublished memoirs (Churchill Archives Centre, Cambridge, PRID 2/2)

Rea, The Rev Edgar, *A Curate's Egg* (Durban: Knox Printing Co, c1967)

Williams, Leonard Charles, *Gone a Long Journey* (Bedhampton, Hants: Hillmead Publications, 2002)

Wartime

Arthur, Max, ed, *The Navy: 1939 to the Present Day* (London: Hodder & Stoughton, 1997)

Beardmore, The Rev Harold, *The Waters of Uncertainty: A Book for Naval Chaplains* (London: A R Mowbray, 1944)

Davis, Admiral Sir William, Unpublished memoirs (Churchill Archives Centre, Cambridge, WDVS 01/002)

Iago, Lt John, *And Home There's No Returning: Letters Home from HMS Hood, 1939–1941*, ed Bee Kenchington (Fleet Hargate, Lincs: Arcturus Press, 2004)

Jenson, Cdr Latham B, *Tin Hats, Oilskins & Seaboots: A Naval Journey, 1938–1945* (Toronto: Robin Brass Studio, 2000)

La Niece, Rear Admiral P G, *Not a Nine to Five Job* (Yalding, Kent: Charltons Publishers, 1992)

Pertwee, Jon, *Moon Boots and Dinner Suits* (London: Elm Tree Books, 1984)

Wellings, Rear Admiral Joseph H, USN, *On His Majesty's Service: Observations of the British Home Fleet from the Diary, Reports, and Letters of Joseph H Wellings, Assistant US Naval Attaché, London, 1940–41*, ed John B Hattendorf (Newport, RI: Naval War College Press, 1983)

Index